Dig... ...with
Pho...shop CS2 ALL IN ONE

FOR
DUMMIES

Camera Cont...

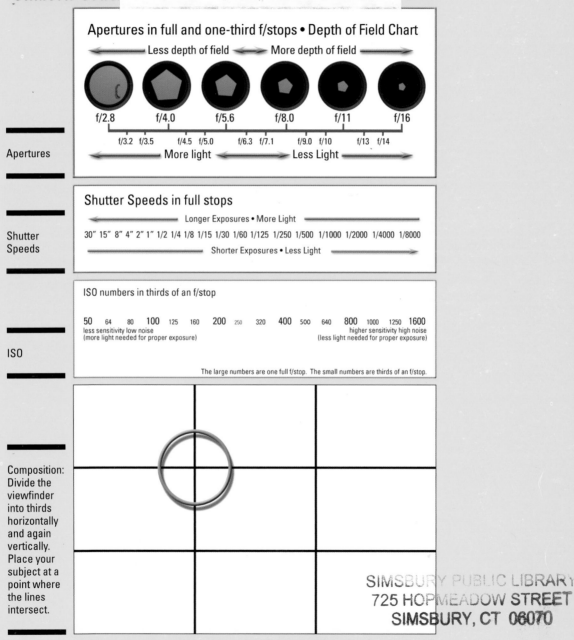

Apertures in full and one-third f/stops • Depth of Field Chart

← Less depth of field ⟷ More depth of field →

f/2.8   f/4.0   f/5.6   f/8.0   f/11   f/16

f/3.2 f/3.5   f/4.5 f/5.0   f/6.3 f/7.1   f/9.0 f/10   f/13 f/14

← More light ⟷ Less Light →

Apertures

Shutter Speeds in full stops

← Longer Exposures • More Light →

30" 15" 8" 4" 2" 1" 1/2 1/4 1/8 1/15 1/30 1/60 1/125 1/250 1/500 1/1000 1/2000 1/4000 1/8000

← Shorter Exposures • Less Light →

Shutter Speeds

ISO numbers in thirds of an f/stop

50 64 80 100 125 160 200 250 320 400 500 640 800 1000 1250 1600

less sensitivity low noise
(more light needed for proper exposure)

higher sensitivity high noise
(less light needed for proper exposure)

The large numbers are one full f/stop. The small numbers are thirds of an f/stop.

ISO

Composition:
Divide the viewfinder into thirds horizontally and again vertically. Place your subject at a point where the lines intersect.

For Dummies: Bestselling Book Series for Beginners

Digital SLR Photography with Photoshop® CS2 ALL-IN-ONE For DUMMIES

Exposure

1. **Find a gray value, like green grass or worn asphalt pavement.**
2. **Take the light reading.**
   Light meters in cameras see the light reflected from the subject.
3. **Reframe and shoot.**
   On a bright, clear, sunny day, use the ISO setting as the shutter speed at f/16. (100 ISO would mean a shutter speed of ¹⁄₁₀₀ second at f/16.) Silhouettes: Take the light reading from a clear area of sky (no sun), reframe your subject, and shoot.

Kevin's Essential Bridge Keyboard Shortcuts

Task	Mac Shortcut	Windows Shortcut
New Bridge Window	⌘+N	Ctrl+N
New Folder	⌘+Shift+N	Ctrl+Shift+N
Select All Images	⌘+A	Ctrl+A
Deselect Images	⌘+Shift+A	Ctrl+Shift+A
Select Labeled Images	⌘+Option+L	Ctrl+Alt+L
Select Unlabeled Images	⌘+Option+Shift+L	Ctrl+Alt+Shift+L
Invert Selection	⌘+Shift+I	Ctrl+Shift+I
Batch Rename	⌘+Shift+R	Ctrl+Shift+R
Ratings		
No Rating	⌘+0	Ctrl+0
★	⌘+1	Ctrl+1
★ ★	⌘+2	Ctrl+2
★ ★ ★	⌘+3	Ctrl+3
★ ★ ★ ★	⌘+4	Ctrl+4
★ ★ ★ ★ ★	⌘+5	Ctrl+5
Labels		
Red	⌘+6	Ctrl+6
Yellow	⌘+7	Ctrl+7
Green	⌘+8	Ctrl+8
Blue	⌘+9	Ctrl+9
Show Thumbnails with/without Labels	⌘+T	Ctrl+T
Refresh	F5	F5
General Controls		
Pause or Play	Spacebar	Spacebar
Increase Display Time by 1 Second	S	S
Decrease Display Time by 1 Second	Shift+S	Shift+S

Task	Mac Shortcut	Windows Shortcut
Play in Window or Play Full Screen	W	W
Captions Full, Compact, Page Number, or Off	C	C
Continuous Loop or Play Through Once	L	L
Fill Screen, Centered, Scale to Fit	D	D
Navigation		
Previous Page	←	←
Next Page	→	→
Editing		
Rotate 90° Counterclockwise	[	[
Rotate 90° Clockwise	]	]
Image Rating		
★	1	1
★ ★	2	2
★ ★ ★	3	3
★ ★ ★ ★	4	4
★ ★ ★ ★ ★	5	5
Decrease Rating	,	,
Increase Rating	.	.
Clear Rating	0	0
Toggle Rating On/Off	'	'
Image Labeling		
Red	6	6
Yellow	7	7
Green	8	8
Blue	9	9

Copyright © 2006 Wiley Publishing, Inc. All rights reserved.
Item 9577-6.
For more information about Wiley Publishing, call 1-800-762-2974.

For Dummies: Bestselling Book Series for Beginners

Digital SLR Photography with Photoshop® CS2

ALL-IN-ONE

FOR

DUMMIES®

Digital SLR Photography with Photoshop® CS2

ALL-IN-ONE

FOR DUMMIES®

by Kevin Ames

Wiley Publishing, Inc.

Digital SLR Photography with Photoshop® CS2 All-in-One For Dummies®

Published by
Wiley Publishing, Inc.
111 River Street
Hoboken, NJ 07030-5774
www.wiley.com

Copyright © 2006 by Kevin Ames

Published by Wiley Publishing, Inc., Indianapolis, Indiana

Published simultaneously in Canada

Library of Congress Control Number: 2005935143

ISBN-13: 978-0-7645-9577-6

ISBN-10: 0-7645-9577-6

Manufactured in the United States of America

10 9 8 7 6 5 4 3 2 1

1K/RW/RS/QV/IN

WILEY

About the Author

Kevin Ames grew up in the orchards of Emmett, Idaho, now a bedroom community of the state's capital, Boise. Both his parents were avid amateur photographers and their love of the hobby transferred and found him making money with his Kodak camera early in life. Kevin has worked as a radio announcer, television news videographer, and in the photographic industry in retail, as a technical representative, and as a district sales manager. He has had a commercial photography business since high school. He has become a recognized leader in the fast-evolving world of digital photography and post-production.

"I love light! I love to model it, fashion it, and sculpt it so my camera will capture the light's magic," Kevin says. "Beautiful light reflected by a beautiful subject captured with my camera is a perfect experience. Any day that I am making photographs is a perfect day!"

Kevin created his current business, Ames Photographic Illustration, Inc., in the early eighties to "serve corporate and advertising clients by crafting evocative photographs to communicate their ideas and to sell their products and services." Kevin describes himself as "a dreamer of pictures (thanks to Neil Young for the line!) who fashions images to make effective photographs for my clients."

Kevin's work has appeared in *The Wall Street Journal* and *Time Magazine,* as well as numerous other magazines, brochures, and catalogs for clients like Westin Hotels, AT&T, Carter's Atlanta, Spanx, and La-Z-Boy.

In addition to his full-time commercial studio, Kevin is much in demand as a speaker on matters digital. He has spoken at numerous national events for the Professional Photographers of America. He is a Photoshop World Dream Team instructor for the National Association of Photoshop Professionals and a presenter at Software Cinema events. He has presented classes at international conferences in Canada, Ireland, and Italy. Domestically, he has spoken at Photo Plus East, the NAB Post-Production Conference, the Mac Design Conference, and has just wrapped up an eight-city tour on pre-production and creative workflows for Blue Pixel. In his adopted home of Atlanta, Georgia, Kevin teaches lighting and digital classes at the Creative Circus and local camera clubs and is a frequent presenter on Pro Day at the Apple Store.

"Teaching is a way of giving back," Kevin explains. "Great Photoshop can only happen when you start with great photography. I love to help people learn this exciting new way of making photographs. I want people who see my programs to think digitally . . . I want to show them how digital photography offers a whole set of problem-solving tools that go way beyond the tips and tricks. I want people who learn from me to be able to apply these techniques creatively to get the images they imagine in their minds out for others to see and enjoy."

Kevin is also an accomplished writer. He writes the *Digital Photographer's Notebook for Photoshop User* magazine. His articles and reviews have appeared in *Studio Photography* and *Design, Photo > Electronic Imaging, Professional Photographer, Digital Output,* and other magazines. He authors the Software Cinema titles "Compositing a Digital Portrait" and "Preserving Pixels— Non-Destructive Editing in Photoshop."

His credentials include being a Certified Professional Photographer, Certified Electronic Imager, Photographic Craftsman, and an Approved Photographic Instructor. He has served as Co-Chairman of the Digital Imaging and Advanced Imaging Technology Committee and Chairman of the Commercial Advertising Group for the Professional Photographers of America. Kevin is a member of ASMP, NAPP, PIDA, and PPA.

He is the author of *Photoshop CS: The Art of Photographing Women* from John Wiley & Sons, which was named the number-five Digital Life book by Amazon.com for 2004. He is a coauthor of the *Photoshop World Dream Team Instructors Book* from Peachpit Press. *Digital SLR Photography with Photoshop CS2 All-In-One For Dummies* is his second full-length book.

Keep up with Kevin's activities on his web site: www.amesphoto.com.

Dedication

For David Chapman — friend, advisor, and inspiration.

Author's Acknowledgments

The acknowledgements are the most important and scariest writing an author ever undertakes and probably the least read. Don't leave the theatre before the credits roll. Please take a moment to know who the wonderful, generous, inspirational people are who have helped me in ways large and larger to write the book you hold in your hands.

Once again for support and understanding way above and beyond the call, I extend my heartfelt gratitude and love to Starr Moore. As with the previous book, I could not have written this one nor would I have wanted to without you.

To David Chapman, who manages Professional Photo Resources in Atlanta. He has helped me and countless others over the years make the transition to digital, which has changed our lives forever. He's the one who kept our early Macs running, selflessly and with lots of love.

Thanks and love again go to Jim DiVitale, who is my brother in digital photography and life if not by blood. And to his new wife, Helene Glassman: Welcome to the family.

Appreciation goes as well to my publisher, Barry Pruett, and my acquisitions editor, Tom Heine, both of whom continue to go to bat for the important things; to Tonya Cupp, my editor and guide through Dummiesworld, and to my technical editor (again!), the amazing Joan Sherwood.

To the models and friends who posed for me for the photographs in this book: Tucker Berta, Cheryl Blair, Tiffany Dupont, Adelina Guerrero, Tia Hinton, Rachel Keller, Amy Lucas, Christina Parfene, Elizabeth Shuttle, and Carrie Thomas.

Deep and continued gratitude to Eddie Tapp, who insisted I join him on his first steps into digital land those many years ago.

Gratitude in huge measure goes to my friend Scott Kelby, who asked me to write for *Photoshop User* and encouraged me to write books as well. His work, guidance, counsel, and humorous prodding have meant so much. He is a one-man inspiration.

To Dave Moser, Kathy Siler, Felix Nelson, Chris Main, Dave Cross, Matt Kloskowski, Larry Becker, Kleber Stephenson, Melinda Gottelli, Mary Laurenitis, and everyone at the National Association of Photoshop Professionals who make Photoshop World and *Photoshop User* magazine such great resources for us all; thanks for all you do.

To the amazing Barbara Thompson, my editor at *Photoshop User* magazine; huge kudos and thanks for helping with ideas, many of which are in this book.

Gratitude and thanks as well to the tremendously talented and generous people who have contributed so much to my learning about the ins and outs of digital photography and Photoshop: Ben Willmore, Jack Davis, Katrin Eismann (Photoshop diva extraordinaire), Bert Monroy, Vincent Versace, Peter Bauer, Rod Harlan, Richard Harrington, Joe Glyda, Julieanne Kost, Daniel Brown, Russell Preston Brown, Bruce Fraser, Jeff Schewe, Barbara Rice, Addy Roff, Kevin Gilbert, Reed Hoffman, Ken Reddy, Lachie O'Bey, Larry Rose, Ron Pierce, and all those who deserve my thanks whom I have inadvertently omitted.

For reading the rough drafts and making helpful comments and suggestions that have saved me from potential embarrassment, thanks to Cheryl Blair and Leann Campbell.

Thanks goes to Dave Metz, David Sparer, Barbara Ellison, Amy Kawadler, Alyssa Cohen, and Les Brown for arranging for some of the gear shown in the book and on the cover.

To Gary Burns, Than Clarke, Chris Lang, and David Burns of Software Cinema: The work I do with you makes this book so much better.

To the photographers who have left us recently, including my mother Janette Guthmann Ames, Dean Collins, Richard Avedon, Helmut Newton, and Eddie Adams.

Words fail when I think of how much Dean Collins has meant to the photographic industry, digital photography, and to me as well. I would not be writing this if not for Dean's teaching, encouragement, gentle spirit, and willingness to always change what works just fine. We all miss you Dean.

Last and without doubt most important, thank you for reading these words. As you enjoy this book, and if you find it is helpful to you in the enjoyment of digital photography, you have these people to thank as well as your humble author.

Publisher's Acknowledgments

We're proud of this book; please send us your comments through our online registration form located at www.dummies.com/register/.

Some of the people who helped bring this book to market include the following:

Acquisitions, Editorial, and Media Development

Project Editor: Tonya Maddox Cupp

Acquisitions Editor: Tom Heine

Technical Editor: Joan Sherwood

Editorial Manager: Robyn Siesky

Media Development Manager: Laura VanWinkle

Media Development Supervisor: Richard Graves

Editorial Assistant: Adrienne Porter

Cartoons: Rich Tennant (www.the5thwave.com)

Composition Services

Project Coordinator: Adrienne Martinez

Layout and Graphics: Lauren Goddard, Denny Hager, Joyce Haughey, Lynsey Osborn, Melanee Prendergast, Heather Ryan

Proofreaders: Leeann Harney, Jessica Kramer, Carl William Pierce, Evelyn Still

Indexer: Sherry Massey

Publishing and Editorial for Technology Publishing

    Richard Swadley, Vice President and Executive Group Publisher

    Barry Pruett, Vice President and Publisher, Visual/Web Graphics

    Andy Cummings, Vice President and Publisher

    Mary Bednarek, Executive Acquisitions Director

    Mary C. Corder, Editorial Director

Publishing for Consumer Dummies

    Diane Graves Steele, Vice President and Publisher

    Joyce Pepple, Acquisitions Director

Composition Services

    Gerry Fahey, Vice President of Production Services

    Debbie Stailey, Director of Composition Services

Contents at a Glance

Table of Contents

Introduction

*G*reat Photoshop goes hand in hand with great photography. You really can't have one without the other. The book you hold right now is designed to help you make great photographs with your new digital single lens reflex (DSLR) camera and edit them with the most versatile image-editing software on the planet . . . Adobe Photoshop CS2. So welcome. Welcome to *Digital SLR Photography with Photoshop CS2 All-In-One For Dummies*.

Photography has changed completely in the last five years. Everything is (or soon will be) digital. Kodak had stopped making black and white paper for traditional prints made in the darkroom. Manufacturers of film are scaling back production. Why? Because making photographs digitally is easy, instant, and inexpensive, and they can be much, much better than prints made traditionally from film.

You might ask why a digital photograph is better than one made on film. The answer is that your DSLR camera records the photograph on pixels *of the original scene*. Film fixes light on grain. A digital print is made with those original pixels. A print from film is made from grain. That's not to say that film is bad. To the contrary. Film delivers extraordinary results. And digital capture, done well, is better.

A decent black and white darkroom costs what a middle-of-the-line computer with Adobe Photoshop and a color printer cost. The darkroom requires dark, chemicals, and plumbing. The digital side runs on electricity — in the light no less — and delivers full color. Woohoo! If you have a laptop, you can take your darkroom on an airplane. Amazing.

About This Book

There have been lots of books written about Photoshop and how to use it. The buzz in photography for the last 10 years or so has been Photoshop. Digital cameras have progressed to the point where a good one with interchangeable lenses is affordable. So how do you understand photography? This book is a great place to start.

Comic genius Will Rogers once said, "Everybody is ignorant, only on different subjects." That's why you are holding this book. The subjects you are a genius in don't include photography or Photoshop. This book is a primer, a starting point, a jumping-off place, the first step of an amazing, long, strange (Thanks, Jerry Garcia!), and rewarding trip called photography. This might lead to you making better photographs that get posted on the refrigerator door, to a great hobby, or to a completely new career.

Foolish Assumptions

My greatest peeve when I read a book for beginners is that often an assumption exists in the author's mind that I know something about the subject. The problem is that I most likely don't know anything at all other than I want to know more and from a beginner's point of view.

This book is written with an assumption too. I assume you have this brand new *digital single lens reflex (DSLR)* camera that you have just bought and you wonder what to do next. My best advice is this: *Read the camera's instruction manual!* Then start reading this book. *Digital SLR Photography with Photoshop CS2 All-In-One For Dummies* is designed to get you started assuming you have never had an SLR camera, film or digital, in your hands before. I tell you about how photography works and when to refer to your camera's manual for details. When you work with this book, keep your camera manual handy.

DSLR cameras have more computing power in them than Apollo 11 did when it took Neil Armstrong, Buzz Aldrin, and Michael Collins to the moon and back. Today's cameras have a lot to them. I carry my instruction manual in my camera bag. You'll want to too.

I would love to tell you that you can jump around in this book and pick and choose what you want to learn. Okay, I will. You can do that. You will do much better (especially in Books III, IV, and V) to go through them in order, especially if you are new to working with Photoshop. If you have some experience with the software, do feel free to pick and choose. If you find you aren't able to "get" a project, start with earlier ones. I designed this book as a project-by-project, step-by-step tutor.

The books on Adobe Photoshop CS2 have conventions too. Just as each manufacturer has his very own idea of where controls on the camera ought to be and ought to work, so too do the makers of the two operating systems that Photoshop runs on. Photoshop CS2 runs on Macintosh OSX from Apple Computer, Inc., and on Windows XP and Windows 2000 from Microsoft. I have to assume you know how to use a mouse, create a new folder, drag and drop — in short, that you have basic computer skills.

Conventions

Books I and II cover photography. They use standard words like *f/stop, shutter speeds, ISO, aperture,* and the like. Each new word is italicized and explained . . . what it is, what it means, what it does, and how to use it creatively. Oh. And you also want to know that the stuff in these books works with (whisper) film. Anytime you type something in, it's boldfaced (unless the text around it is boldfaced; then the words you type are not boldfaced).

For all practical purposes Photoshop is identical in operation on both Macintosh and Windows operating systems. The big difference is in the cosmetic appearance of the screens displayed and a few (about four) keys on the keyboard. Keyboard conventions are simple. They appear in alphabetical order by operating system name or manufacturer (the first for the Apple Macintosh, followed by Microsoft Windows). The Windows combinations trail in parentheses. For instance, if you see "Press ⌘+Option (Ctrl+Alt)," and you use Windows, you press Ctrl and Alt at the same time. If you use a Macintosh, you press the ⌘ and Option keys at the same time.

The screen captures shown in *Digital SLR Photography with Photoshop CS2 All-In-One For Dummies* are made with Photoshop running on a Macintosh. The content of the screens and dialog boxes is identical on Windows. It will look different is all.

Sample files are available for download from www.amesphoto.com/learning. Each chapter that mentions files for projects, especially in the books on Photoshop, gives you specific instructions. A one-time registration and email verification process for files protects my copyrights. Your username is your valid email address. Please add learning@amesphoto.com to your address book so your authorization link doesn't wind up in your spam folder. The files you download are compressed in the cross-platform .zip format.

The goal of photography is to be able to make a print that is close to the scene you photographed. At a bare minimum you will want to get a monitor calibration system from either X-Rite or Gretag MacBeth. When you get to that point, check out Book V, Chapter 4 and Appendix A. This relatively inexpensive investment will eliminate lots of frustration throughout your digital work on computer.

How This Book Is Organized

Digital SLR Photography with Photoshop CS2 All-In-One For Dummies holds for your photographic and pixel-manipulating pleasure six mini books. They take you through your introduction to your new DSLR camera, through exposure, composition, lens choice, pixel pushing, and lots lots more. Do you want specific info on white balance? Book II, Chapter 3 covers for the camera, while Book III, Chapter 5 does it if you shoot RAW files, and Book IV, Chapter 2 shows you how if you shoot JPEG. Book III, Chapter 1 answers the question, "What are RAW and JPEG?"

Take a look at the mini books and the *CliffsNotes* version of what's inside each one. (This is, of course, a shameless plug for John Wiley & Sons, who publish both *CliffsNotes* and the *Dummies* books.)

Book I: The Digital Single Lens Reflex Camera: Photography is recording light. The DSLR camera's sole job is to record the light that you see through the viewfinder. Book I introduces you to the DSLR. It guides you through the controls that make the exposure just right. It helps you understand exposure and how to make good ones. This book also shows you how the world looks through the interchangeable lenses that are the DSLR camera's eyes on the world.

Book II: The Digital Photograph: Making outstanding photographs takes a lot more than clicking the shutter. Book II takes you inside photography. It shares what professionals do that sets their work apart. You see how to hold your DSLR camera and why using a tripod is so critical to great work. You read how to clean the camera's sensor, how data is stored in the camera, and the care and feeding of the storage media. You discover the color of light, how sensors see light, the importance of white balance, and composing a successful photograph.

Book III: The Digital Negative: Choosing the right digital format for your DSLR camera to record light is critical. This book explains the pros, the cons and, for that matter, what JPEG and RAW formats mean. You create bulletproof archives of your original digital negatives, catalog them to avoid the photos-in-the-shoebox-on-the-closet-shelf syndrome, and you share them with your family, friends, and the world using the Internet. This book is your introduction to Adobe Camera Raw version 3, only the finest RAW converter on the planet. You experience the power, contained in a RAW file, that your DSLR camera has captured and how to release it visually.

Book IV: Working with Photographs in Photoshop CS2: Adobe Photoshop CS2 is your color darkroom without the dark, the chemicals, the film, the (messy) processing, or even the water. This remarkable software is also your digital light box, where you sort, rename, rank, and label your images. You discover how to control color in Photoshop and refine your exposures there, too. You command color using Photoshop features that create color and allow you to apply it creatively wherever you want.

Book V: Preserving Pixels: This book guides you through nondestructive image editing in Photoshop. You discover how to retouch portraits, whiten teeth, brighten eyes, and smooth lines under and around the eyes. You do it in ways that always allow you to change your mind no matter when you change it. You also create stunning black and white from your color digital photographs. You create an easy way to preview conversions for your own black and white photographs. You have a peek into how to get the color on your screen to be the color on your print.

Part VI: Appendixes: These are the parts of a book that nobody reads and you are going to want to read them anyway. Here is where you find the essential keyboard shortcuts that make using Photoshop fast and efficient. You find links to the manufacturers and resources you read about in this book.

Icons, Sidebars, and Tips . . . Oh My!

There is always some good-to-know stuff that doesn't fit in the body of the material. *Digital SLR Photography with Photoshop CS2 All-In-One For Dummies* makes note of it with these special icons.

This is the good stuff! It is so cool that I want to make a special note of it. The tips are golden little gems that make your photographic and Photoshop experience really worth living.

Eyes up! There be dragons! Be careful! There aren't many of these and the ones you see are very important. Usually they are things that I have learned the hard way — by losing data and the like — that are unrecoverable and will cause you pain. This is where you can get burned. Please, please heed the warning before it's too late!

These gems in the text of this book are so golden that they shine brighter by repetition. In other words, when you see this icon you know it is something that I want you to know by heart. You'll be tested later.

This is the back story. Think of it as the last three *Star Wars* movies; you already knew that Luke's father would become Darth Vader and you went to see them anyway. This is some relevant history or information that can be really useful later in your hobby or career as a photographer. One day you'll run across some of this stuff and the light bulb will burn brightly in your mind. You'll say, "Oh yeah! That's familiar! I want to learn more."

And Wait . . . There's More!

Okay, dig in and get started with the greatest hobby ever. Who knows? This book might even lead you to a new career! As you work through the projects, remember that photography has a very rich history and there is no way you'll ever be able to learn everything about it. You will be able to explore it, poke it, prod it, dive into it, and know that when you wake up the next day there will still be something new to discover and learn. This keeps you young. Occasionally check in with me on www.amesphoto.com. A news section tells you about upcoming events. The training link has tips, techniques, and opportunities for you to further your photographic and Photoshop skills.

Good shooting!

Book I
The Digital Single Lens Reflex Camera

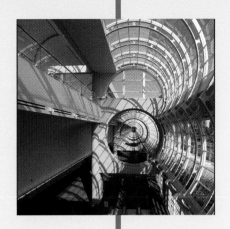

*P*hotography is recording light. That is exactly what the digital single lens reflex camera does. Its sole job is to record the light that you point it toward. The DSLR camera is an amazingly versatile tool. Book I introduces you to the DSLR. It guides you through the controls that make the exposure just right. It helps you understand what exposure is and how to make a good one. Interchangeable lenses are the DSLR camera's eyes on the world. This book shows you how the world looks through them.

Chapter 1: Taking a Shot at the Digital Single Lens Reflex Camera

In This Chapter

✏ **Defining the single lens reflex**

✏ **Pulling apart the parts of the DSLR**

✏ **Understanding sensor sizes**

This chapter introduces you to the *digital single lens reflex (DSLR)* camera. You get an overview of this incredibly versatile light-recording tool and the advantages you can only have with it. You explore the parts of the camera common to all. You read about how sensors work, their physical sizes, and their pixel dimensions. You also gain an understanding of resolution and megapixels and why they're so important. Lens magnification factors help you get even more out of your telephoto lenses. You discover why they're important and how they also affect wide-angle lenses. Welcome to the fascinating world of photography through the amazing eye of the digital single lens reflex camera.

The camera used for the illustrations may not be the model you own. Please refer to your camera's instruction manual for the exact location and operational details of the controls listed in this section.

Introducing the Digital Single Lens Reflex Camera

The digital single lens reflex has, at its heart, a what-you-see-is-what-you-get attitude. When you look through the viewfinder you're seeing right through the lens. So you see what the digital sensor sees when the shutter button is pressed. One big and often overlooked advantage is the impossibility of leaving the lens cap on a DSLR camera. The viewfinder is black when the lens cap is in place. It's very good to know whether the lens is covered or not when making photographs.

Figures 1-1 and 1-2 show typical DSLR cameras and highlight their main parts. The cameras in this case are the Canon Digital Rebel XT and the Canon 20D, shown in Figures 1-3 and 1-4, respectively. A camera made by another manufacturer will be slightly different. Don't worry, though. No matter which DSLR camera you use, all have these parts in common.

Figure 1-1: The back of the Canon Digital Rebel XT.

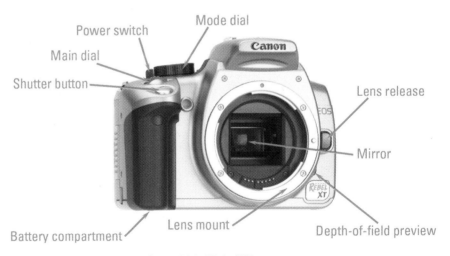

Figure 1-2: Front view of the Canon Digital Rebel XT.

Parts Are Parts

No matter which DSLR camera you have, all of them have these parts. Here are the ones that you use to make your camera dance to whatever your creativity lays down.

On the back and top

Here are the parts you find most often on the back and top of your DSLR:

- ✔ **Viewfinder.** The window on your camera's world. When you look through it you see what your photograph will be, as well as exposure information, autofocus zone in use, flash indicator, and exposure mode. Most DSLR viewfinders have corrective lenses built in so you can adjust them to use without eyeglasses. The rubber eyecup makes the window comfortable whether you're wearing glasses or not.

- ✔ **Dioptic adjustment dial.** Adjusts the focusing of the viewfinder so you can use the camera without glasses or contact lenses.

- ✔ **LCD panel.** A small external display panel shows camera information. It can be located on the back or top of the camera, usually on the right side. It tells you about the exposure, metering mode, number of images taken (or remaining), and other operational facts.

- ✔ **LCD monitor.** A larger full-color display panel that displays your photograph after it's been taken, menu options, and images you play back.

- ✔ **Selector switch.** A rocker switch, set of buttons, or command wheel controls menu selections, autofocus zones, and playback functions.

- ✔ **AE/AF lock.** A button that allows you to lock in an *a*utomatic *e*xposure or *a*utomatic *f*ocus setting.

- ✔ **Power switch.** Twist this one to get the party started.

- ✔ **Mode dial.** Choose the exposure method that suits your style. You can make your DSLR camera work fully automatically, in an aperture or shutter priority or as a thoroughly old-fashioned manual camera. Choice is good!

  DSLRs have many ways of setting exposure. One way is to control how long the sensor is exposed to light. That is the job of the shutter. Another way to set the exposure is by setting the amount of light that goes through the lens. That's what the aperture does. Metering is how the camera tells the shutter and aperture what to do. This can be done automatically or manually. You learn all about these in Book I, Chapter 2.

- ✔ **Main dial.** This one has many names and sometimes there's another dial. The main dial controls either the shutter or the aperture. If your DSLR camera has a second dial, you have one for the shutter and one for the aperture.

✔ **Shutter button.** Press halfway to do lots of things, including setting the focus and exposure. Give it a full press to make the photograph.

✔ **Hot shoe.** Your external electronic flash mounts here.

Figure 1-3: The front of a Canon 20D.

Figure 1-4: Rear view of the Canon 20D.

Up front

Turn your DSLR so the lens faces you. Here is what you will find. Remember that if you are using a camera not pictured here, check the manual that came with it.

- **Depth-of-field preview button.** This one stops the lens down to its working aperture. The smaller the aperture, the darker the scene you see through the viewfinder will be. And if you look very carefully, you can see what will be in focus and what won't.

- **Lens mount.** This flange holds the lens on the DSLR camera. It also sports electronic contacts that allow the lens to send data to the camera about focal length, maximum aperture, point of focus, and working aperture. The camera uses these contacts to tell the lens how to focus and what aperture to use. Don't touch them! The oils on your fingers might keep them from working properly.

- **Lens release.** Press this button to change lenses.

- **Mirror.** Inside the lens mount is a mirror. It reflects the light that comes through the lens into the viewfinder for you to see. When you press the shutter button, the mirror flips up out of the way for the time the shutter is open, sending light to the sensor. After the shutter closes it flips back down into position for viewing. When you press the shutter release to make a photograph, the viewfinder goes black because the mirror covers it up.

- **Port cover.** This handy rubber cover keeps dust out of connectors for video, remote controls, and data transfer cables. Sometimes the external power connector lives here.

- **External power connector.** DSLR cameras love electricity. When you're near an outlet, this port allows you to plug in and give your batteries the day off. This port does not recharge the batteries.

- **Card slot cover.** Behind this cover is where the storage media lives. Depending on your model of DSLR camera, you may use CompactFlash, Microdrive, Smart Media, or Memory Stick. Some DSLRs have slots for two different types of media. You read more about storage media in Book II, Chapter 1.

- **Battery compartment.** Power to the DSLR! Right on! Recharged batteries go here.

- **Function buttons.** All DSLR cameras have these. They control stuff in the menus. Read the manual that comes with your DSLR camera for the inside scoop.

- **Tripod socket.** This is always on the bottom of the camera. I love tripods. More on them and why I love them so much in Book II, Chapter 2.

It seems like these cameras have a huge number of parts. DSLR cameras share the same genetics of their film-using ancestors. Practically everything in digital photography has its roots in film. Periodically I mention the origins of some of the seemingly mind-numbing contradictions of photography itself.

Wondering if Sensor Size Matters

Does size matter? Some would say yes and some would say no and some would say it just depends. And they would all be right. There's a big debate about sensor and pixel size among professional photographers and digital camera manufacturers as well. The Holy Grail is one digital camera that does all of the jobs. The truth is you're lucky to find one that can do 80 percent of them.

Back story

Start with the classic recording medium, film. Film has lots of different formats or sizes. They're classified as large, medium, and 35mm formats. Large format is 4×5 inches and larger. Medium format is 2¼ inches in one direction. 35mm is $1 \times 1½$.

Figure 1-5 shows a comparison of 4×5-inch film and 35mm. The photograph of the Westin Peachtree Plaza hotel in downtown Atlanta was made with a 90mm lens on a 4×5-view camera. I have placed a 35mm film frame to show how much more area the larger format covers. Notice that the 35mm frame has the same size image within. The 90mm lens is wide angle on a 4×5 camera and telephoto on a 35mm camera.

A format's "normal" lens focal length is determined by measuring the diagonal of the film in millimeters. Normal for 4×5 is 150mm, for 2¼ × 2¼ is 80mm, and for 35mm is 50mm. Focal lengths greater than normal are considered *telephotos*. Focal lengths less than normal are called *wide angles*.

Format, grain, and resolution

As film format size increases, there's more grain to record the image, which results in higher resolution. The smaller the grain, the more detail the film is able to record. Fine-grain film offers a tradeoff. The smaller the grain, the more light the film must see to capture the photograph. Films that record images in low light have much larger grain structures and less resolution.

Grain is the clumps of light-sensitive silver halides that are processed to record the image on film. *Resolution* is film's ability to record detail.

Figure 1-5: Comparing 4 × 5-inch film and 35mm.

How digital sensors see

Film records light by fixing it to clumps of grain embedded in the emulsion coated on a plastic base. Digital sensors are made up of precisely aligned rows of pixels. Each pixel in a DSLR camera is equipped with a micro lens and a color filter of either red, green, or blue. The number of pixels in a sensor is its *resolution.* The ability of the sensor to gather light and record it with minimal noise determines its *sensitivity.*

Pixel is made up from the words *picture* and *elements.* A pixel is the smallest part of a digital image. *Noise* is the digital version of grain. As light levels drop, the sensor produces more noise at longer exposure, though in-camera noise reduction can be good. In a well-lit scene there's no visible noise in a photograph.

Adding Up Lens Magnification Factors

Sensor sizes smaller than 36 × 24mm have a *lens magnification factor.* This factor is a number multiplied times the focal length of a standard 35mm full frame lens; it tells you what the effective (equivalent) focal length the lens is for the size sensor in your DSLR camera. For example, a 200mm telephoto lens on a full frame DSLR is the equivalent of a 300mm lens on a smaller sensor with a lens magnification factor of 1.5X. So telephoto lenses become even more telephoto. It also means that wide-angle lenses become longer, too. A 20mm lens on a full frame camera becomes a 30mm lens on one with a 1.5X lens magnification factor.

Sizing up digital sensors

The sensors in DSLR cameras range in size from 8.8 × 6.6mm to a full frame 35mm (36 × 24mm). In between are 18 × 13.5mm, 23.7 × 15.5, 22.5 × 15.1, 23.7 × 15.7, and 28.7 × 18.5. Figure 1-6 shows the three most common sizes. The green frame is a 6 megapixel sensor. It has a lens magnification factor of 1.3X. The red frame is for an 8.2 megapixel sensor from a state-of-the-art Canon EOS 20D. In this case the physical size of the sensor is smaller, while the resolution in pixels is greater. The lens magnification factor for this sensor is 1.6X. A DSLR camera with a full frame sensor (36 × 24mm) is the least common DSLR camera because it's the most expensive.

Freeze those full frames

As a point of interest, as of this writing only Canon makes a full frame digital single lens reflex camera and they make two of them. Cameras equipped with full frame sensors are the only ones that match exactly to lenses made for film single lens reflexes. This doesn't mean that existing lenses won't work with DSLR cameras that sport smaller chips. It only means that they work differently.

Keeping the true focal length

It's important to understand that shooting with a 200mm lens on a full frame DSLR camera or one with a smaller sensor still give you the same size photograph for the area the sensor sees. This is one of those technical parts of photography that can make your eyes roll.

Look at Figure 1-7. It shows a photograph of a young male lion with a female looking on; the photograph was taken with a full frame DSLR camera and a 400mm lens. The boxes inside the frame show the areas for sensors with a 1.3X and 1.6X lens magnification factor. The smaller sensors record *exactly* the same area as in the full frame view, just less of it. The area around the smaller sensors is lost because the chip is smaller. See how the 1.6X magnification size effectively cuts the female out of the shot except for her nose? The effect is the same as cropping the full frame photograph down to the smaller sensor size. The image rendered by the lens does not show a closer view or more detail because of the lens magnification factor.

Figure 1-6: Sensor sizes: Full frame 1X, 1.3X (green), and 1.6X (red).

Figure 1-7: Areas captured by full frame, 1.3X, and 1.6X magnification factor chips through the same lens.

Chapter 2: Revealing Exposure Controls

This chapter begins your journey into what lies behind the *automatic* settings on your *digital single lens reflex (DSLR)* camera. The basics are very useful throughout a lifetime of photographic exploration — even if you decide to shoot some film for old-time's sake. Read how the sensitivity of the camera's sensor to light factors into exposure, what ISO numbers mean, and how ISO numbers form the basis for exposure. I explain what shutter speeds do, how they work, and creative ways to use them. Apertures are the irises of the camera. You'll find out where the term f/stop comes from as well as what importance it has in your photographic experience. This chapter also shows you how to think about what apertures do, creative ways to use them, and how they relate to shutter speeds and ISO in determining exposure. This is one of my favorite parts in all of photography. Get started!

Controlling Your Exposure

Holding your new DSLR camera for the first time can be a daunting task. Look at all of those buttons and knobs. And what about all of the readouts and menu screens? Intimidating? That's an understatement if ever there was an understatement! Don't worry. For all of the stuff that has been tacked on to your digital camera there are two and only two controls used to set the *exposure* (the amount of light it takes to record a photograph). That's right, two: the aperture and the shutter. Once you understand these two players in the game of exposure, you are well on your way to mastering your camera. Or anyone else's camera for that matter. Digital or film. Yep. All of this stuff works on a film camera too.

Here's a way to visualize how exposure works. Substitute water for light for the moment. Now imagine a one-gallon bucket. When it's filled with water, that's "proper exposure." The aperture in the lens is the diameter of the water pipe that fills the bucket. The camera's shutter is the valve that controls how long water flows into the bucket. So the aperture controls the amount of light and the shutter times how long that amount of light hits the sensor.

Say there is a pipe 1 inch in diameter. And it takes 60 seconds to fill a 1-gallon bucket. The full bucket of water represents "proper exposure." In this example the "exposure" would be 1 minute of water flowing through a 1-inch pipe to fill the bucket.

Now double the area of the pipe (the aperture on your DSLR) so twice as much water flows through it. The valve (shutter) would only have to be open for 30 seconds to fill the bucket. Remember "proper exposure" is a full 1-gallon bucket.

Double the area of the pipe once again so it moves four times more water than the 1-inch pipe. The valve (shutter) would be open for 15 seconds. The large pipe puts four times the volume of water into the bucket, so the valve is open only a quarter as long as it would be with the 1-inch pipe. Actual camera apertures are shown illustrating the times to fill the exposure bucket. See Figure 2-1.

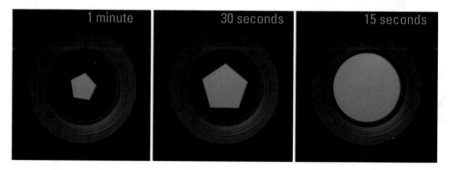

Figure 2-1: Camera apertures.

The only difference between your pipes and valve example of photographic exposure is that the names and numbers change; it's also much drier — unless you like making photographs in a downpour.

Getting to Know Your ISOs

ISO is the acronym for *International Organization for Standardization.* On older cameras the film sensitivity was measured in *ASA.* That stood for the *American Standards Association.* ISO is much more international than ASA. Both numbers represent the same values: the light sensitivity of film. As a rule, the sensor's lowest ISO rating is optimal for the amount of light to make a capture with the best dynamic range and least noise. Now sensors are described the same way using the same numbers. See Figure 2-2.

Capturing, shooting, snapping, clicking the shutter, or releasing the shutter all mean the same thing: *Taking the photograph with the camera!*

Dynamic range is the amount of light from the deepest shadow with detail to the brightest highlight with detail. *Noise* is the digital grain that appears most often in the shadow areas of an image. In a color image like the one in Figure 2-3, it looks like red, green, and blue specks.

Figure 2-2: ISO describes film's sensitivity to light.

Figure 2-3: A photograph full of noise caused by a high ISO setting.

ISO and Measuring Light

Inside the camera is a light meter that measures the amount of light the camera sees and reports back a suggested combination of shutter speed and aperture to record the photograph. The meter must know how sensitive the digital sensor is in order to report back how much light is required to capture the image. The ISO is the starting place for creating a photograph. The best part is it only has to be set once and that happens at the factory. That's right. *Digital* cameras know how sensitive they are right out of the box — one of many pluses the DSLR has over its film-shooting cousins.

The choice of film determines the ISO set on the camera's light meter. Sensor ISO is a subjective, though pretty accurate, approximation of the equivalent Film ISO. And unlike film, you can change the ISO on a DSLR anytime according to the light available.

As you work with your digital camera you will notice its whole range of ISO settings. The lowest number (usually 100 or so) delivers the best quality photograph overall. You may want to sacrifice some image quality for the ability to shoot in low light or freeze action. That's why some ISO settings on your camera are higher than the one for the best quality.

Figure 2-4 shows the ISO range from 100 to 1600 with third f/stops in between. As the ISO numbers decrease, so does the sensitivity. The advantage of a low ISO number is reduced noise.

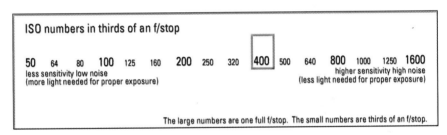

Figure 2-4: ISO from 100 to 1600.

Trading Off with ISO

As the ISO number setting is moved to higher values, the amount of dynamic range decreases and the noise becomes more noticeable. Compare the five photographs of the same scene in Figure 2-5. The first is made with the camera's base ISO of 100. The second is at ISO 200, then ISO 400, ISO 800, and the last at ISO 1600. The noise levels at ISO 1600 are considerably higher than at ISO 100 and very easy to see in this case. Some cameras work better than others in low light, high ISO situations. This changes — usually for the better — as newer models are introduced.

Figure 2-5: Compare the effect of ISOs ranging from 100 to 1600.

Have some fun with ISOs and see what they do.

1. **Set up the shot.**

    If you have a tripod, put your camera on it. This makes these exercises easier to complete. Do your best to frame the photographs the same way every time if you don't have a tripod yet. Compose and focus in the viewfinder a photograph outside of a building that has sunshine and shadows.

2. **Set the camera's mode setting on manual (M).**

    Refer to the instruction manual (like those in Figure 2-6) for details for your specific model. This assures that the exposure settings for the camera remain the same during this exercise.

3. **Set your DSLR camera's ISO to 400, as shown in Figure 2-7.**

    Figure 2-8 shows a typical range of ISOs for a digital camera. Yours may be slightly different from this example.

Figure 2-6: If you don't have this model camera, your instruction booklets will look different.

Figure 2-7: The ISO is 400.

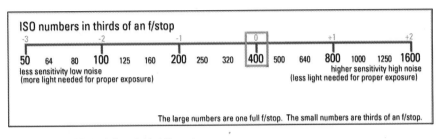

Figure 2-8: ISOs in full and third f/stop increments.

4. Press the shutter button half-way down to get a reading from the light meter and set the shutter speed and aperture at the proper exposure.

The readout looks similar to Figure 2-9. The exposure indicator is in the center of the scale. Leave the exposure where it is for the rest of this exercise. Now is when you change the ISO settings and shoot photographs.

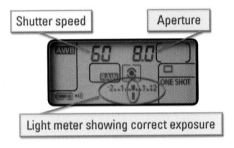

Figure 2-9: The indicator centered in the scale (circled in red) shows proper exposure.

5. Your ISO is 400. Take this exposure for the normal shot.

Now you make the darker, or *underexposed,* photographs.

6. Set the ISO on 200 and release the shutter.

7. Now set it on 100 and make another one.

Now make the overexposed images.

8. Set the ISO on 800 and take a shot.

9. Finally, set the ISO to 1600. Make the last photo.

Doubling the ISO setting (from 800 to 1600 for example) makes the camera twice as sensitive to light. The change means the sensor is now one f/stop more sensitive to light.

You have made a bracket of exposures, each separated by one f/stop. Two exposures are underexposed: ISO 200 (one f/stop underexposed) and ISO 100 (two f/stops underexposed), one exposure normal (ISO 400), and two more exposures overexposed by one, then two, f/stops (ISO 800 and ISO 1600). Figure 2-10 demonstrates the increased sensitivity to light of high-number ISOs.

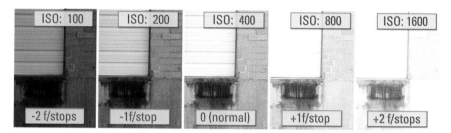

Figure 2-10: Exposure differences caused by changing ISOs on the DSLR.

The ISO 100 image has one quarter of the amount of light as the "normal" one shot at 400. It is two f/stops darker. The image made at 200 ISO is one f/stop darker and received half the amount of light the normal one did. The middle photograph is normal because it received exactly the exposure the meter in the camera called for at 400 ISO. The fourth photograph is twice as bright as the normal one and is one f/stop overexposed. The fifth image has four times the light of the normal one. It is two f/stops overexposed. The ISO 800 and ISO 1600 are much brighter.

Bracketing is making exposures brighter and darker than what the camera's meter says is the correct exposure. Film cameras bracket by changing the shutter speed or the aperture setting. Bracketing with ISOs is a very useful technique unique to digital photography. ISOs can be changed anytime during photography to increase or decrease the DSLR camera's light-gathering sensitivity. Do remember to compensate with the exposure settings to make certain they're right after changing your camera's ISO. Find more information on using ISOs and light meters in Book I, Chapter 3.

The Long and Short of Shutter Speeds

The *shutter* is the camera's valve in the filling-the-bucket example at the beginning of this chapter. Its job is to precisely control how long light strikes the sensor. Usually (not always) the shutter works in fractions of a second. Some digital cameras have shutters that open and close in 1/8000 of a second — very speedy indeed.

A long time ago, in the era just preceding Disco (see, I told you it was a long time ago), shutters were mechanically controlled. They had gears and escapements and cams to make sure they stayed open exactly long enough. They were calibrated so that each speed was either twice as fast or half as fast as the one above or below it, respectively. This meant that the speed above 1/125 of a second was always 1/250 of a second. And the one below 1/125 was always 1/60. (Yes I know. It should be 1/62.5 of a second. That was too hard to say and took up too much room on the dial.) Each increment either increased or decreased the exposure by one f/stop.

Today's shutters are electronically timed and are much more accurate and long lasting than their mechanical counterparts of yestercentury. And they have a whole range of speeds *in between* the twice-as-fast or half-as-slow settings.

Shuttering in Creativity

Fast shutter speeds stop action. Slow ones allow time to flow into the sensor. Slow speeds are also used for shooting in low light or recording bursts of fireworks or creatively interpreting illuminated glass or thousands of colored lights during the holidays. The shutter is a creative tool as well. The speed you choose for it makes flowing water a cloud, or freezes it into an apparent ice sculpture. Figure 2-11 is an example.

Figure 2-11: A high shutter speed has frozen the water shooting from a fountain.

The photograph in Figure 2-12 of an installation by glass artist Dale Chihuly in Atlanta's Botanical Garden was made with a very slow shutter speed. The bubbling water becomes a lacy cloud amidst the standing red glass cylinders.

The shutter is the camera's time machine. It can freeze a young Masaai warrior's hair in mid-leap as he performs the traditional Ipid jumping dance. Long exposures and intentional camera movement make holiday lights become a multicolored abstract. Figure 2-13 and 2-14 are just such shots.

A shutter speed *always* has its corresponding aperture setting that maintains proper exposure. Extreme ranges of shutter speed can mean extreme measures with lighting or filters on the lens to keep everything in balance.

Figure 2-12: The long two-second exposure makes the fountain flowing mist.

Figure 2-13: A dancer frozen off the ground by a high shutter speed.

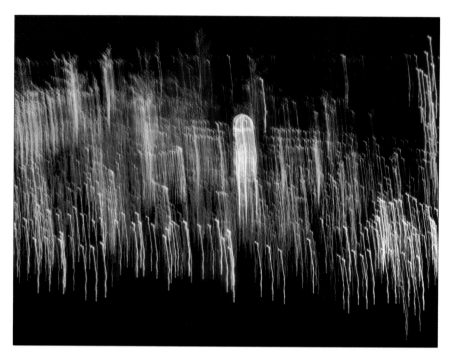

Figure 2-14: This was made with a one-second shutter speed and moving the camera while the exposure was being made.

Figure 2-15 is a listing of the common shutter speeds from slow to fast. These are found on most DSLR cameras. The chart starts at 30 full seconds down to $\frac{1}{8000}$ of a second. As the shutter speeds get faster, each speed is twice as fast as the one before it. Each one lets in half the amount of light as the one before it. The amount of light controlled by each of these shutter speed settings (double or half) is referred to as a *one stop change*. Again, you know that half of 15 is not 8 and that half of $\frac{1}{60}$ is not $\frac{1}{125}$. That's the way shutter speeds were standardized when they were mechanical.

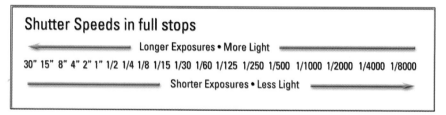

Figure 2-15: This chart shows a typical range of shutter speed in full stops. DSLR cameras (depending on model) also have half-stop or third-stop speeds in between.

While the slower shutter speeds let in more light, they make the result much more susceptible to moving the camera. Your heartbeat, your breathing, and the general swaying back and forth that your body does affect a handheld camera. It moves and the result is a soft or blurry photograph. At slow speeds, use a tripod or at least lean on a wall or brace against a tree. Walls and big trees are much steadier than people.

Exercising the Shutter's Genius

Stopping rushing water or making water into a flowing cloud is all controlled by the DSLR's shutter. Here's how to do it yourself:

1. **This afternoon, just before dusk, take your DSLR and tripod (this one really works better with a tripod, believe me) to a flowing water fountain or waterfall.**

   Compose a photograph with lots of water rushing by.

2. **Set the ISO to 100 and the mode to Shutter Priority.**

3. **As soon as the sun dips below the horizon, take a light reading.**

   It should be somewhere around $\frac{1}{60}$ of a second at f/8.

   Light can vary greatly. Trust your DSLR's light meter, not the numbers I mention here. This is about you getting the concept of what fast and slow shutter speeds do to moving subjects.

4. **Shoot a photograph with the highest shutter speed you can without getting an underexposure or low-light warning.**

   As it gets later your exposures will get longer. Set your aperture on its largest setting.

5. **Slow the shutter speed one whole f/stop and press the shutter release.**

   Your camera may read $\frac{1}{15}$ of a second at f/2.8. If the reading was $\frac{1}{15}$ second at f/2.8, it now reads $\frac{1}{8}$ second at f/4. As the shutter slows by an f/stop, the aperture automatically closes down one f/stop to maintain proper exposure.

6. **The third exposure is with the shutter speed at $\frac{1}{4}$. The aperture in this example is f/5.6**

7. **The fourth exposure is at $\frac{1}{2}$ second and the aperture is f/8.**

8. **Turn the shutter to 1 second and make the fifth and final photograph of the series: f/11.**

   When you get to 1 full second as your shutter speed, your viewfinder may give you an overexposure warning because the lens you're using only goes to f/16.

9. **Open the photographs in Adobe Bridge or your camera's viewing software.**

   You get into Photoshop soon enough. Right now look at the photographs in Adobe Bridge, which comes with Adobe Photoshop CS2. All of the photographs are very uniform because Bridge uses the automatic settings that optimize RAW files and their previews for exposure, shadow, brightness, and contrast. You can see the uniformity in Figure 2-16.

   The automatic exposure enhancement in Adobe Bridge only works on photographs recorded in the RAW format. For more on the RAW format, see Book III, Chapter 4.

10. **Notice that the water from the fountain is almost frozen in the photograph at ¹⁄₁₅ of a second. Figure 2-17 reveals this.**

11. **As the series progresses, see how the water (in Figure 2-18) becomes more and more dreamlike.**

   When the shutter speed finally reaches one full second, the water is more of a heavy cloud pouring into the fountain.

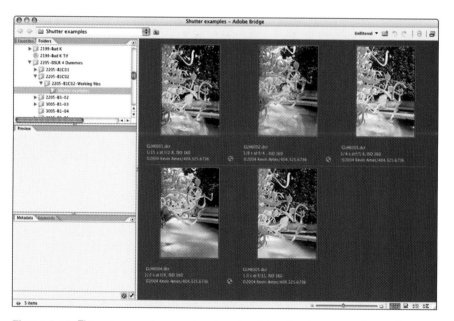

Figure 2-16: The water goes from moving drops to mist as the shutter speed gets slower.

Figure 2-17: Shutter speed of ⅟₁₅ shows some movement of the water.

Figure 2-18: The 1-second shutter speed makes the falling water into falling mist.

Closing the shutters

The electronic shutters in DSLR cameras are very accurate. They can do speeds unheard of in their mechanical forbears. Some are calibrated in half stops, others in thirds of an f/stop. Don't let the strange numbers confuse you!

Opening Apertures

The *aperture* is another name for the iris that lives in the lens. And like the pupil in your eye, it controls the amount of light that reaches the sensor by increasing or decreasing its diameter. *f/stop* is another name for the aperture. It's also called the *diaphragm*. The aperture itself is made of several curved blades that can form circles of varying diameters. You see this effect in the opening of every 007 James Bond movie.

The full f/stops from f/2.8 to f/16 are shown on the top line in Figure 2-19. The bottom line displays the less familiar one-third of an f/stop and two-thirds of an f/stop that are becoming known due to the accuracy of DSLR cameras. Notice that the smaller the number (f/2.8, for example), the larger the aperture. And as the numbers increase to f/16, the smaller the opening becomes. The lens on your DSLR may have different aperture ranges.

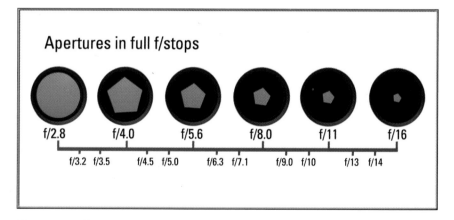

Figure 2-19: Apertures in full and third stops.

Aperture sizes and positions in a lens depend on the lens itself. Some aperture mechanisms are behind the lens. In modern lenses the placement is determined by the lens' job. The physical size of an aperture f/8.0 in a 20mm wide-angle lens is much smaller than the size of an f/8.0 aperture on a 300mm telephoto. Yet they both let the same amount of light reach the imaging sensor.

Holding Your Focus — or Not

You've seen the dreamy portrait where the subject is sharp and surrounded by blurred, pastel, dappled highlights. Ever wonder, "How did they *do* that?" The answer lies in the aperture setting and a term called depth of field. *Depth of field (DOF)* is a property of a lens' aperture setting, which controls the size of the circle of confusion of the light hitting the imaging sensor or film. The smaller the *circle of confusion,* the more depth the focus has. *Circle of confusion* is made of scattered or unfocused light rays. The smaller the circle of confusion, the sharper the image appears. Small apertures (toward f/16) produce smaller circles of confusion than do large ones. Figure 2-20 breaks this down.

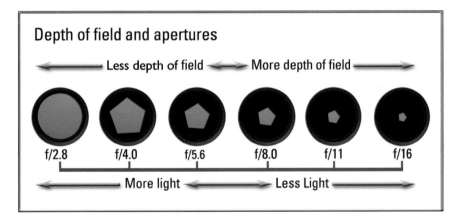

Figure 2-20: This chart shows the relationship of depth of field to different aperture settings.

The smaller the opening letting light through the lens, the more in focus in front of and behind the actual point of focus. The rule for most situations is that one third of the depth of field is in front of the point of focus and two thirds falls behind it. Look at the street scene on the left in Figure 2-21.

At f/2.8 on a 200mm lens, the Stop sign and the pedestrian signs are points of focus. And they are sharp. The sign naming the restaurant in the background is soft. At f/2.8 the depth of field is said to be *shallow.* Compare it to the image shot at f/22 on the right. All of the signs, including the restaurant's name, are sharp. You can even see details reflected in the window. This characteristic of lenses varies with the focal length and the size of the image sensor. I explore that in greater detail in Book I, Chapter 4.

Figure 2-21: Compare the objects in focus in these two photographs. This illustrates depth of field at maximum (f/2.8) and minimum (f/22) apertures.

Using small apertures for greater depth of field has a tradeoff: You have to let in a lot more light. Each f/stop between f/2.8 and f/16 cuts the light in half. In this example, five stops *less* light reaches the sensor. If the shutter speed started at ⅟₁₂₅ of a second, it would now have to be at ⅛, allowing light to hit the sensor for a much longer period of time. This is too slow to hand-hold. Also, the subject has to hold still as well. Photography is a balancing act between creativity and the physics of exposure.

In the preceding example, determining the number of f/stops between f/2.8 and f/16 might include counting the numbers and getting five stops. Count the *spaces* between the f/stops on the chart in Figure 2-20 and you get the right number of stops. The first stop is between f/2.8 and f/4.0. The second is between f/4.0 and f/5.6. The third is between f/5.6 and f/8.0, the fourth is between f/8.0 and f/11, and the fifth is between f/11 and f/16.

TECHNICAL STUFF

The-more-than-likely-way-more-than-you-really-want-to-know-department

The widest f/stop or aperture is the ratio of the focal length of the lens to the diameter of its front element. So a 50mm lens with a maximum aperture of f/2.0 would have a *front element* (that's the piece of glass you see in the front of the lens) 25mm in diameter. The lens designation would be 50mm 1:2. Logic would say that measuring the aperture diameter and expressing it as a ratio would determine the f/stop. Logic (as with most everything in photographic thinking) would be wrong.

What's important is the area of the aperture at a given f/stop. Using the formula for the area of a circle — Πr^2 (yes I *know pies* are round) — it works out this way: Π is 3.14159. The radius of the maximum aperture is 12.5mm (half of 25mm, the diameter of the front element). So the formula is 3.14159×12.5^2 or 156.25; that equals 490.87 square millimeters. The area of the aperture at f/2.0 is about 491 square millimeters. Step down one stop to f/2.8. Work the math again. 50mm divided by 2.8 (this is a ratio 50 ÷ 2.8) gives an aperture diameter of 17.85mm. Half of 17.85 is 8.9. (Radius is half of the diameter.) 8.9^2 is 79.21 $\times 3.14159$ (Π) = 248.85 square millimeters. So the area of the aperture at f/2.0 is 490mm² and the area at f/2.8 is *half* that of f/2.0 at 249 mm². f/stops are really all about the *area* of the opening, not the diameter. Figure 3-20 is a chart of f/stops and their approximate areas for a 50mm f/2.0 lens. (The numbers are rounded for simplicity's sake for goodness' sake.)

As the aperture dial is turned to the next smallest f/stop (largest number), the area of the aperture decreases by one half. Go from f/11 (16mm² aperture area) to f/16. The aperture area is now 8mm², or half of that of f/11. Moving from f/11 to f/8 doubles (almost) the area to 31mm². This lets in twice the amount of light as f/11 with only 16mm² of open area.

See, I *told* you it was probably way more than you wanted to know. The point to all of these numbers is to help you understand that there actually is a method behind the seeming illogic of the workings of things photographic. When you get the feeling that apertures are exactly the opposite of what you think they ought to be, it's all right. All photographers feel that way about this stuff most of the time.

f/stop	aperture area in mm²
f/2.0	490
f/2.8	249
f/4.0	123
f/5.6	63
f/8.0	31
f/11	16
f/16	8
f/22	4

Focusing in on Depth of Field

Grab your DSLR and shoot an example of how DOF works:

1. **Mount the camera on a tripod.**

2. **Put on a telephoto lens or zoom to about 100mm to 200mm.**

   Again, I recommend a tripod.

3. **Set the camera's mode to Aperture Priority.**

   This allows you to set the f/stop and have the camera choose the appropriate shutter speed for proper exposure.

4. **Choose the minimum (smallest) aperture with the aperture control on your camera.**

   This control's location on your camera varies according to the make and model.

5. **Set the ISO on the lowest available on your camera.**

   The minimum aperture is the *largest* number. On a zoom lens it is somewhere around f/16 to f/22.

6. **Focus the lens on some flowers about 6 feet away.**

   As you look through the viewfinder, the subject is sharp. The background is out of focus.

7. **Press the DOF preview button to see what effect the small aperture has.**

   The DOF preview button stops the lens down to the aperture that's used when you take the photograph. The viewfinder gets very dark. Look through the darkness and note that the background is much sharper than it is when the lens is wide open for normal viewing.

8. **Make the photograph by pressing the shutter release.**

   Look at the LCD screen on the back of the camera. The subject is sharp and the background is sharp. It looks just like it did through the viewfinder.

9. **Stop down to the maximum aperture by moving the aperture control to the smallest number (usually f/3.5 or f/4, depending on the lens).**

   Don't change the point of focus. Notice that the shutter speed speeds way, way up.

10. **Press the DOF preview button.**

    Nothing happens because the lens is already set to its widest aperture.

11. Make the photographs.

Now the scene through the viewfinder looks exactly the same as the image on the LCD shows. The background is very soft.

In Figure 2-22, compare these photographs of flowers against a background of green shrubbery. At f/22 the flowers are in focus and the background is soft (yet not so soft you don't know what it is). When the same scene is photographed at f/2.8, only a small section of the flower is sharp. The background is a complete pastel blur.

The proper exposure for the photograph with the shallow depth of field where only a few flowers are sharp is f/2.8 at $\frac{1}{250}$ of a second. The proper exposure where all of the flowers are sharp and the background is recognizable is f/22 at $\frac{1}{8}$ of a second. Both let exactly the same amount of light reach the camera's imaging chip. The setting reflects the photographer's interpretation of the subject.

Figure 2-22: The shallow depth of field in the photograph made at f/2.8 isolates the subject. The eye naturally goes to the sharp areas of the image.

Depth of field is a very useful tool for isolating a subject from the background. Creatively, this technique is great for making viewers look exactly at what you want them to see.

In this chapter you have read how ISO ratings are important to establishing base exposure for a DSLR camera. You have an overview of how exposure works and its relationship to the shutter and aperture. You have been introduced to the two controls that determine exposure — the shutter and the aperture. You know how each works and relates to the settings of the other. Whew. You *have* taken in a *lot!*

Chapter 3: Understanding Exposure's Overs, Unders, and Right-Ons

In This Chapter

- Understanding your DSLR camera's light meter
- Measuring reflected light
- Applying light readings for better photographs

This chapter helps you get a basic knowledge of how light is measured inside your *digital single lens reflex (DSLR)* camera. It explains how the light metering system works and gives you information you want to make better exposures. In addition, exercises you can do for yourself help you see how what the meter tells you translates in a digital photograph.

Knowing Your DSLR's Light Meter's Limitations

Every DSLR camera has to answer these questions before taking a photograph: How much light is in the scene and is there enough of it to make this a well-exposed photograph? And that is also a question you want to always ask yourself, too. A lot of number crunching goes on inside your DSLR camera when the mode is set on one of the automatic settings. The computer inside a modern DSLR is many times more powerful than the one that took men to the moon a few decades ago. It reads the light, measures the brightness values, and then makes an educated guess at the proper settings — and a lot of the time does a pretty good job of it. See Figure 3-1.

Having the basic concepts of what's going on in that powerful chip can only improve your results. Usually the problem with a photograph that "didn't turn out" lies with the camera not understanding what the photographer wants. That is the downfall of "automatic." This smart program can't read your mind. DSLR cameras are tools to record light. Your job as a photographer is to interpret what you see and then *tell* the camera what to do. This is always better than "auto" and will be until they come up with a mode labeled "C" for creative. And then cameras won't need photographers, will they?

Figure 3-1: The DSLR in action.

Thinking Like Your Light Meter

Think gray. Think only one tone of gray. Think that everything you look at is translated into a single tone called *middle gray.* Now you're thinking like your light meter. What happens when you aim your DSLR camera at a subject? Your light meter takes it all in and returns settings for the shutter and aperture of your camera that give a middle gray value when you make the photograph.

Telling Horse Tales of Black, White, and Gray

Consider this tale of three horses — a black stallion, a white mare, and a rather plain-looking horse whose coat was the color of old, gray asphalt. You are their stable boy (or girl) and you really love these three horses, each being wonderful in its own way. One day you decide you want to make a photograph of them. You have your brand-new DSLR, so you walk up to the black stallion, fill the frame with the sleek coat of his side, and take a careful light reading. You step back and make the photograph. On the monitor of your DSLR the black stallion is gray; the white mare is so white all you see are her nostrils and eyes. The gray horse is white.

You think your camera is broken. You decide to make another photograph. You walk up to the white mare again, filling the viewfinder with her coat and making another careful light reading. You once again move back and frame the three horses. You slowly press the shutter release and take the photograph. This time when you consult the LCD monitor on the back of your camera, the black stallion is completely black, with only his teeth showing! The white mare is middle gray and the asphalt horse is black! Now you are very concerned that your camera is not working at all well. You give the project one last effort. You walk up to the asphalt-colored horse, fill the viewfinder with his medium-gray coat, and make a light reading. You compose the photograph of all three and press the shutter. Hesitantly, almost fearing the result, you look at your camera's monitor. To your delight, the three horses are as you always see them off camera. The black stallion, the white mare, and your plain old asphalt-gray horse are each perfect in the photograph. And you know your new DSLR camera works just fine!

Light meters are consistent. No matter where you point one, the resulting reading turns out an exposure that produces a middle gray tone when you convert it to black and white. So that's the answer to the problem you experienced as a stable girl (or boy). When the meter read the light reflected from the black stallion, it gave a reading to make it middle gray. The reading was about two full f/stops brighter than the proper exposure. When aimed at the white mare the meter once again wanted the mare to be gray so the reading was almost two stops darker. With the meter pointed at the asphalt-gray horse all was well with the world because old, worn asphalt is almost a perfect middle gray.

Shades of gray in a colorful world

The world of color has a lot of middle gray. Worn asphalt is middle gray; so is green grass. The palm of a human hand is between a stop and a stop and a half brighter than middle gray. Once you know that light meters return a middle gray value for whatever they see, you can use that creatively.

Middle gray is a tone that reflects 18 percent of the light, hitting it back to the viewer. There's some controversy that the tone is really 12 percent. And it doesn't really matter. Light meters are calibrated to return a reading that reproduces middle gray. See Figure 3-2.

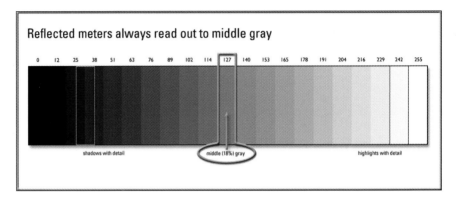

Figure 3-2: This grayscale shows steps between black and white. Middle gray is outlined in red.

Light meters come in two flavors: reflective and incident. The meter in your DSLR camera is a *reflective meter*. It measures light that's already hit the subject and is on its way to the sensor. *Incident meters* measure the amount of light falling on the subject. You read more about incident meters in Book II.

Metering practice

Now that you have the theory about metering with the reflective meter in your DSLR camera, put it into practice. Here's how: Do some scouting on a bright sunny day between 10 in the morning and 2 in the afternoon. Find a white car, SUV, or van in a parking lot whose surface hasn't been freshly refinished. Make sure the sun is behind you so that the vehicle is lit by the sun. Your readings may not be the same as those you see here. That's all right. Work with your DSLR camera's readings.

Step one: The first exposure

Take the first exposure of the black stallion. See Figure 3-3.

1. **Set your DSLR camera's mode to Manual.**

2. **Set the ISO (sensor's light sensitivity) to the lowest setting your camera offers.**

   See Book I, Chapter 2 for more ISO information.

3. **Walk up to the car and fill the frame halfway with the tread and halfway with the black sidewall of the tire.**

4. **Move the aperture dial to f/8.0, and adjust the shutter speed until the indicator in the viewfinder indicates proper exposure.**

5. **Back up and frame the photograph so it looks like Figure 3-3.**

Figure 3-3: One-and-a-half f/stops overexposed. The meter makes the black tire gray. Everything else is way too bright.

Step two: The second exposure

Now for the white mare. See Figure 3-4.

1. Walk up to the vehicle. Fill the frame with the white side.

The White Mare

Figure 3-4: One-and-a-half f/stops underexposed. The meter makes the shutter much too fast to bring the white down to gray. Everything else is now too dark.

Again, make sure that you only see white in the viewfinder.

2. **Adjust the shutter speed to make the readout in your viewfinder indicate the proper exposure.**

3. **Back up and frame the photograph as close as you can to the first exposure.**

You're going to continue through the next section from here. Stay put!

Step three: The third exposure

And finally, the old asphalt-colored horse. See Figure 3-5.

1. **Without moving, aim the camera at the pavement, making sure that you see only pavement in the viewfinder.**

This won't work if you see your shadow in the viewfinder. Turn either to the left or right if you see your shadow.

2. **Take a light reading and adjust the shutter speed until a proper exposure is indicated.**

3. **Reframe the photograph and make the exposure.**

Figure 3-5: Everything is just right! The tire is black, the van is white, and the asphalt is good old middle gray.

Reviewing the results

Now copy the files to your hard drive and review your results in Adobe Bridge.

1. **Take your storage media card back to your computer and plug it in to the card reader attached to your computer.**

   If you don't have a card reader, follow the instructions that came with your DSLR camera to plug it into your computer using the cable packaged with your camera.

2. **Copy the files to a folder on your hard drive.**

   The next series of steps introduces and shows you how to set up Adobe Bridge to read RAW files.

   Data on removable storage media used in DSLR cameras is easily corrupted. It's never a good idea to work directly off of the card. Copy the data to your hard drive and work from those files. Additionally, the process runs faster off a hard drive as opposed to a card in a reader or one in the camera tethered to the computer.

3. **Click the Bridge icon in Photoshop's options bar, which is shown in Figure 3-6.**

   This launches Adobe Bridge, the file-browsing application included and installed with Photoshop CS2.

Figure 3-6: Click the icon circled in red to launch Bridge or switch to it when it is already running.

4. **In the folders section, navigate to the storage media used by your DSLR camera.**

5. **Click the disclosure triangle and then spin down the one on the folder name DCIM.**

6. **Click the folder inside.**

   You see thumbnails of your photographs appear in the light box panel in Bridge; see Figure 3-7.

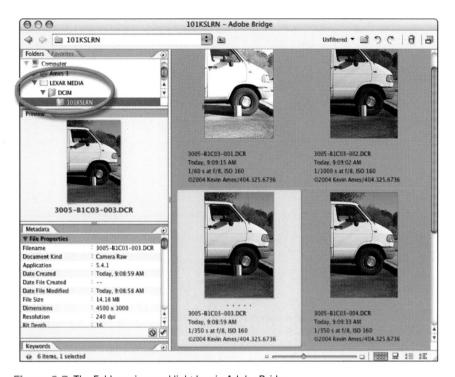

Figure 3-7: The Folders view and light box in Adobe Bridge.

If you are shooting in the JPEG format, skip over the next section. If you are shooting the RAW format, congratulations. (More on why later, in Book III.) Adobe Bridge automatically uses Adobe Camera Raw 3 (ACR3) to build previews and displays them in the light box panel in Bridge.

7. **⌘+click (Ctrl+click) each of the three photographs that were made in the beginning of this exercise.**

   The three RAW files are highlighted in the light box panel of Bridge.

8. **⌘+R (Ctrl+R) to open the Adobe Camera Raw dialog shown in Figure 3-8.**

   The first selected photograph appears at the top of the filmstrip view and in the large preview pane. The other two photos appear as thumbnails below the first in the filmstrip.

When an instruction says, "⌘+R (Ctrl+R)," the R is not capitalized when you type. It is capitalized in the instruction to make it easier to read.

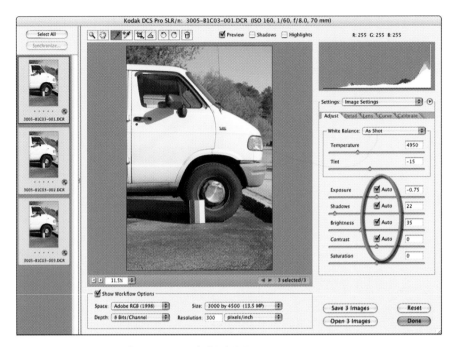

Figure 3-8: The Adobe Camera Raw 3 (ACR3) dialog.

Turning Off ACR3 Auto Adjustments

Continue going through the steps from the previous section.

1. **Look at the right side of the dialog.**

   Four checkboxes labeled Auto appear for exposure, shadows, brightness, and contrast. See Figure 3-8. The Auto settings (circled in red) are
   on by default. And all of the photographs look the same. Auto settings
   can be very useful for quickly reviewing photographs without having
   to apply Adobe Camera Raw settings to every shot as you've had to do
   in previous versions. The Auto settings are not useful for the exposure
   exercise because they do their very best to calculate a good exposure in
   spite of intentions otherwise. This is the Camera Raw equivalent of the
   Program mode setting on DSLR cameras.

2. **Click the checked Use Auto Adjustments in the drop-down menu to
   turn it off, as shown in Figure 3-9.**

3. **Click the flyout menu again and choose Save New Camera Raw
   Defaults, illustrated in Figure 3-10.**

Figure 3-9: Turning off the Auto adjustments.

Figure 3-10: Saving new Camera Raw defaults to keep the Auto settings turned off.

This makes the turned-off Auto settings the default. The Auto settings can be toggled on with the keyboard shortcut ⌘+U (Ctrl+U) while the ACR3 dialog is open.

4. **Click the Select All button at the top of the filmstrip column on the far left of the ACR3 dialog.**

   The Select All button is circled in red in Figure 3-11. These next steps apply the Auto off settings to the remaining files.

5. **Click the Synchronize button underneath it.**

6. **Click OK when the Synchronize dialog (shown in Figure 3-12) appears.**

7. **Click Done in the lower-right corner of the ACR3 dialog to close it, then continue to the next section.**

Figure 3-11: Applying the Auto off setting to the rest of the files in ACR3.

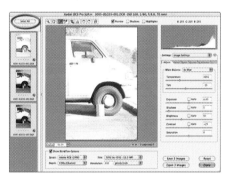

Figure 3-12: ACR3's Synchronize dialog.

Setting the Preferences in Bridge

Set these preferences to display exposure information.

1. **Type ⌘+K (Ctrl+K) to open the Preferences for Bridge, as you see in Figure 3-13.**

   Instead of the shortcut, you can choose Preferences from the Bridge menu on the Mac (Edit Preferences in Windows).

2. **Click the second drop-down menu under the Additional Lines of Thumbnail Metadata section.**

3. **Select Exposure.**

   A check appears in the Show checkbox like you see in Figure 3-13.

4. **Click OK.**

   The exposure information appears under the name of the file when you view it on the light table in Bridge.

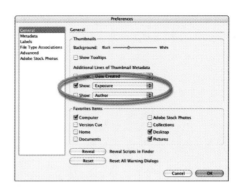

Figure 3-13: The general Preferences screen in Adobe Bridge.

Seeing what the meter sees

Now that you have set up Bridge and ACR3 to provide accurate uninfluenced feedback, look at your work. The first photograph in the series is overexposed as predicted in the "Horse Tales" story. Metering off the black tire causes more light to be called for to make it light enough to be middle gray. Everything else is brighter too. The second photo is underexposed. The reading was made of the white fender so the light meter told you to reduce the amount of light to make the white gray. Everything else is dark. The third photograph was metered by pointing the camera at the asphalt in front of the van. Sure enough, the right amount of light was set to produce middle gray and everything is as it should be: The van is white, the tires are black, and the pavement is gray. The three photographs are two-and-a-half stops underexposed, one-and-a-half stops overexposed, and properly exposed, respectively, as you see compared in Figure 3-14.

Figure 3-14: Your version of Horse Tales will look similar to this.

Putting it together

The light meter in your DSLR camera is very literal in its interpretation of scenes. Understanding how it sees and reacts helps when you are creating your prize-winning photographs. Figure 3-15 has an example of a photograph that benefited from an exposure that differs from what the light meter said.

Figure 3-15: Lucky Peak Reservoir outside Boise, Idaho.

Everyone *knows* that snow is white. Yet when you look at it you *see* detail. Your brain looks at bright objects and tells the irises in your eyes to close a little bit so you can see any detail there. This photograph of snow on a frozen reservoir is slightly underexposed to bring out the detail in the snow. This makes the photograph more interesting. The lower exposure reveals detail that otherwise you would miss, like the footprints where someone or something walked across the frozen lake, as you see in the enlargement shown in Figure 3-16.

Figure 3-16: An enlargement of the snow field reveals footprints where people have crossed the frozen reservoir.

Interpreting a scene creatively happens naturally for you as you practice with your DSLR camera. Consider this scene of the lonely tree in the distance. How do you see it in your mind with your creative vision?

Normal, as in Figure 3-17? Overexposed, as in Figure 3-18? Underexposed, as in Figure 3-19? Or black and white, as in Figure 3-20? These examples show that "correct" exposures are often in the creative mind of the photographer.

Figure 3-17: This one is a normal exposure.

Figure 3-18: This one is about a stop overexposed.

Figure 3-19: And this one is about a stop underexposed.

Figure 3-20: This is Figure 3-17 in glorious black and white. Read more in Book V, Chapter 3.

Chapter 4: Working with Lenses, the Camera's Eye

In this chapter

✓ Understanding how lenses see

✓ Using selective focus

✓ Working with depth of field

✓ Understanding the difference between digital and regular lenses

This chapter takes you on an exploration of your DSLR camera's eyes: interchangeable lenses. You find out how wide-angle lenses differ from normal and telephoto lenses. You can do practical exercises to discover more about selective focus and depth of field. A section explains how exclusively digital lenses are different from those designed for film or full-frame DSLR cameras.

Doing That Thing They Do

The only job a lens has is focusing the light reflecting off the subject on the plane where the digital sensor is. Sounds simple, doesn't it? And like so much of the rest of photography there is a lot more to it than meets the eye. The lens' design can be relatively simple, as with fixed focal-length telephotos, or extraordinarily complex, as with a wide-angle-to-telephoto combination. The combination of elements and their grouping is a complex design project that optical engineers work out on computers before even touching a piece of glass.

 Fixed focal-length lenses have only one angle of view. Cut a rectangle in a piece of cardboard. Hold it at arms' length from your eyes. That is an angle of view similar to a telephoto lens. Bring the cutout closer, say, to 6 inches in front of your face. That is a wide angle of view. As you bring the card from arms' length to 6 inches from your eyes, that is the effect of a zoom lens. A 200mm telephoto has one angle of view. Zoom lenses cover all the angles of view between their shortest and longest range. A 70–210mm covers all of the views possible between 70mm and 210mm.

A lot of things go on inside lenses. Since visible light is made of a spectrum of colors, the lens has to focus all the colors in the same plane. Different colors of light have their own specific wavelength. This makes the work of the lens designer a challenging one.

Chromatic aberration is the result of some colors of light falling into focus either behind or in front of the sensor. The artifact that appears in the files is a *color fringe,* usually red/cyan or blue/yellow. Adobe Photoshop CS2 has correction tools built in for both RAW files and regular ones. See Figure 4-1.

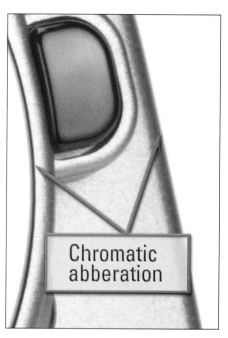

Figure 4-1: The color fringe shown by the arrows is caused by light focusing behind or in front of the sensor instead of directly on it.

Understanding focal lengths

The focal length of lenses tells you how much or how little of the subject will be in the photograph. *Focal length* is the distance from the lens to its focal point (the sensor) when the lens is focused at infinity. Wide-angle lenses show more of the subject. Telephoto lenses have narrow angles of view. They bring distant objects in close.

The smaller the number is when it comes to focal lengths, the more you get in the photograph. These lenses are called *wide-angle lenses.* They provide a wider than normal angle of view. Larger numbers are called *telephoto lenses.* They give a narrower than normal angle of view. They actually magnify the image, bringing far-away objects closer.

Doing the math on focal length numbers

Figure 4-2 shows the image sensor and the lens. The light, indicated by red lines, crosses inside the lens at the nodal point. The *nodal point* is the place where the lens inverts the image, literally turning it upside down. The distance from this point to the sensor — measured in millimeters — is the focal length of the lens. The lens has to be focused on infinity to measure focal length so the nodal point is as close as it can be to the sensor.

Infinity is the focus setting where the groups of lenses are closest to the image sensor. With all lenses — except for some extreme telephotos — an object a city block away (or the length of a football field) is at the infinity setting.

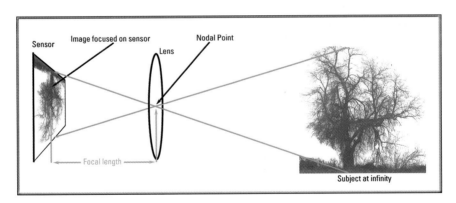

Figure 4-2: The image sensor and lens.

Broadening Your View from Telephoto to Wide Angle

The range of lenses available for DSLR cameras is truly amazing. Most camera manufacturers offer a complete array of standard (lenses that work with full-frame 36mm × 24mm sensors) and digital lenses for the smaller-sized sensors. Sigma, Tamron, and other manufacturers make lenses for the popular camera bodies from Canon, Fujifilm (Nikon mount), Konica-Minolta, Nikon, Olympus, Pentax, and Sigma. The number of choices is huge. This section helps in the decisionmaking process.

Figure 4-3: A red and a white lens mount index on the Canon EOS Digital Rebel XT shows it accepts both digital and full-frame lenses.

When shopping for digital lenses, keep in mind that they don't work with full-frame DSLR cameras. The area of coverage for digital lenses is much smaller than for the 36 × 24mm format. If you see yourself making the jump to a professional full-frame camera in the future, you might want to only purchase full-frame–compatible lenses. Only Canon manufactures full-frame cameras at the time of this writing. Canon signifies which lenses work on their Digital Rebel XT and 20D bodies with the lens mount index marks shown in Figures 4-3 and 4-4. The white dot is for digital lenses. The red dot is for full-frame lenses.

Figure 4-4: Red and white lens mount indexes show that the Canon EOS 20D is compatible with both digital and full-frame lenses.

Normal lenses

A *normal lens* reproduces the approximate perspective of the human eye. Normal lens focal lengths are determined by the sensor format. Normal is considered the focal length closest to the diagonal measurement of the format.

Figure 4-5 shows the three digital formats discussed in Book I, Chapter 1. Normal for full-frame 35mm (36 × 24mm) is 43.27mm. Nobody makes a 43.27mm lens! Normal lenses for the full-frame 35mm digital sensor are usually 50–65mm in focal length. The 27.8 × 18.5 sensor gives a normal focal length of 33.4mm, while 27.3mm is normal for the 22.7 × 15.1mm chip.

Figure 4-6 shows a view of a stream, trees, and grass in the Massai Mara in Kenya. The photograph made with a 50mm normal lens on a full-frame sensor DSLR would look the same as 38mm lens on a camera with a smaller sensor that has a 1.3X magnification factor.

Wide-angle lenses

The wide-angle lens is one whose focal length is less, or shorter, than the normal lens for a given format. The wide-angle lens offers a wider field of view than the normal one does. Extreme wide-angle lenses can have angles of view of 180° or more. Imagine a lens that can see the palms of your hands when you stretch your arms out horizontally, stretching as wide as you can. Now that's w i d e!

36 X 24 format — Normal = 43.27mm

27.8 X 18.5 format — Normal = 33.4mm

22.7 X 15.1 format — Normal = 27.3mm

Figure 4-5: Three common digital formats: their normal lens focal length and relative size difference.

50mm
(full frame)

38mm
(1.3 lens factor)

Figure 4-6: Shot with a full frame camera, the normal lens is 50mm. With a 1.3X camera, the normal focal length is 38mm.

Photographers often want to make their photographs look different, even dreamlike. The spacious field of view offered by wide-angle lenses is great for landscapes. The fact is they're great for getting the big picture of a scene. Figure 4-7 shows a comparison of two different focal lengths of the same African scene in Figure 4-6.

Figure 4-7: Get more of the scene in the photograph. Go wide angle!

Wide-angle lenses push the view back from the scene, letting you see more than ever. These lenses also have amazing depth of field. Some of them, when set to smaller apertures like f/11 to f/16, can hold focus from something one foot in front of the lens all the way to infinity.

Depth of field (DOF) is the area of focus in front of and behind the actual point of the camera's focus.

One of the properties of wide-angle lenses is spreading out the dimensions of objects or people close to the lens. The subject in the foreground can be wildly distorted. This distortion can add interest and make the photograph striking. You can do this exercise to show how much fun your wide-angle lens can be.

1. **Put your wide-angle lens on your DSLR camera.**

   Or if your zoom lens has a wide angle built in, zoom to the smallest number.

2. **Move in close on the face of a friend.**

   Do this outside in open shade or on an overcast day. Direct sunlight is too harsh.

3. **Take the light reading, then shoot the photograph.**

   In this exercise it's alright to use automatic settings.

4. **Play! Shoot some with the camera at your friend's eye level.**

   Take some from below and the head will be small. Make some from above and the head will be huge and the body will be thin, receding into the background.

Figure 4-8 was shot in my studio on a roll of yellow background paper. I was standing on a ladder aiming my camera down on the model. The wide-angle lens makes her head so large it is almost the width of her shoulders. The forced perspective makes her body look very thin. She looks like a cartoon caricature.

Telephoto lenses

Telephoto lenses have focal lengths longer than normal lenses. A short telephoto (on a full-frame camera) is considered to be between 70–105mm. Medium telephotos range from 105–300mm. Super telephotos are longer than 300mm. The longer the telephoto lens, the higher the magnification provided. A 100mm short telephoto delivers two times (or 2X) magnification for a full-frame sensor camera, which has a 50mm focal length.

Figure 4-8: Forced perspective from a wide-angle lens up close makes a photographic caricature.

Magnification is determined by dividing the normal focal length of the camera into the focal length of a telephoto lens: 100mm × 50mm = 2X.

A medium telephoto lens 200mm in focal length has a 4X magnification factor. A 400mm super telephoto gives the same effect as a pair of 8X binoculars. The job of the telephoto lens is to bring distant objects closer.

Figure 4-9 shows a couple of male lions. It was taken with a 160mm medium telephoto on a full-frame camera. The equivalent for a camera with a 1.3X magnification factor is almost 210mm. The 400mm version in Figure 4-10 brings the foreground lion up close and almost personal. The eight times magnification is equal to an 8 power pair of binoculars. You would get the same frame with a lens zoomed to 307mm on a 1.3X lens factor camera.

Figure 4-9: Two kings of the jungle.

Figure 4-10: Closer than you'd ever want to be to a free-roaming lion!

Getting picky with selective focus

One of the characteristics of telephoto lenses is their apparent shallow depth of field compared to normal or wide-angle lenses. The effect is extremely useful in isolating a subject from the background. Apertures with smaller numbers and larger openings show much less in focus in front and behind what you're focused on than do apertures with large numbers and small openings. For more on depth of field, check out Book I, Chapter 2.

Telephotos actually have the same depth of field as wide-angle lenses at a given f/stop if you were to measure the distance of the areas in focus in front and behind the point of focus. Since this category of lenses covers a much deeper zone from their closest focus point to infinity as compared to wide angles, the illusion is that they have less depth of field.

Figure 4-11 shows a great example of selective focus. This young lioness was resting on a hillock when our Land Cruiser happened by. She mustered up enough energy to look my way and I made her photograph with a 400mm lens at f/8. This aperture was small enough to make sure all of her detail was crisp. At the same time it was large enough to make the grass in the foreground and the acacia trees on the horizon soft.

Selective focus isolates the lioness and forces your attention to her. The out-of-focus areas give you plenty of information about her surroundings without hitting you over the head by being sharp. You recognize the trees and rolling plains and your brain fills in the rest of the story while you concentrate on the subject.

Figure 4-11: Selective focus.

Now it's time for you to go make some wildlife photographs. If an African safari is not in your immediate plans, make a trip to your nearest zoo. Take your DSLR camera, telephoto zoom lens, and tripod along for the ride. Find your vantage point and follow along.

1. **Compose the photograph.**

   If your animal of choice is behind a chain link fence, move in as close to the fence as you can. You want to shoot between one of the squares formed by the links. Have the edges of the chain resting on the front of the lens. The filter flange will protect the glass.

2. **Set your camera on Aperture Priority.**

   This means you choose the aperture and the camera sets the shutter speed. You may also work in Manual mode if you choose. If the background is very bright or very dark, use Manual and compensate. For more information, see Book I, Chapter 3.

3. **Zoom all the way in by setting your lens at the highest focal length setting it has.**

4. **Set the biggest number available on your lens as the aperture.**

   It lets in the most light, allows you to use the fastest shutter speed, and gives you the shallowest depth of field.

5. **Make the shot.**

   Shoot several images at these settings. The shallow depth of field blurs the edges of the chain link fence and they disappear. There may be some darkening on the edges. That's not a problem.

6. **Experiment and play!**

   Make a series of photographs using progressively smaller apertures. You quickly see how smaller apertures give you more depth of field.

A myth says that changing focal length changes perspective. It does not. The only times perspective changes are when the camera moves closer or farther away from the subject.

Comparing Focal Lengths

You have an overview of the three primary types of focal-length lenses. The next section shows you a comparison of focal lengths from extreme wide angle to super telephoto. The photographs shown in Figures 4-12 through 4-25 were made on a level tripod with the same exposure. The only thing that changes is the focal length of the lenses. The location is the San Diego Convention Center. The most popular focal lengths are illustrated.

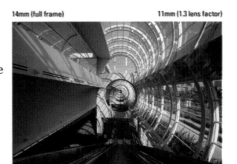

Figure 4-12: Extreme wide-angle lens, 14mm (full frame) or 11 mm (1.3 lens factor).

17mm (full frame) · 13mm (1.3 lens factor)

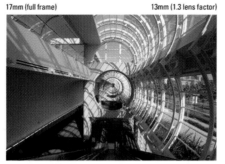

Figure 4-13: Extreme wide-angle lens, 17mm (full frame) or 13mm (1.3 lens factor).

20mm (full frame) · 15mm (1.3 lens factor)

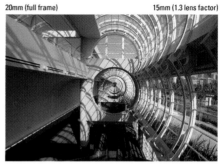

Figure 4-14: Extreme wide-angle lens, 20mm (full frame) or 15mm (1.3 lens factor).

24mm (full frame) · 18mm (1.3 lens factor)

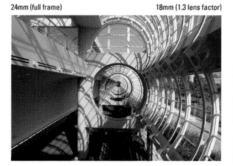

Figure 4-15: Extreme wide-angle lens, 24mm (full frame) or 18mm (1.3 lens factor).

28mm (full frame) · 22mm (1.3 lens factor)

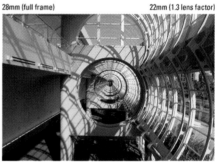

Figure 4-16: Wide-angle lens, 28mm (full frame) or 22mm (1.3 lens factor).

35mm (full frame) · 27mm (1.3 lens factor)

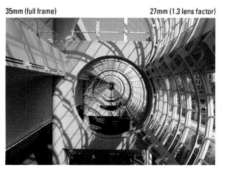

Figure 4-17: Wide-angle lens, 35mm (full frame) or 27mm (1.3 lens factor).

50mm (full frame) · 38mm (1.3 lens factor)

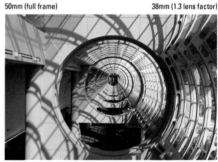

Figure 4-18: Normal lens, 50mm (full frame) or 38mm (1.3 lens factor).

80mm (full frame)   62mm (1.3 lens factor)

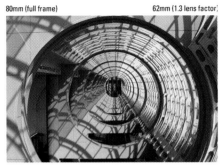

Figure 4-19: Short telephoto lens, 80mm (full frame) or 62mm (1.3 lens factor).

105mm (full frame)   81mm (1.3 lens factor)

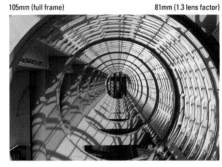

Figure 4-20: Short telephoto lens, 105mm (full frame) or 81mm (1.3 lens factor).

135mm (full frame)   104mm (1.3 lens factor)

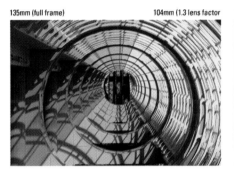

Figure 4-21: Telephoto lens, 135mm (full frame) or 104mm (1.3 lens factor).

200mm (full frame)   154mm (1.3 lens factor)

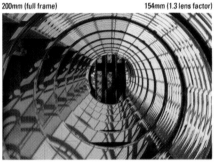

Figure 4-22: Telephoto lens, 200mm (full frame) or 154mm (1.3 lens factor).

210mm (full frame)   162mm (1.3 lens factor)

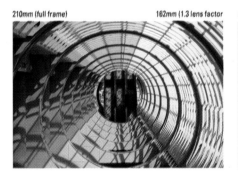

Figure 4-23: Telephoto lens, 210mm (full frame) or 162mm (1.3 lens factor).

400mm (full frame)   308mm (1.3 lens factor)

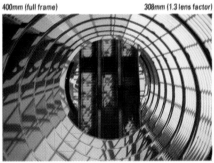

Figure 4-24: Extreme telephoto lens, 400mm (full frame) or 308mm (1.3 lens factor).

Lensbaby

Figure 4-25: Lensbaby: One of the coolest creative lenses going!

Pampering Your Lensbabies

One more lens really must be explained: the Lensbaby. Lensbabies are one of the most fun, innovative, and just plain creative accessories ever made for a digital camera. Basically it's a lens on a bellows-like tube. Figure 4-26 shows you what it looks like.

Focus the Lensbaby by moving the collar in and out with your fingertips until the image looks sharp in the viewfinder. Selective focus and creative distortions are made by tilting the collar right, left, up, down, or in a fluid combination. When it looks good, shoot it!

Figure 4-26: Shooting with the amazing Lensbaby.

Wrapped Sandwich

Morning Coffee

Figure 4-27: A new way of looking at lunch!   Figure 4-28: Morning coffee . . . yummmmmm.

Stripes and Stars

Figure 4-29: Old Glory.

ON THE WEB

I love my Lensbaby! When I find myself in a creative funk, I get it out and shoot for a couple of hours. The results are amazing. They give you a whole new way of using a DSLR. Lensbabies are available in mounts for popular DSLR cameras. Check them out at www.lensbaby.com. Figures 4-27 through 4-30 exhibit some of my Lensbaby photographs of everyday objects, including a sandwich wrap, a cup of coffee, an American flag, and an Open for Business sign. This is a new way of looking at the world. Photography is fun!

Open for Business

Figure 4-30: Neon never looked better.

Book II

The Digital Photograph

The 5th Wave — By Rich Tennant

"I've got some new image editing software, so I took the liberty of erasing some of the smudges that kept showing up around the clouds. No need to thank me."

*M*aking outstanding photographs takes a lot more than clicking the shutter. Book II takes you inside photography and shares the things professionals do that sets their work apart. It tells you about how to hold your DSLR camera and why using a tripod is so critical to great work. You discover how to clean the camera's sensor, how data is stored in the camera, and the care and feeding of the storage media. You also read about the color of light, how sensors see light, the importance of white balance, and composing a successful photograph.

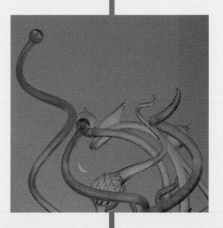

Chapter 1: Storing Your Images from the Camera and Beyond

In this chapter

✐ **Caring for and feeding your camera's storage media**

✐ **Formatting media**

✐ **Using card readers**

✐ **Using external hard drives**

✐ **Recording on CD or DVD**

This chapter is about the care and feeding of your digital files. Digital cameras create data — digital files — that must be stored. DSLR cameras have some common storage methods. Storage cards have important dos and don'ts that you explore here so you ensure the safety of your photographs as you shoot. I show you how to format storage cards the right way for your DSLR camera and the easy way to use external card readers. I also help you manage files, including backing up and archiving.

Exploring Storage for DSLR Cameras

The best part of shooting digital is that the storage media is almost infinitely reusable. Once your DSLR camera, storage media, and accessories are paid for, practicing the craft of photography costs practically nothing. That's quite a change from spending between a dollar and a dollar and a half for every photograph made on film. Figure 1-1 shows digital storage media in the foreground, traditional film in the background.

Digital cameras have lots of choices of removable storage media for temporarily holding photographs:

✐ Memory Sticks

✐ CompactFlash

✐ Secure Digital (SD) cards

✐ mini SD cards

- xD-Picture cards
- MultiMedia Cards (MMC)
- Reduced-Size MCC (RS-MMC)
- SmartMedia cards

Figure 1-1: Memory cards are the new film.

Whew. That's a lot of choices. It reminds me of the media wars: VHS versus Beta, 8-track versus cassette, albums versus CDs. Everyone wants to be the one to introduce the next "best" format for storing digital photographs. Fortunately for DSLR camera shooters, none of this applies. You have only two choices: CompactFlash or SD cards. Figure 1-2 shows both.

And all DSLR cameras use Compact-Flash cards. Some cameras use both CompactFlash and SD cards. None of them use SD cards alone. So when you come right down to it there's really only one choice: CompactFlash cards or their hard-drive equivalent, IBM/Hitachi Micro-drives (a miniature spinning hard drive that conforms to the CompactFlash format).

Figure 1-2: A CompactFlash card, a Microdrive, and an SD memory card.

IBM/Hitachi Microdrives

Invented and originally manufactured by IBM, the business was sold to Hitachi Global Storage Technologies in December of 2002. The drives are available in sizes from 512MB to 1-, 2-, 4-, and 6GB. These very solid, dependable drives (I have taken these rugged drives on safari in African heat and dust) fit in DSLR cameras just like flash memory cards.

The big story is price and speed. A 6GB Microdrive costs $285 (versus a 4GB CompactFlash card for $485). Microdrives are miniature hard drives in the CompactFlash type II size. They are thicker than standard CompactFlash cards. DSLR cameras have media slots wide enough to handle both. As of summer 2005, the 4GB Microdrive comes in at $180. The Microdrives read and write over 7MBps. See Figure 1-3. Flash memory cards read and write data faster than Microdrives.

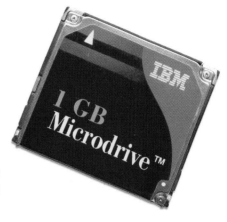

Figure 1-3: A 1GB Microdrive.

CompactFlash Cards

CompactFlash cards use a type of permanent memory called *flash memory.* Flash memory retains data until it is erased. All of the storage media mentioned so far — except, of course, the Microdrives — are made up of huge numbers of flash memory chips. This kind of memory doesn't need power to remember what's been written to it. This is important because if the cards required power to retain data, they would be much larger and more prone to data loss. CompactFlash cards, one of which is in Figure 1-4, were introduced by SanDisk Corporation in 1994.

Figure 1-4: A 1GB CompactFlash memory card.

Getting inside

Flash memory cards contain no moving parts. They have lots of flash memory chips inside. The more chips, the more data they can store. They have a controller chip inside that tells the card how to write and read data stored on it.

The cards are very rugged. Documented accounts of CompactFlash cards tell of surviving one-story drops to the pavement and even a trip through the washing machine and dryer with image files intact and readable. While it's nice to know that they're tough little storage devices, this treatment is not recommended.

Showing some speed

CompactFlash cards read and write at between 12–20MBps, depending on the card speed and the camera's write speed. At the time this is written camera's write speed is slower than the memory card. As DSLR camera file sizes increase due to higher and higher sensor pixel counts, the time it takes to write the data to the card becomes a consideration. Faster write times mean less waiting for the camera's buffer to transfer files to the card. The *buffer* is temporary storage in the camera's on-board memory that stores digital photographs while they are written to the memory card. Without the buffer, you would have to wait several seconds before you could shoot again.

Sizing things up

Currently, CompactFlash cards are available in sizes from 32MB to 8GB. Figure 1-5 gives an approximate number of 8MB RAW files that can be stored on each size.

The 8GB large-capacity CompactFlash cards can store 1,000 or more images. If one high-capacity memory card should fail, an entire shoot could be lost.

CompactFlash® card size	8MB files per card
32MB	4
64MB	8
128MB	16
256MB	32
512MB	64
1GB	125
2GB	250
4GB	500
8GB	1,000

Figure 1-5: How many 8MB files does your memory card hold? Find out here.

Durability

Flash memory cells do have a life span somewhere in the hundreds of thousands of write-read cycles. When a cell fails in a CompactFlash card, the control automatically works around it. Cards last a very long time thanks to this feature. Some cards are designed to quit when the number of cycles reaches a preset number — again, somewhere in the hundreds of thousands. That's way more than you would ever expect to shoot. Think about filling a 1GB card 100,000 times — let's see, 125 shots times 100,000 is 12,500,000 photographs. Think about how long it would take to shoot 12.5 million images. Mind boggling to say the very least!

When flash cards fail

Sometimes the data that tells where individual images are on the card gets scrambled. When this happens, the card is unreadable. Image recovery programs like Lexar Media's Image Rescue (see Figure 1-6) bypass the data catalog and recover the image files. Image Rescue can also find photographs still on the card after it's been formatted.

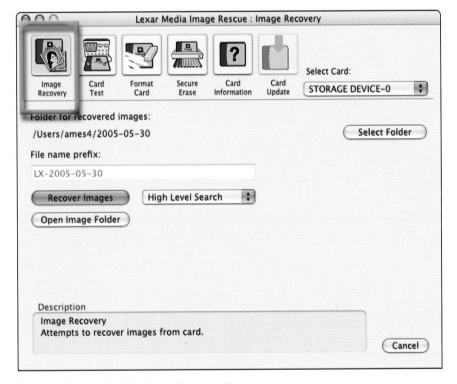

Figure 1-6: Lexar Media's Image Rescue software.

You can minimize the possibility of flash memory card failure by following this advice:

- **Reformat the card.** Every time you have finished copying and archiving your image files, reformat the card in your camera.

- **Carry your cards with you when you go through airport security.** The stronger x-rays used for checked luggage is likely to damage them.

   🖝 **Wait a few seconds before either removing the memory card from the camera or turning the camera off.** Waiting ensures that photographs being written to the card will not be lost.

   🖝 **If a card starts being finicky, stop using it immediately.** Get your photographs off of it using recovery software. The best practice is to replace it.

Formatting CompactFlash cards

The very best place to format your flash memory card is in your camera. *Formatting* creates a new file allocation table that tells the camera exactly where to write each image. Formatting flash memory cards is different for each DSLR camera. Refer to your instruction manual for details. As a second choice, Windows XP users can also format flash memory cards. Their file allocation systems are the same as those in digital cameras. DSLR cameras purchased before 2003 are unable to format 2GB cards. Cards 2GB or larger require a file system called FAT32. Newer cameras can format cards up 8GB.

Flash memory cards must not be formatted directly on Macintosh computers. To format cards with a Mac, use a CompactFlash utility program like Lexar's Image Rescue. The program's shown in Figure 1-7.

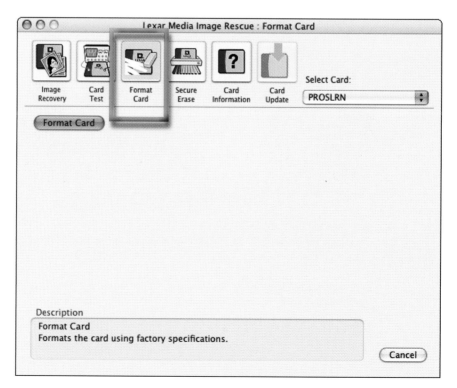

Figure 1-7: Mac users want to use a card-formatting program like Lexar Media's Image Rescue.

Caring for CompactFlash cards

Keep your flash memory cards in a wallet designed to hold them. I use one made by Lightware (www.lightwareinc.com) and shown in Figure 1-8. Other manufacturers of wallets are Lowepro (www.lowepro.com) and Tamrac (www.tamrac.com). The wallets have clear compartments stitched for individual cards. Freshly formatted cards are stored with their labels showing. Full cards are returned to the wallet face in. That way a glance tells me how many cards I have left at any give time. You can see my organization system in Figure 1-9.

Figure 1-8: Lightware's memory card wallet folded up and ready to go.

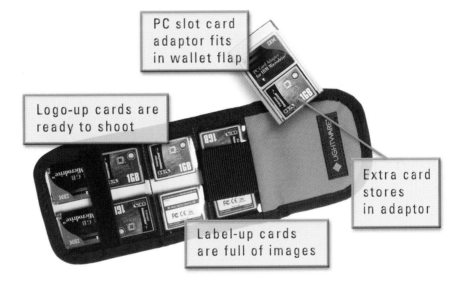

PC slot card adaptor fits in wallet flap

Logo-up cards are ready to shoot

Extra card stores in adaptor

Label-up cards are full of images

Figure 1-9: Organizing memory cards the easy way.

The Lightware wallet carries the eight cards in separate compartments and one in a card reader that fits into the PC slot of most laptops (Mac and Windows). That gives me about 60 17MB RAW exposures per card, or 600 shots with a wallet of nine cards and one in the camera. (And yes, I *am* a resolution freak.) I only shoot 1GB cards. This spreads the risk of loss over many cards. If one of them fails completely (rare, and it does happen), only a portion of the shoot is lost. On commercial jobs I have an assistant downloading the cards onto a laptop, burning them to discs, and proofing the discs. Once that's been done, the card is reformatted in a backup camera and returned face out to the wallet. Read how to safely archive digital negatives in Book III, Chapter 2.

Copying Images from CompactFlash Cards

Once you've finished shooting, you have two ways to get images from the card onto your computer: connect the camera to your computer with a FireWire (IEEE 1394) or USB cable or use a card reader. The very best way is with a dedicated card reader. Card readers are faster than with the camera connected to the computer. And card readers don't drain the camera battery. Using a card reader allows you to download a card and still be shooting onto another card. When the camera is downloading over a cable you can't shoot with it.

Seeing a psychic: Card readers

Card readers are named by what they read and how they connect to your computer. CompactFlash card readers are called CF readers. In order of fastest to slowest:

- **FireWire.** These readers use the IEEE 1394 standard for high-speed data transfer. Figure 1-10 shows the reader.

- **USB 1.0/2.0.** Multicard readers have slots for several types of media, which you can see in Figure 1-11. They connect to a USB 1.0/2.0 port on your desktop or laptop.

Figure 1-10: Lexar Media's FireWire CompactFlash reader.

- **PC slot adaptors.** These adaptors work only with laptops that have PC slots (technically known as PCMCIA Type 1 slots). This adaptor fits the CF card (Type I or II) into the PC slot on a laptop. See Figure 1-12.

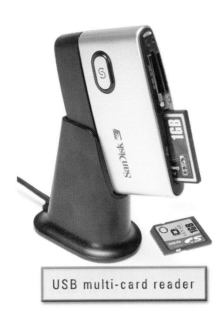

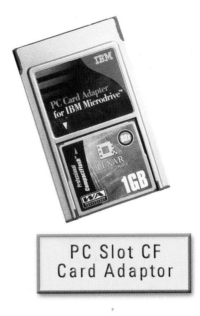

PC Slot CF
Card Adaptor

Figure 1-12: A PC slot (PCMCIA) card
adaptor for Type I and II memory cards.

Figure 1-11: SanDisk's multicard reader.

Copying your images

Downloading your digital photographs from your CompactFlash memory
card is easy. Follow these steps:

1. **Connect your card reader to your computer following the instructions
   that came with it.**

2. **Insert the CompactFlash card or connect your camera to your computer
   with the CompactFlash card already in the camera.**

   Read your DSLR's instruction manual for details.

3. **Navigate to your CompactFlash memory card and double-click to
   open it.**

   Inside is a folder named DCIM.

4. **Open DCIM to find the subfolder holding your images.**

   The name of the subfolder depends on the DSLR camera you use.

5. **Make a folder on your desktop named with a simple description of the
   subject of your photos.**

6. Highlight the folder of image files.

7. Drag the highlighted folder of images to the folder you created on the desktop. See Figure 1-13.

For Windows, right-click the highlighted folder and select Copy from the menu. Figure 1-14 shows this being done. Navigate to the desktop, right-click the folder you created, and choose Paste. See Figure 1-15 for this step.

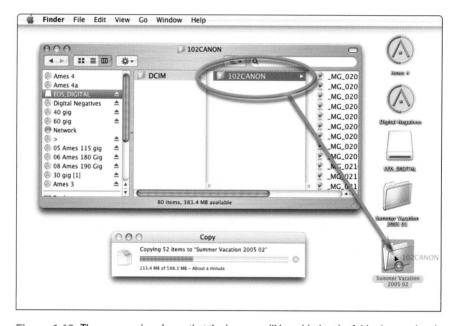

Figure 1-13: The green + sign shows that the images will be added to the folder by copying them.

Figure 1-14: Right-click the folder inside the DCIM folder and choose Copy from the menu in Windows.

Figure 1-15: Right-click the folder you want your images copied to and choose Paste.

A dialog (shown in Figure 1-16) indicates the copy process as started. When the copying process is completed, your image files are on your desktop.

If you're copying several folders of images, they need to have unique names. Rename the copied folder by clicking it, pausing, then clicking again (Mac). Right-click and choose Rename in Windows. Type in a name that tells you what's in the folder. (Summer Vacation 2005 01, for example.) The 01 tells you it's the first folder of images. Continue renaming the folders with the same name, changing the 01 to 02. The third folder of images is 03, and so on. For more information on archiving your digital photographs, read Book III, Chapter 2.

Figure 1-16: Windows shows this dialog as it copies files to another folder.

Backing 'em up

Backing up images is where a lot of digital photographers trust to luck. They refuse to back up their image files to a separate hard drive. Most of the time they get away with it, too. Then one day the hard drive in the computer checks out permanently and refuses to open the photographs. You should hear them moan, groan, and cry. I hate to see a grown photographer cry, don't you? A simple, inexpensive, and downright smart solution: Back up the files to an external hard drive. External hard drives are inexpensive and easy to connect to desktop, tower, or laptop computers. Great external hard drives are available from LaCie (www.lacie.com) and Other World Computing (www.macsales.com).

Windows computers can only read external hard drives formatted in FAT or FAT32 and NTFS. Macintosh computers can read Mac HFS-, FAT-, and FAT32-formatted drives. Mercury Elite Pro FireWire and USB drives from Other World Computing are compatible with both Mac and Windows computers.

Follow these steps to back up your images to a hard drive:

1. **Highlight the folder of images on your computer's desktop.**

   Now you copy the folder to an external hard drive. This is done exactly the same way as copying the folder of images from the CompactFlash memory card.

2. **Mac: Drag the highlighted folder onto the external hard drive icon, as done in Figure 1-17.**

   Windows: Right-click the highlighted folder and choose Copy, as done in Figure 1-18.

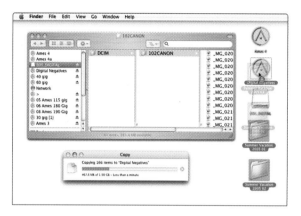

Figure 1-17: Dragging the folders of photographs to an external hard drive (Mac).

A green plus sign like that in Figure 1-18 indicates the folder will copy to the destination. The green plus goes away as soon as the copy process begins, when you release the mouse button, or when you take your finger off a touch pad.

3. Drop the folder on the icon.

In Windows, find the external hard drive on My Computer. Right-click the drive and choose Paste, as done in Figure 1-19.

You now have a backup of your precious digital photographs. This is a very good thing.

Figure 1-18: In Windows, right-click the two highlighted folders and choose Copy.

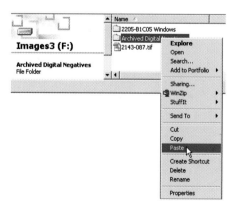

Figure 1-19: Go to your external hard drive, right-click, and choose Paste.

Making a permanent archive

Once you have all the folders from your shoot on your desktop and backed up to the external hard drive — You did back them up, didn't you? — you're ready to burn them to a CD or DVD. I know what you're thinking: "If my photographs are on two hard drives, why would I want to burn them to a disc?" The answer: ALL HARD DRIVES FAIL . . . eventually. The disc is a permanent backup of your digital photographs. With it you'll always have the photographs, no matter what happens to your hard drives over time. Follow the instructions for the disc-burning software on your computer.

Find out how much storage space your folders require by highlighting them. Choose File⇨Get Info in the Mac Finder's Menu or in Windows by right-clicking them and choosing Properties. If the folder size is less than 690MB, they will fit on a CD. For groups of folders over 690MB, burn them to a DVD or multiple CDs.

**Book II
Chapter 1**

**Storing Your Images
from the Camera
and Beyond**

Deleting files

Copies of your digital photographs are in four places: the flash memory card, your computer's desktop, the external hard drive, and either a CD or DVD. The files on the cards and desktop can now be deleted. You don't want to clutter up your startup drive or C:\ drive.

Figure 1-20: Click and hold on the trash icon on the Mac. Then choose Empty Trash.

1. **Mac: Highlight the folders and drag them to the trash can in the Dock.**

   Windows: Right-click the highlighted folders and send them to the Recycle Bin.

2. **Empty the trash (see Figure 1-20) or the Recycle Bin (see Figure 1-21).**

   Once the CD or DVD of your digital image files has been burned, you should reformat the CompactFlash cards. The best place to reformat the card is in your camera.

3. **Put the card in the camera and follow the instructions in the camera manual for reformatting the card. See Figure 1-22.**

4. **Put the card face up in your card wallet or case.**

   You're ready to go make more digital photographs.

Figure 1-21: Right-click the Recycle Bin and choose Empty Recycle Bin in Windows.

Light my FireWire

FireWire was developed by Apple. Sony calls it i.Link. The electronics industry has assigned it the name IEEE 1394. It's a very efficient means of moving data from one storage device to another. Some DSLR cameras use it to connect directly to a computer. There are two types of camera cable 1394 plugs: 6 pin and 4 pin. The 6-pin plugs not only carry data, they supply power directly to the device they're connected to, eliminating the need for an external power supply.

Apple computers, including PowerBooks and iBooks, have 6-pin connectors. Windows computers use add-on cards for FireWire. Windows laptops that have it built in use 4-pin plugs. PC slot FireWire adaptors with 6-pin plugs are available for laptops.

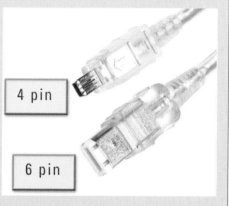

The digital images on your external hard drive are the ones you edit and work on in Adobe Photoshop CS2. Store the digital files archived on CDs or DVDs in a safe place, in another location. Off-site storage gives you another level of file security if a catastrophe strikes and your computer is wiped out. You never know when that errant soft drink might get spilled on your hard drive. And remember this quote from Dan Burkholder: "The most important photographs are the ones on the refrigerator."

Figure 1-22: Reformatting a CompactFlash card takes three steps on a Canon 20D.

Chapter 2: Supporting Your Local DSLR

In This Chapter

✔ **Holding your digital single lens reflex camera**

✔ **Using a tripod vertically and horizontally**

✔ **Using time lapse to your advantage**

*T*his chapter takes you through hand-holding your DSLR camera. You read about the don'ts. You see what you may have been doing that causes blurry photographs. You discover the really useful dos, including tucking your elbows and leaning into your shot. Finally, you get the inside information that separates the pro from the amateur using a tripod. You discover that tripods come in all sizes and some odd shapes. You explore why using a tripod is so worth all of the apparent trouble.

Hand-Holding Your DSLR Camera

Okay. I know your DSLR camera has all kinds of very smart electronics for taking care of exposure, storing files on CF cards, and generally needing very little from you other than creativity. So I am not really talking about that kind of hand-holding. I know you love your DSLR camera and if it had hands you would hold them. What I'm talking about here is how to physically hold the camera so it's as steady as it can be.

Amateurs with wings

Take a look at the less-than-optimal ways of holding a DSLR camera. All right, enough of the political correctness; this is just wrong. . . .

When someone holding a camera looks like a bird in flight, that person just can't be called a real photographer. The camera in Figures 2-1, 2-2, and 2-3 has no stability. It's just hanging out there, flapping in the breeze. The photographs will be blurry because the camera can't be held still this way. This stance presents these problems:

- The camera is hanging from the right hand. The lens has no support.

- The left hand is blocking the left eye. The shooter can't see what's moving into the frame.

- The elbows (wings, if you will) are spread wide, forcing the shoulder and biceps to create a stable platform. This is like pectoral exercises that lift a weight to the eyes, with the elbows out to strengthen the arms. It doesn't take long for those muscles to tire and start to shake.

- The "photographer" (note the quotes!) is standing square to the camera. The at-ease stance, with the elbows out, causes the body to rock front to back. Neither a horizontal nor a vertical camera orientation is effective when in flight mode.

Figure 2-1: The how-not-to-hold-a-DSLR-horizontally pose is shown here.

Showing the right stuff

Steady support is the name of the game when holding your DSLR camera. If you've been through the military or have learned to target practice, holding a camera steady and squeezing the shutter release so that it surprises you when it fires is the same thing you learned about handling firearms. The stance for holding your camera is coincidentally the same for a rifle or shotgun. Imagine shooting a gun standing like the woman in Figure 2-3. She would wind up sitting on the ground from the recoil caused by shooting. She has no front-to-back stability. Standing this way, she tends to rock back and forth.

Take a look at the right stuff. Figure 2-4 shows her at a ¾ stance to the angle of the camera, with her weight shifted forward. Her elbows are tucked into her ribs. Her left hand is under the lens, cradling it. Figure 2-5 shows the fingers and thumb of her left hand facing away from the camera and giving her a grip on the lens's zoom ring.

Figure 2-2: This is the vertical version of the horizontal pose.

Figure 2-3: Standing shoulders parallel to the camera lacks front-to-back stability.

Figure 2-4: Lean into the direction of the photograph.

Figure 2-5: Hand-holding a horizontal DSLR the right way.

Gripping vertically

Turning the DSLR camera 90° to shoot a vertical composition presents a whole other problem. The photographer's stance has her weight forward. Her left hand position is correct in Figure 2-6.

She can also keep track of action outside of the viewfinder by having her left eye open. The problem here is her right wrist, which is bent at an unnatural angle. It loses stability in this position. Once again, the camera is hanging instead of being supported. The answer lies in getting an accessory battery grip with a vertically oriented shutter release. This allows her right wrist to remain straight by providing a shutter button under her right index finger, circled in red in Figure 2-7. And believe it or not, the added weight of the batteries and grip adds to the overall steadiness when hand-holding a DSLR camera.

Figure 2-6: The "broken" wrist reduces the stability of a vertical camera position.

Figure 2-7: The battery grip with vertical release is a more stable way to hold the DSLR.

Supporting Your Local Camera

All the talk of how to hand-hold your DSLR camera is well and good. And no matter how steady you are, you can't beat a good tripod. Tripods come in lots of sizes, weights, brands, heights, and materials ranging from metal, carbon fiber, and plastic.

Let me eliminate plastic as a choice right now. Tripods have to be strong. That means that a lightweight tripod is something of a contradiction. It is an oxymoron for the most part. Yes, "lightweight tripod" is just like "jumbo shrimp." They're just words that don't make sense when used together.

Tripods have really only one job: to hold your camera exactly where you want for as long as you want it there. The classic use for a tripod is the time exposure. Other ways a tripod comes in handy is in shooting extreme close-ups or reaching out with a long telephoto lens.

Picking a tripod

There's no such thing as a camera support that's too big, too heavy, or too expensive. For proof of this statement, I offer my studio stand: a 12-foot high Foba holding a Canon 20D and shown in Figure 2-8.

Okay. It just might be a little bit 'o overkill. I got this behemoth when I was shooting 4×5 inch film and the camera was big too. And this shot is *not* a joke. As a matter of fact, all of the studio shots (with the exception of this one) in this book were shot with a camera mounted on this stand. As I said: There's no such thing as too tall, too big, or too heavy. If you ever have the chance, check out one of these monsters. Once you experience how easy it is to raise, lower, or move the camera side to side, you see what a great tool studio stands really are.

Figure 2-8: The studio stand does a great job of holding the Canon 20D stock-still.

ON THE WEB

Stay warm

REI stores (www.rei.com) have great cold-weather clothing. Their fingerless gloves are perfect for keeping most of your hands warm and still letting you work a camera.

Opening the closet of disappointing tripods

Every photographer has several tripods that languish in a closet or studio corner. They are there because they didn't fulfill the needs of the photographer using them. I cleaned out my old (un)used tripods a few years ago when it became clear I would never put a camera on any one of them again.

Before you make your tripod purchase, ask around. Find out what other photographers are using. Ask the key question, "How long have you been using your tripod?" Any answer over five years is a good one. The next question to ask is, "May I see it please?" (Of course you'll say please. I put that in to prove I'm polite.) When it's in your hands, check to see if it is well worn. Are there nicks on the legs? Chips in the paint? Are the bottoms of the legs worn? If you answered yes to these questions, you can rest assured that this tripod has not only been with the photographer a long time, it has been well used. Check out this close-up of a leg of my heavy-duty Gitzo in Figure 2-9. It carries the scars of almost 20 years in the field — and it has never needed repair.

**Book II
Chapter 2**

**Supporting Your
Local DSLR**

Figure 2-9: A well-worn tripod is the mark of a serious photographer.

The rule of tripod buying

I may sound as if I'm contradicting myself, and to a degree maybe I am. Here's my Rule of Tripod Acquisition: Go shopping. Find the biggest, heaviest tripod you can imagine ever carrying and buy the next largest model. I have lived by this maxim and have not been disappointed. Figure 2-10 is a full-sized view of my all-purpose Gitzo. I am not suggesting you get a tripod so heavy that you have to have three Sherpas carry it for you. It's a way of thinking that will serve you well over time. Clearly, don't buy a tripod that is so heavy you won't use it.

Figure 2-10: My all-purpose, expands-to-over-nine-feet-tall-or-hugs-the-ground, heavy-duty Gitzo tripod.

Cashing a reality check

There's a difference between us. I make my living creating photographs. I have to have the tools to do the job. You're on the amazing quest to either become a pro or a really advanced amateur — a *prosumer,* if you will. Buy the best gear you can afford; you won't be disappointed. This is especially true for your tripods. After all, tripods don't become obsolete every couple of years like computers and digital cameras. Buy a good one. It will last. Get a heavy-duty one and later add a smaller one — maybe even one made of carbon fiber, like you see on the right in Figure 2-11.

Figure 2-11: My two lighter Gitzos: metal on the left and its lightweight carbon-fiber brother on the right.

Yes, you will more than likely wind up with at least two or three. The one on the left went with me on safari in Kenya. The other tripod is slightly shorter, fits crosswise in a suitcase, and is very light because it's made of carbon fiber. I used it to shoot the lens comparisons in Book I, Chapter 4. I firmly believe a good tripod is the best single purchase a photographer makes.

Good and really good tripods

Several really good brands of tripods are available today. Manfrotto (also know as Bogen) tripods are good (www.bogenimaging.us). So is Giottos (www.hpmarketingcorp.com/giottos.html). My personal all-time favorite portable tripods are Gitzos. (I rarely take the studio stand out of the studio. There's a reason it's called a *studio stand* for goodness' sake.) Gitzo is also distributed by Bogen Imaging. I have had at least one Gitzo in my kit since the mid-eighties. In my humble and accurate opinion, Gitzo is the best tripod available in the United States. (David Chapman helps me keep up-to-date on photo gear — digital and otherwise — and upholds the accuracy of my opinion. David is the digital department manager of Professional Photo Resources here in Atlanta and is to whom this book is dedicated. See the PPR site at www.ppratlanta.com.)

Your tripod is also an invaluable help in composition and special effects shooting. I like tripod heads that have a quick-release system like you see in Figure 2-12. A plate is attached to the bottom of the DSLR. It mounts onto the head and is ratcheted down tightly with a lever making the camera tight on the tripod. When it's time to move to a new location, a flip of a locking lever releases the camera and off you go. I have a base plate on each of my DSLR bodies.

Taking time exposures

Time exposures are made with the camera's shutter open for several seconds to record a scene in very low light.

Marching time

Figure 2-13 shows three views of the Idaho State Capitol in Boise during the holidays. The photographs were made over time from late afternoon until it was completely dark. Every photograph is in exactly the same position as the others. The only change is the light. As the sun gets lower in the sky you can see the shadow move across the building. By just before 7:00 pm the sun is so low in the sky that the color of the light turns to amber. Recording the march of time is nearly impossible without a tripod.

Figure 2-12: The parts of a quick-release head. The cork on the plate and the ball bearing help prevent the DSLR from rotating when it is vertical.

Figure 2-13: Changing angles and color of light made possible by your friendly neighborhood tripod.

Tethered

A *tethered* DSLR camera is connected to and controlled by a computer. Tethering software comes with most DSLR cameras and works on both Macs and Windows computers. Check your manual to find out if your camera supports direct-to-computer operations. Shooting through a cable into a laptop has several advantages. The camera settings are changed from the computer, eliminating the need to touch, and possibly move, the camera. The shutter is released from the computer, too. And the image appears for review right away. When shooting a series of photographs that might be composited later, this is a great way to work.

Make your own March of Time series of photographs with these steps:

1. **Check www.weather.com for the sunset time for the day you plan to do this project. Arrive at the location two hours before sunset.**

2. **Frame your shot.**

3. **Make sure all of the leg locks on your tripod are tight.**

   Tighten down the head of the tripod as well. Rock steady is the name of the game (and yes, I listen to No Doubt).

4. **Choose the lowest ISO available on your DSLR. Make a light reading. Set your exposure.**

5. **Check your light readings.**

6. **Bracket by making additional photographs:**

   • **One shutter speed faster than the camera's reading**

   • **Two shutter speeds faster than the camera's reading**

   • **One shutter speed slower than the camera's reading**

   • **Two shutter speeds slower than the camera's reading**

This gives five exposures every 15 minutes. If the light reading through the camera is $1/60$ at f/8, your series of five photographs will be made as follows: $1/60$, $1/125$, $1/250$, $1/30$, and $1/15$.

7. After the sun sets completely, make another series of exposures.

Be very careful not to move your camera when you release the shutter.

A full f/stop change using the shutter speed control is either twice as long (more light) or half as long (less light).

Remote shutter releases are available for your DSLR camera as an accessory. If you don't have one or if you left it at home, use the self timer setting on your DSLR camera. The self timer releases the shutter for you without movement.

The photographs in Figure 2-13 were made Christmas afternoon and evening. I wanted the least amount of traffic so I chose a time when most people were home. I had lots of warm clothes and a thermos of coffee. I waited another half an hour and made the hero photograph in Figure 2-14. The exposure is 15 seconds at f/8.0. The *hero* is the favorite of the shoot. Think of it as the pick of the litter.

Figure 2-14: The Idaho State Capitol Building, Christmas night 2004.

The setup for this series is shown in Figure 2-15. The tripod is my Gitzo carbon fiber. See how one leg is shortened to rest on the abutment of the parking garage? Versatility in the way the legs can be set is key in choosing a tripod.

The camera is linked to a 12" PowerBook. The camera is controlled from the computer. The images appear on the computer's screen as the exposure is made. Being able to preview the photography in Photoshop as you shoot it is a huge help in making certain you got the shot.

Tripods go swimming

A good tripod goes everywhere. Mine has been on top of buildings, in the surf, deep in sand, and almost completely submerged in water on several occasions. One instance, shown in Figure 2-16, of a swimsuit fashion shoot at a swimming pool in Florida shows a water top angle.

The camera is just above the level of the water and below the concrete skirt of the pool. It was shot with an 80mm to 200mm f/2.8 lens on a 1.3 magnification camera. The equivalent focal length is 260mm. This is impossible to hand-hold — especially when the photographer (yours truly) is chest deep in water, like you see in Figure 2-17.

Figure 2-15: Here's where I spent Christmas afternoon and evening.

Figure 2-16: Tia and Adelina of Elite Models/ Miami show off the latest swimwear.

After you take your tripod swimming, be certain to take it completely apart and dry it out thoroughly. If you use it in salt water, rinse it thoroughly in fresh water several times before drying and reassembly. Make sure that there is no sand in any of the joints before reassembly. If you find some, keep cleaning until it is completely removed.

Figure 2-17: My heavy-duty Gitzo and I go swimming in Florida. Models don't have all the fun.

Chapter 3: Making Better Photographs

*W*hite balance is how your camera delivers great color. Here you explore the colors of light, how they differ, and how to tell your DSLR camera what color white is for the photographs you're making. You read about white reference cards and how they can help you balance color in Adobe Photoshop. You get insight into a white balancing filter called the ExpoDisc. And finally, you see examples of dust on a sensor and discover Adobe Photoshop techniques that find dust in your images. Ways to clean the inside of your camera and sensor are revealed at last.

Finding White's Color

Color is made of the entire spectrum of visible light. Outdoors, the color of light depends on the time of day, the weather, and even if you are shooting in sunlight or shade. The color of light at dawn and dusk is very blue, or cool, in tone. Figure 3-1 shows a morning skyline in downtown Calgary, Canada. See the difference a half an hour makes in the color on the buildings?

Bright sunshine between 10 in the morning and 2 in the afternoon is considered *true daylight*. At dawn and at late afternoon just before dusk, the color of the light is a warm amber. As the afternoon progresses, the light becomes warmer, more and more orange until the fiery decent of sunset. *Open shade* areas illuminated by the sky without sunlight hitting them is bluer than daylight. Light's color on an overcast day is blue, too. Fluorescent has a strong green bias. Flash is close to daylight, though not exactly like it.

Dawn: 6:35am 7500°Kelvin   Sunrise: 7:07am 3550° Kelvin

Figure 3-1: This is Calgary at dawn and sunrise.

Feeling the heat

A burning candle has a color temperature of around 1850° Kelvin. Daylight is 5500°k. Sunrise or sunset (the same as far as photography goes, except in really polluted areas like LA or Atlanta) falls between 2000–3000°k. A 100-watt light bulb radiates a color

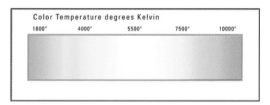

Color Temperature degrees Kelvin

| 1800° | 4000° | 5500° | 7500° | 10000° |

Figure 3-2: Color temperatures can get hot.

of 2870°k. Shade is bluer than daylight at 7100–8000°k and sometimes higher. A truly blue sky can be as hot as 20,000°k. (Figure 3-2 reveals more color temperatures.) And you thought that blue is a cool color. Sheesh. No wonder photography is confusing. So what does all this Kelvin temperature stuff mean, anyway?

White and gray matter

Our brains compensate for color on the fly the same way they do for exposure; see Book I, Chapter 3. This evening, sit down in your favorite chair, turn on your reading lamp, and open a newspaper. What color is the paper? White. Right? Yes. And no. You "know" that paper is white, so your brain compensates for the color of the 100-watt bulb in the lamp so the paper looks white. The light's orange, for heck's sake. Look at Figure 3-2 again and look up the color for the bulb. Yep. 2870°k is quite a bit shy of true white (5500°k). Your brain automatically performs a white balance so color under this orange-colored source still looks right.

White balance is an adjustment to compensate for the color of the light to make white white under the light.

TECHNICAL STUFF

Color me lucky

Color temperature really is a temperature. British physicist William Thompson, who became the first scientist ever granted peerage, was ennobled as the first Baron Kelvin of Largs. He explained the color of light by heating a theoretical black body radiator. To give you an idea of the numbers, water boils at 100° Celsius, 212° Fahrenheit, or 373° Kelvin. Imagine heating a horseshoe. Even after it becomes too hot to touch, the horseshoe is black. After a while it starts glowing a dull red at about 900° Kelvin.

The color shifts to an orangish glow at around 1750° Kelvin. Continued heating to over 3000° Kelvin gives a yellow color (about the color of a tungsten filament in a light bulb). By the time the horseshoe reaches 5000° Kelvin it is close to white hot, or the color of daylight. Now here is where the theoretical part comes in: In life, if you could get a horseshoe to 5000° Kelvin (that's 8540° Fahrenheit or 4726° Celsius), it would be a melted puddle. The accompanying chart shows the correlation between degrees Kelvin and their color.

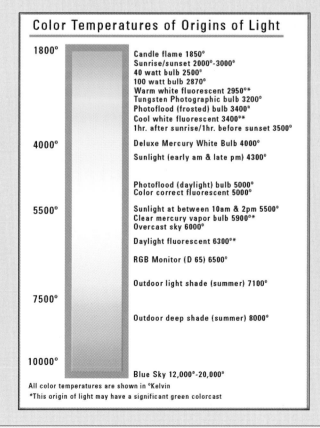

Color Temperatures of Origins of Light

1800°	Candle flame 1850°
	Sunrise/sunset 2000°-3000°
	40 watt bulb 2500°
	100 watt bulb 2870°
	Warm white fluorescent 2950°*
	Tungsten Photographic bulb 3200°
	Photoflood (frosted) bulb 3400°
	Cool white fluorescent 3400°*
	1hr. after sunrise/1hr. before sunset 3500°
4000°	Deluxe Mercury White Bulb 4000°
	Sunlight (early am & late pm) 4300°
	Photoflood (daylight) bulb 5000°
	Color correct fluorescent 5000°
5500°	Sunlight at between 10am & 2pm 5500°
	Clear mercury vapor bulb 5900°*
	Overcast sky 6000°
	Daylight fluorescent 6300°*
	RGB Monitor (D 65) 6500°
	Outdoor light shade (summer) 7100°
7500°	Outdoor deep shade (summer) 8000°
10000°	Blue Sky 12,000°-20,000°

All color temperatures are shown in °Kelvin
*This origin of light may have a significant green colorcast

Taking white and digital photography

Digital single lens reflex (DSLR) cameras have white balance settings in their menus. These settings help the computer in the camera determine the color of the JPEG files it produces. RAW files have the white data embedded in them so Adobe Camera Raw (part of Adobe Photoshop CS2) can turn them into Photoshop-editable files. (You read more about white balance and RAW files in Book III.) The camera wants to know the light's color temperature so it can calculate the colors in the photograph. (At this point the DSLR camera's theme song is, "If I Only Had A Brain.")

Most cameras have automatic white balance settings. The setting is pretty good at figuring out the color temperature at least some of the time. Auto white balance is a poor choice if consistent color is important. Since it is automatic, colors shift as the camera tweaks the white balance, which leads to inconsistent color results from one photograph to the next. I show you three methods of white balance here: One way is in the camera and two are post-production techniques in Adobe Photoshop CS2.

Setting the white balance

Pressing the WB button on the four-way selector of the Canon Digital Rebel XT brings up the white balance choices shown in Figure 3-3. Each time you press the button, the white balance setting advances. Refer to the instruction manual for details on how to apply them to your camera. What you want to know is what the settings are and how they work so you choose the right one. The most common choices are Daylight, Cloudy, Shade, Tungsten, Fluorescent, and Flash.

- ✔ **Daylight** is white light. You choose it when the photographs you are making are lit with bright sunshine.

- ✔ **Cloudy** is the setting for overcast days.

- ✔ **Shade** is used when your subject is standing in the shade on a sunny day.

- ✔ **Tungsten** is for indoor scenes lit with lamps and light bulbs.

- ✔ **Fluorescent** applies to those lit with fluorescent tubes (offices, for example).

- ✔ **Flash** is correct if you are shooting with electronic flash.

Figure 3-3: The white balance menu on the Canon Digital Rebel XT.

Sticking out your tungsten

Figure 3-4 shows two different colors of light: daylight and a warm tungsten color from a sodium vapor bulb. *Tungsten* is the color of an incandescent light bulb. Daylight is the predominant light source. Take note of the white clouds, the gray of the lamp housing, and the gray of the transformer above it. The white balance on the DSLR camera is set on Daylight.

Compare Figure 3-4 to Figure 3-5. The only difference is that the camera's white balance is changed to tungsten. The light that was warm orange light (Daylight white balance) is now almost neutral. Notice that the clouds now have a blue cast, as does the gray case around the light and the transformer.

It's not easy being fluorescent

With apologies to Kermit the frog for paraphrasing his famous line about being green, shooting under fluorescent light means your photograph will be green. This is one of those undisputable facts of life. Just like white shirts are

Figure 3-4: White balance is daylight. The clouds are white and the bulb is orange.

Figure 3-5: White balance is tungsten. The bulb is almost white and everything else is blue.

tomato sauce magnets in Italian restaurants, fluorescent light is green. That's why DSLR cameras have a setting for this type of light. Figure 3-6 is of a trauma center lit with fluorescent light. The white balance is set on Daylight. And the photograph is green. Don't believe me? Take a look at Figure 3-7. It has the white balance set to Fluorescent. The difference is subtle until you compare them side by side.

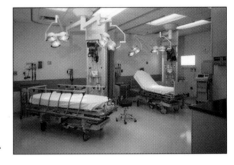

Figure 3-6: Fluorescent light shot with a Daylight setting.

Fluorescent tubes come in all kinds of colors. Except for the full-spectrum true color tubes, all have a green cast that you can't see because your brain "knows" what white is. When making photographs under fluorescent light on film, a magenta filter had to be put in front of the lens to eliminate the green cast.

Seeing the green

Here is a way you can see the green without even being Irish. Go to an office or any building lit with fluores-

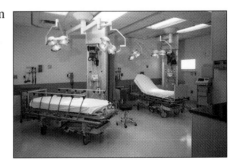

Figure 3-7: Fluorescent light photographed with a Fluorescent setting.

cent tubes. The best choice is one where fluorescents are the only source of light. An office after dark is ideal. That way no other color of light contaminates your efforts.

1. **Put your DSLR camera on a tripod.**

   Yes, I know it seems like every exercise starts this way. I do like my tripods and you will too.

2. **Set your DSLR camera's white balance to Daylight.**

   Refer to the manual that came with your camera to learn how to make this setting.

3. **Place something white in the shot.**

   A piece of white paper works. A GretagMacbeth ColorChecker Gray Scale reference card is even better. It is a great investment and you read more about this invaluable tool later in this chapter.

4. **Set your camera on Aperture Priority. Set the aperture at f/8.0.**

   The shutter changes automatically according to the light.

5. **Take the photograph.**

6. **Change the white balance to the Fluorescent setting.**

   This setting is an electronic magenta filter-equivalent that neutralizes the green cast of the fluorescent tubes.

7. **Take another photograph.**

8. **Set the white balance on Auto.**

   This is just for fun. It gives you an example of what your camera thinks the setting ought to be for a clean white with no color cast.

9. **Take the photograph.**

10. **Open the photographs in Adobe Bridge and compare.**

    The first one shot with the DSLR camera's white balance on Daylight will be distinctly green, like the trauma room in Figure 3-7. The second shot with the white balance set for fluorescent light will look close to right. I am not certain how well the auto setting will work. Like I said, the third shot is just for fun.

**Book II
Chapter 3**

**Making Better
Photographs**

Playing your neutral reference card

In the previous example, I mentioned the GretagMacbeth ColorChecker Gray Scale reference card. I carry this amazing tool in my camera case everywhere I go. It is the first thing I shoot before committing a scene or set up to bits and bytes.

I've already pointed out that your brain makes up for different colored light in everyday situations. The camera is not so sophisticated nor nearly so agile in its abilities with light's color casts. A *color cast* is a predominate color in the neutrals, like the gray transformer in Figure 3-6. It has a blue color cast. Having a reference of what white, gray, and black really is extremely useful. The reference is invaluable when you want to correct color in Photoshop CS2.

ColorChecker charts and other references

Color references are calibrated cards or filters that have a known value of color or reflectance of white, gray, and black. Make a habit of photographing a color reference chart every time the light changes. It makes color correction in Photoshop easy.

A lot of different color references are available on the market today. They range from the venerable Kodak 18% Gray Card to the 24-patch GretagMacbeth ColorChecker Chart, Mini ColorChecker, and the ColorChecker Gray Scale Balance Card. (If you don't believe me, look closely at Figure 3-8 — the name is on the card's edge. Whew. That's a mouthful!) Figure 3-8 shows the GretagMacbeth offerings, as well as the ExpoDisc and the WhiBal references. The gold standard of color references are the ColorChecker charts. They are expensive and worth every penny.

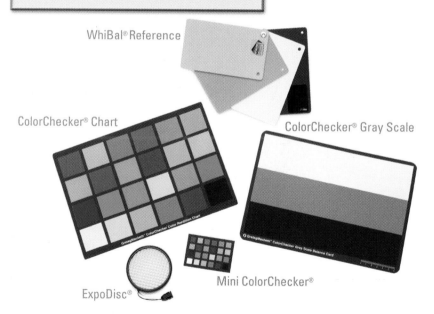

Figure 3-8: Color references.

For more information on the color references visit these Web sites:

- **ColorCheckers** at www.gretagmacbeth.com/indes/ products_color-standards.htm
- **ExpoDisc** at www.expodisc.com
- **WhiBal** references at www.whibal.com

Putting the color reference in the shot

Having a color reference in your camera bag is not enough. Use it! Every time the light changes, shoot another frame of your chart (aka take another picture of it). You use this reference in Photoshop to tweak exposure and color. Here is a good rule to follow: Shoot the ColorChecker first. Put it in the scene, hand it to your model, or hold it yourself. When you want to do critical color work you will be *very* glad you did. Take a look at Figure 3-9. After a while you'll have a collection of photos featuring your reference cards too.

**Book II
Chapter 3**

**Making Better
Photographs**

Figure 3-9: Some of my collection of reference card photographs.

Using an ExpoDisc

The ExpoDisc does the same job as the gray section of the Gray Scale Balance Card. It works differently. The ExpoDisc is a filter that snaps onto the front of the lens. It takes all of the light and scrambles it into an 18-percent neutral gray. This gray file can be used to create a custom white balance setting for the given lighting conditions. The camera analyzes and neutralizes the color cast of the ExpoDisc file. The ExpoDisc is easy to have with you. It comes with a lanyard so it can be worn around your neck. The quick disconnect shown in Figure 3-10 makes it fast and easy to snap on to your lens for creating a white balance file.

Figure 3-10: The ExpoDisc.

Check your camera's manual for details on creating custom white balance settings.

Composing Some Basics

Kodak defines composition as the "pleasing arrangement of the elements within a scene — the main subject, the foreground and background and supporting subjects." This is well and good and says nothing since you don't know what a "pleasing arrangement" is really. The Minneapolis Institute of Arts offers this description: "The arrangement of shapes, forms, colors, areas of light and dark, and other elements in a work of art." This one works a lot better. *Composition* is the arrangement of the things you see in your DSLR camera's viewfinder.

Schooling on composition principles

These easy-to-understand rules help make your photographs more pleasing. There's that word again. Remember that *pleasing* is in the eye of the beholder, and it is *your* photograph after all is said and done. Or as that great philosopher (okay, he was a musician) Ricky Nelson once said, "You can't please everyone so you got to please yourself. . . ."

Reading from left to right

English is read on the page from the upper-left corner of the page to the lower right. That means your eyes track automatically from the left to the right and constantly seek to reach the lower-right area of the page. Advertisers use this principle by placing the call to action in the lower-right corner of a printed ad. Sometimes place your subject to the right of the frame. Your viewer eye is drawn to it naturally and will linger there.

The darkness and the light

In a *low-key,* or dark, scene, your eye automatically goes to the lightest area. Your eyes are programmed to look for light. As a matter of fact, this programming overrides the eye's tendency to seek the lower right. Where does your eye land in Figure 3-11? Even though the white dot is on the lower left, your eye immediately finds it.

Figure 3-11: What catches your eye?

In a *high-key* image where the dominant tone is white (or almost white), the eye goes to the darker areas. Once again, where does your eye go in Figure 3-12? It finds the black dot in the field of white. Your eyes want to find areas of contrast. Since white is the contrast of black in Figure 3-11, the eye finds the white dot. On the other hand, black is the contrast carrier against the white background in Figure 3-12. The eye is drawn to the black dot.

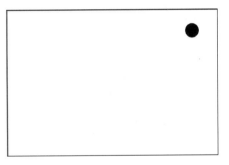

Figure 3-12: You see the black dot in the upper-right corner.

Applying the rule of thirds

The viewfinder of your DSLR camera is a rectangle. Mentally divide the area into thirds. (Some viewfinders already have a rule-of-thirds grid on them.) Where the lines intersect are the best focal points of the space. Figure 3-13 shows a rule-of-thirds grid with a focal area circled in red.

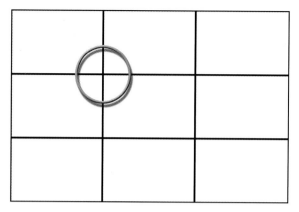

Figure 3-13: The lines cross at the points of interest in the composition.

Figure 3-14 shows a boat on the water in Nantucket Harbor. For the most part, the boat is perfectly centered in the frame. It falls right through the middle part of the rule-of-thirds grid. The photograph lacks tension and interest. Compare it to Figure 3-15, where the buoy in the boat exactly intersects one of the focal points. The photograph has much more interest now that it's off center.

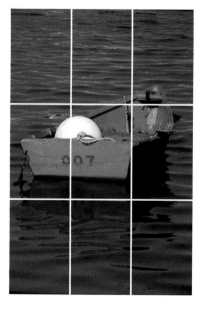

Figure 3-14: A boat centered in the frame.

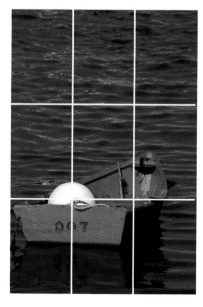

Figure 3-15: A boat ready to head off on an uncharted adventure.

Okay, so much for theory. Look at some photographs. Figure 3-16 is part of the Tampa, Florida, skyline. The major buildings are positioned right through the middle of the grid. The circular high rise is dead center. The white building to the left looks like it is part of the circular building.

Figure 3-16: The round structure merges with the one to its left.

I moved my camera position about 100 feet to the left for Figure 3-17. The white Bank of America building is now separated from the round high rise. I also moved the building to the left third of the frame. The buildings are still in the middle of the center third of the grid from top to bottom.

Finally, in Figure 3-18 the buildings have been moved so that they are in the focal point on the intersection of the rule-of-thirds grid. The strong diagonal of the railroad tracks leads the eye into the shot. The final version, without circles and grids, is shown in Figure 3-19.

Figure 3-17: A better composition, though still centered.

Figure 3-18: Now the buildings are at an interest point where the lines cross.

Figure 3-19: The final, or hero, composition.

See what you are looking at

At first glance this statement, "See what you are looking at," sounds silly. When you think about it oftentimes all you do is center the subject in the frame, set the exposure (or let the camera do it), and shoot. The results are often not the best they could be. Practice actually seeing what you are looking at in the viewfinder. Be aware of the elements in the scene. Ask yourself these questions:

- What's in the foreground?
- What's the subject of the photograph?
- What's the background?
- How do these elements work together?

Question everything. Shoot a photograph. Look at it. Change something. Shoot another photograph. Look at it. Remember that when you are photographing digitally it costs nothing to shoot one more frame. That is a decided advantage over film, where each image cost at least a dollar and took a lot of time to reveal results — Polaroids notwithstanding.

Your tripod is the greatest accessory ever made for improving composition. It helps you get horizon lines straight. It holds the camera in exactly the same place while you pick up that soda can in the foreground. It keeps still while you zoom in or out. It maintains the scene in the viewfinder while you take the memory card out of the camera and look at the photograph on your computer screen. Shooting on location, your laptop is second only to your tripod as a compositional tool. No matter how well you see through your camera, nothing beats looking at the actual pixels.

Dusting in the Wind: Your Sensor

The *sensor* in a DSLR camera is many things. It receives light, converting it to electrons recorded as images. Mostly, though, it is a dust magnet. That's right. DSLR camera sensors collect dust the way dogs do fleas, kids do toys, and supermodels do shoes.

Dust does not adversely affect your photograph if you can see it through the viewfinder. Dust in the viewfinder is sitting either under or on top of the viewing screen. When a photograph is made, the mirror flips up out of the way and the sensor sees the image. At that point, the sensor sucks up any dust in the camera chamber. It happens. This section is about what dust looks like on an image and how to clean your sensor.

Sensing what dust does

If you are looking at a photograph and see a dark, fuzzy bowling ball, that is dust on the sensor. A dust particle is huge when compared to the tiny pixels that make up a sensor. A speck of dust may block or just obscure the view of a bunch of pixels.

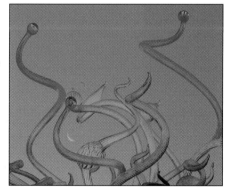

Figure 3-20 is a photograph of a Chihuly glass sculpture outside of the Atlanta Botanical Garden just before sunrise. Look between the arms of glass framing the center of the shot. See the three black specks? (The white one is the moon.)

Figure 3-20: Chihuly in the Atlanta Botanical Garden, June 12, 2004.

Figure 3-21 is a zoomed-in version. The dust motes are circled in red. These little intruders cause issues with the quality of the photograph. When against a plain background, they are relatively easy to get rid of in Photoshop. When they overlay a texture like the glass itself, retouching that is a whole other story.

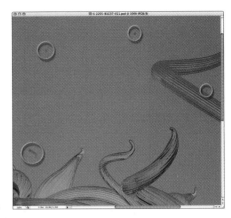

Figure 3-21: Dust on the sensor. Yuck!

The sensor in a DSLR camera is its heart. Damage the sensor and the camera is ruined. The next section shows you the methods that I use to clean my sensors. I am not suggesting you clean yours. I am showing you how I clean mine. If you decide that you want to clean the sensor in your DSLR camera, that's fine with me. Just as I am responsible for any damage I cause my sensor in cleaning it, so are you responsible for any damage done to yours. I am not responsible. The publisher of this book is not responsible. Finally, before you do anything about cleaning your sensor, read your instruction manual about how to do it. Once again, READ YOUR INSTRUCTION MANUAL FIRST. Okay.

If you are squeamish about cleaning your sensor, don't clean it. Take it to the camera store where you purchased it. They will be glad to help. That's why buying at your local camera store is a really great idea. If you bought it mail order or through the Internet, don't be surprised if your local camera store either won't help you or charges for showing you how to clean your sensor. They are professionals at this stuff. They are worth patronizing, and if you don't buy from them, their knowledge is still worth paying for.

Choosing cleaning tools

I use the tools manufactured by the folks at www.visibledust.com. They have good tutorials on their Web site for using their products. The other tool I use is the Giottos Rocket-Air blower, available at www.giottos.com. This blower is shaped like a space ship in the movies from the 50s, complete with fins! The nose of the Rocket is a solid tube with a hole in the tip. Squeeze the body hard to get a blast of clean air.

Blowing dust off your camera's sensor

The simplest method of cleaning a sensor is blowing it off with the Rocket.

1. **Mount your camera on your tripod.**

   Extend the tripod's legs so the camera is just above your eye level. Tilt the camera so the lens points down toward the floor.

TIP

If your tripod isn't tall enough to get your camera as high as your eyes, pull up a chair and sit down. Most tripods reach higher than a person sitting down.

2. Remove the lens.

Put the *back cap* that came with the lens on the lens mount. The front of your DSLR camera is now open. Look up into the mount. You can see the mirror and the bottom of the viewing screen (as shown in Figure 3-22). Now you prepare the Rocket.

3. Point the tip of the Giottos Rocket away from the camera. Squeeze the bulb a half dozen times as hard as you can.

This clears any debris that might have drifted into the nozzle.

Figure 3-22: The viewing screen's mirror and bottom.

WARNING!

4. Carefully blow out, with the Giottos Rocket, the inside of the lens mount. Avoid touching the mirror with the nozzle.

Squeeze the Giottos Rocket body with as much pressure as you can and still keep the nozzle from jumping around. See Figure 3-23.

5. Gently lift the mirror with the fingertip of your free hand. Blow out the camera chamber with the Giottos Rocket.

The mirror is being lifted in Figure 3-24.

6. While holding up the mirror, blow off the underside of the mirror and the shutter.

Refer to Figure 3-25. See why the camera wants to be on the tripod? This process gets out dust that might be attracted to the sensor in the next step.

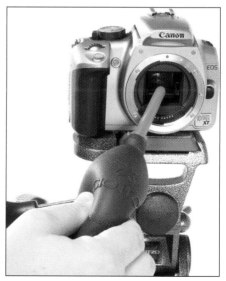

Figure 3-23: Blowing out the camera chamber.

Figure 3-24: Use a finger tip to gently lift the mirror out of the way.

Figure 3-25: Blow out the rest of the camera. This removes dust that might be on the shutter.

7. Open the shutter.

Normally the sensor is safely covered by the shutter. Opening the shutter exposes the sensor. Check your instruction manual for how to open the shutter properly for sensor cleaning. Be sure to follow these instructions to the letter to avoid potential damage to your camera. Notice that the mirror stays up by itself while the shutter is open. See Figure 3-26.

8. Carefully — very carefully — put the tip of the nozzle close to the sensor.

9. Squeeze the body of the Giottos Rocket to push air through the nozzle.

Figure 3-26: Be very careful when the sensor is exposed for cleaning.

Be extremely careful not to touch the sensor with the nozzle. Squeeze several times, moving the nozzle back and forth across the area above the sensor, as shown in Figure 3-27.

Figure 3-27: Carefully blow over the sensor. Avoid touching it with the Rocket's nozzle.

10. Close the shutter and reattach the lens.

Your instruction manual tells you how to close the shutter.

11. Shoot a photograph of a plain wall or one of a clear sky.

Check the resulting photograph in Photoshop for those fuzzy bowling balls. If you still see some, remove the lens again and repeat Steps 7 through 10.

Using the Visible Dust Sensor Brush

Dr. Fariborz Degen and the staff at Visible Dust in Edmonton, Alberta have made a science of cleaning dust off sensors. The tools listed on their Web site — www.visibledust.com — are invaluable. Based on the principle of ionic attraction, the Sensor Brush actually attracts and holds dust that has settled on a digital image sensor. Complete instructions are on the Visible Dust web site. I use the following steps with my digital cameras.

Before using a Sensor Brush, thoroughly clean (or have professionally cleaned) the camera chamber, as shown in the previous steps.

1. **Mount the camera on your tripod.**

   Consistent, aren't I? Extend the legs so the tripod holds the camera above eye level. Tilt the camera down at about 45°.

2. **Remove the lens.**

   Take the lens off the camera and cover the back lens mount with the cap that came with the lens. It is a good idea to first use the Giottos Rocket to blow off the lens' back glass element, as well as blow out the cap.

3. **Open the camera shutter.**

   Again, refer to your instruction manual to find out how.

4. **Charge the Sensor Brush.**

   a. **Hold a can of compressed air level.**

   b. **Pull the trigger to clear the nozzle.**

   c. **Pull the trigger again and blow air through the bristles of the sensor brush. This also cleans any dust off the bristles.**

   Or use the new self-cleaning, self-charging Sensor Brush. Spin the Sensor Brush by pressing its button for 10 seconds to charge it. The spinning motion also cleans any dust that might have settled into the bristles; see Figure 3-28.

5. **Using one stroke, pull the Sensor Brush across the face of the chip as shown in Figure 3-29.**

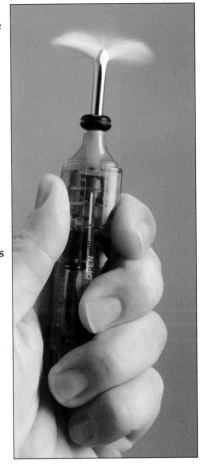

Figure 3-28: The spinning Sensor Brush.

Figure 3-29: Use one stroke of the brush, then recharge it.

6. **Close the shutter.**

   See your instruction manual for details.

7. **Reattach your lens and photograph a plain wall or clear sky.**

8. **Open the photograph in Photoshop.**

9. **Zoom in 100% by choosing View⇨Actual Pixels from the Photoshop menu.**

10. **Scroll the entire photograph looking for those pesky, fuzzy bowling balls.**

    Repeat Steps 3 through 7 if necessary.

Book III
The Digital Negative

"Remember, your Elvis should appear bald and slightly hunched. Nice Big Foot, Brad. Keep your two-headed animals in the shadows and your alien spacecrafts crisp and defined."

*C*hoosing the right digital format for your DSLR camera to record light is critical. Book III explains the pros and cons and, for that matter, what JPEG and RAW formats mean. You read how to create bullet-proof archives of your original digital negatives and share them with your family, friends, and the world using the Internet. This book is your introduction to Adobe Camera Raw version 3, the finest RAW converter in the land. You experience the power contained in a RAW file that your DSLR camera has captured and discover how to release it visually.

Chapter 1: Choosing the Best Format: JPEG or RAW

In this Chapter

✓ **Understanding bit depth**

✓ **Getting familiar with the JPEG format**

✓ **Compressing digital images**

✓ **Reading about the RAW format**

This chapter helps with some of the technical aspects of how digital photographs are recorded and includes a simple explanation of bit depth. This chapter also helps you decide which format to choose when using your *digital single lens reflex (DSLR)* camera. You read about the popular JPEG format — its good points, some downsides, and why it has become a standard. Finally, I introduce you to the RAW format, exploring the positives of digital negatives and comparing it to JPEG capture. You use the Layers palette and Curves adjustment layers on low- and high bit-depth files to see how each is affected. The Histogram palette introduces the damage that can happen to a file when working in low bit depths.

Diving into Bit Depth

Bit depth is the amount of data that a digital sensor can capture. The higher the bit depth, the more visual information gets recorded.

It's all about the number of tones

Bit depth is concerned with the number of tones each pixel records. The more tones a pixel sees, the better the quality of the final photograph. High bit depths are better and as you see later, lower bit depths are not so good. An image that is 1 bit has only black and white: two tones. You know people to whom 1 bit (as in on or off, right or wrong) applies as a great description of their personalities. Teenagers come to mind, for example. A 2-bit file has black, white, and two shades of gray: four tones. A 3-bit file has black, white, and six shades of gray: eight tones. The list goes on.

Figure 1-1 is a 1-bit digital photograph. All you can see is black or white. There is no detail. Figure 1-2 is a 2-bit image. Detail appears because there are two shades of gray in addition to black and white. Look at the 4-bit photograph in Figure 1-3. It reveals even more detail with 14 gray tones plus black and white. Now consider the 8-bit black and white photograph in Figure 1-4. It has continuous graduations between black and white. The 254 shades of gray really make a difference in the detail. Now you can see texture in the woman's skin.

Figure 1-1: A 1-bit photo.

Figure 1-2: A 2-bit image.

Figure 1-3: A 4-bit photo.

Figure 1-4: An 8-bit picture.

Playing the numbers game in a digital photograph

An 8-bit file has 256 steps. Each step is represented by a number between 0 and 255. Black is 0 and white is 255. There are 254 shades of gray. Each shade has a number assigned to it from 1 through 254. And the numbers have meaning. Each number represents one single tone. Once you work with them enough and become familiar with what they mean, you can use them to know that your photograph is properly exposed. More importantly you will know what will print and what won't. Figure 1-5 shows a pair of gradational gray scales.

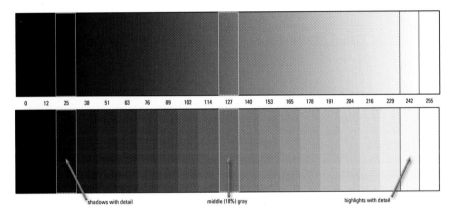

| 0 | 12 | 25 | 38 | 51 | 63 | 76 | 89 | 102 | 114 | 127 | 140 | 153 | 165 | 178 | 191 | 204 | 216 | 229 | 242 | 255 |

shadows with detail   middle (18%) gray   highlights with detail

Figure 1-5: Know your numbers.

The gray scale on top is continuous in tonality, with each step one number higher than the one before it. The scale on the bottom has been broken into wedges. Between the two are the numbers for each wedge. The important numbers to remember are 25 and 242. They represent the darkest and lightest values that a properly set up photo-quality printer can reproduce. The numbers vary from printer to printer. In general this is a very good rule.

Relating numbers to a photograph

Figure 1-6 shows a gray scale chart under a black and white photograph of actress Tiffany Dupont. The red arrows point from the number to the area of that tone. Her shirt reads 255 and that is pure white. It is overexposed. There is no detail present. Her cheek bone is 242 — white with detail. The skin under her right eye is middle gray. It reads 127. The shadow area on the right side of her forehead is 38; it prints with some detail. Her hair reads 12 and will be a solid area with no detail.

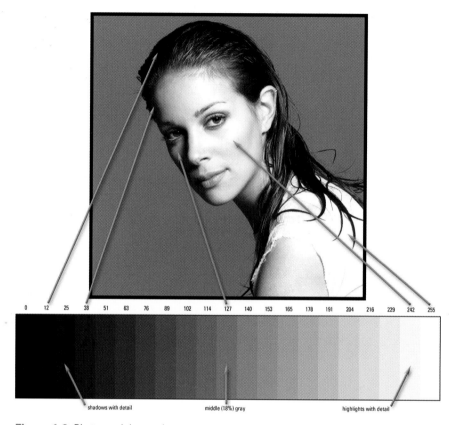

Figure 1-6: Photograph by numbers.

The close up of Tiffany's face in Figure 1-7 shows the detail in her skin and the shadow area around her right eye. There is almost no detail in the hair on top of her head.

The close up of her t-shirt in Figure 1-8 shows no detail at all in most of the white areas and the skin just below the sleeve of her shirt. Understanding the numbers is key to producing good photographs.

A highlight area that is overexposed and shows no detail is said to be *blown out*. A blown-out highlight has numbers above 249. Shadow areas that read below 25 and have no detail are said to be *blocked up*.

Figure 1-7: Looking closely.

Figure 1-8: Looking even more closely.

Gathering all the bit depths and tones

Figure 1-9 is a chart of the tones for each bit depth, from 1 to 16 bits. Every increase in bit depth doubles the number of tones. The bit depths commonly used in DSLR photography are asterisked. 8 bits is the standard for digital output. Printers and printing presses use 8-bit files. Most DSLR cameras record 12 bits. Photoshop can work in either 8 bit or 16 bit.

Adobe Photoshop works in the 16-bit space, though it only has 15-bit space. To get to 16 bits, Photoshop adds 1 bit to the 15-bit space. While this may seem a bit iffy and maybe a slick way to technically be 16 bit, a very good reason exists. By adding the extra bit of data and moving to the 16-bit space, the mathematics behind the scenes is a whole lot easier. That means that computers

Bit-Depth Chart

Bits	Tones
1	2
2	4
3	8
4	16
5	32
6	64
7	128
8	256
9	512
10	1024
11	2048
12	4096
13	8192
14	16384
15	32768
16	65536

Figure 1-9: Bit-depth chart.

Book III
Chapter 1

Choosing the
Best Format:
JPEG or RAW

run a lot faster. Kudos to the Adobe Photoshop team for being straight up with their customers and for making computers more efficient!

Doing some 8-bit and 16-bit math

How much difference is there between 8 and 16 bits? If you said "Eight," you'd be right, of course. There's a whole lot more to it than that. If you said "128 times more tones," you know exactly how much more a "whole lot" more is. It's important that the more tones you have, the more creative you can be while maintaining the integrity of the image.

8-bit files don't have a lot of room to play with their pixels without potentially damaging them. The photograph of Tiffany you've seen is an 8-bit, slightly underexposed, black and white file. Her face wants to be brighter. Photoshop can easily make the image brighter and it does it at a cost to the image. Follow the steps to make it better.

Inserting a color sampler

When working with pixels made with a DSLR camera, use the largest sample size. This reduces dramatically the errors that could occur by reading a single pixel, especially if it were noise or an unexpected white or colored pixel. Noise is digital grain. *Noise* happens in the shadows of a digital photograph, especially when the camera is set to higher ISOs.

1. **Download the Book III, Chapter 1 folder at www.amesphoto.com/learning.**

   To download files for this and other tutorials in the book, you have to register a valid email address. Don't worry — no one other than I will use your email. Choosing to register gives you the benefit of receiving updates and special tutorials that show the latest digital photographic and Photoshop CS2 techniques, as well as information about where you can see one of my live sessions.

2. **Open 8-bit.psd.**

   Navigate to it in Bridge and double-click it. It opens in Photoshop. Refer to Figure 1-10 to locate the Photoshop palettes and tools mentioned in this exercise.

Taking a shortcut

Adobe Photoshop CS2 offers many ways to accomplish a task, select a tool, or open a palette. Using the mouse is the slowest way. If you want to become a Photoshop power user, work with keyboard shortcuts. Throughout the book I show you the shortcut and alternative methods of getting around. Appendix B, "Kevin's Essential Photoshop Shortcuts," enhances your Photoshop experience.

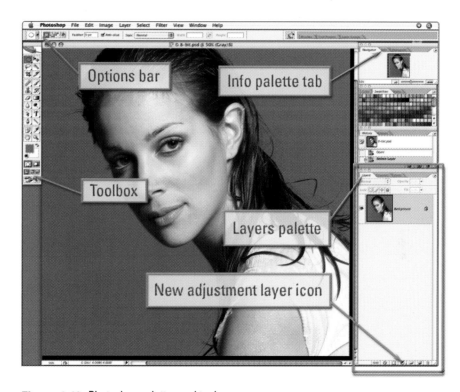

Figure 1-10: Photoshop palettes and tools.

3. **Click the triangle at the bottom of the Eyedropper and select Color Sampler from the flyout menu.**

   You are going to place a Color Sampler on the photograph's mid tone. See Figure 1-11 for the menu. A *color sampler* allows you to dynamically see the changes you make to the RAW file in the Info window. Camera Raw supports up to nine discreet color samplers.

4. **In the options bar, click the Sample Size drop-down menu and select 5 by 5 Average (as in Figure 1-12).**

5. **Position the sampler on the illuminated skin under Tiffany's right eye, as shown in Figure 1-13, and click to place the sampler.**

   Continue with the next section.

Choosing the Sample Size option from the drop-down menu (see Figure 1-12) is important because it allows accurate data to be displayed in the Info palette. Point Sample reads a single pixel; 3 by 3 and 5 by 5 sample a grid of either 9 pixels or 25 pixels, respectively, and averages them.

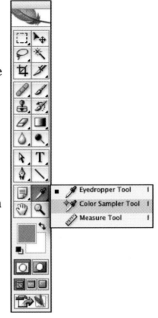

Figure 1-11: Choose the Color Sampler.

Setting up the Info palette

The Info palette is where you read the values of the pixels in your photograph. Set it up this way:

Figure 1-12: Choose 5 by 5 Average for a sample area.

1. **Reveal the Info palette by clicking its tab, choosing Window⇨ Info, or pressing the F8 function key.**

2. **Click the eyedropper, circled in red in Figure 1-14.**

   A drop-down menu appears. Now you're going to make a curves adjustment layer.

3. **Choose RGB Color, as you see in Figure 1-15.**

4. **Repeat this step for the #1 Sampler reading in the Info palette.**

   Find the Layers palette. At the bottom is a series of icons that let you do different things to an image. The one you want looks like a half-black, half-white circle. This icon lets you add new adjustment layers.

Figure 1-13: Place a sampler here.

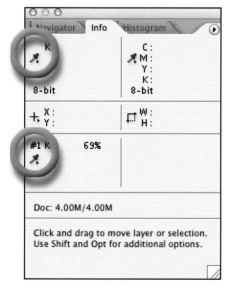

Figure 1-14: Click the eyedropper to set up each readout in the Info palette.

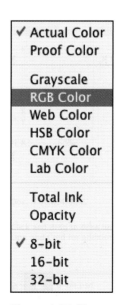

Figure 1-15: Choose RGB Color to set up this readout.

5. **Click the New Adjustment Layer icon⇨Curves, as shown in Figure 1-16.**

The New Adjustment Layer icon is the fourth one to the right, counting the trash icon, at the bottom of the Layers palette. Now you adjust the Curve to brighten the skin tones.

6. **⌘+click (Ctrl+click) above the color sampler.**

A circle briefly appears on the curve and is replaced by a dot.

7. **Press the ↓ key until Sampler #1 reads 128 for R, G, and B.**

8. **Move the cursor over the brightest area on her left cheek.**

Your curve and Info palette look similar to Figure 1-17.

9. **Click OK.**

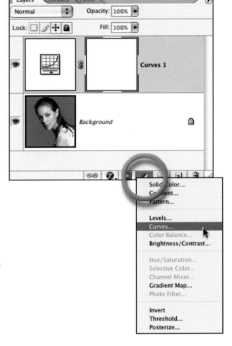

 Caucasian skin tones are usually a stop to a stop and a half above middle gray when measured in the highlights. This image was underexposed. The middle gray tone on the properly exposed version earlier in this chapter shows 127 under her right eye. You have used the Curves adjustment layer to brighten that area. It also brightens the skin on her cheek (in this case to 246).

Figure 1-16: Clicking the Add New Adjustment Layer icon shows the menu.

10. **Click Window⇨Histogram. Click the triangle in the upper-right corner of the window.**

This refreshes the readout. Notice the gaps in the graph in Figure 1-18. If your Histogram does not show the additional information in the bottom half of the palette, click the flyout menu in the upper-right corner and choose Expanded View.

Figure 1-17: The results of the Curves adjustment displayed in the Info palette.

11. **In the Layers palette, hide the Curves layer by clicking the eye icon.**

12. **Click the triangle on the Histogram once more.**

    You can see in Figure 1-19 that no gaps appear when the curve is turned off.

13. **Click the Curve layer again and refresh the Histogram.**

    The graph is broken. The appearance of gaps in a Histogram's graph is called *combing* because it looks like a hair comb. In severe cases of combing the photograph may print with posterization or banding artifacts.

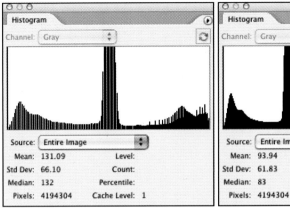

Figure 1-18: Gaps in the histogram are caused by the Curves adjustments.

Figure 1-19: A solid histogram with the Curves layer hidden.

14. **Click the Move Tool, which is circled in red in Figure 1-20.**

15. **Choose Window⇨8-bit.psd.**

16. **Click+drag the Curves 1 layer from the Layers palette onto 16-bit.psd.**

    The layer is copied to 16-bit.psd and appears above the Background palette in the layers stack. 16-bit.psd is as bright as 8-bit.psd.

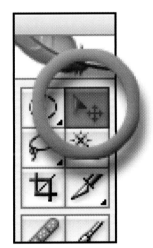

    Adjustment layers can be dragged between files to apply the settings the layers already carry. This speeds the process of adjusting several images to the same settings.

17. **Refresh the Histogram with 16-bit.psd active.**

    The graph in the Histogram window is solid even though the Curves adjustment layer is on! This is living proof of the power of high bit depth in maintaining image quality.

Figure 1-20: Choose the Move Tool.

18. **Save both of your files for future reference.**

The versatility of 16-bit files carries a file size burden. The high bit-depth photographs are twice the size of their 8-bit counterparts. The red circles in Figure 1-21 show that 16-bit.psd is 8 megabytes (MB) and 8-bit.psd is only 4MB.

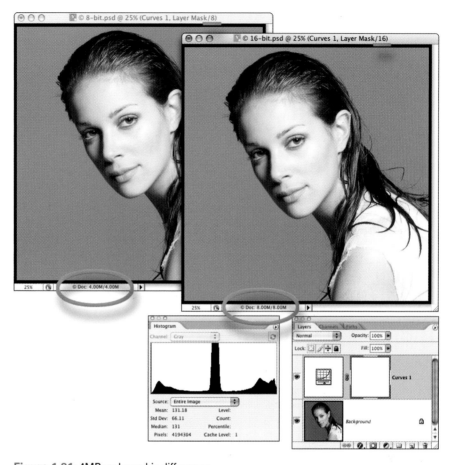

Figure 1-21: 4MB makes a big difference.

Making digital color happen

DSLR cameras capture three channels of color information. One channel is Red, one is Green, and one is Blue. A computer inside the camera either sends the RAW file to be saved on the CompactFlash card or processes the data received from the chip into a JPEG file. (You can read more about storage media in Book I, Chapter 5.) The sensor in your DSLR is made of pixels with *color filters* (dye layers) over the *micro lenses* that concentrate the light on each pixel in specific locations. The camera's built-in computer knows what color each pixel is assigned and its exact location on the sensor. With that information, it can calculate what a scene's proper color is.

To dye for

One DSLR camera available today does not use color dye layers on individual pixels: SD10 from Sigma. Its chip is manufactured by Foveon, Inc., and uses technology that allows every pixel to see every color. It's called the X3F sensor.

This color scheme for pixel layout on a digital sensor is called a *Bayer Array* and is a common form of color pixel array. You can see one in Figure 1-22. Not all manufacturers use a Bayer Array or even square pixels, for that matter. It really doesn't matter what shape or color arrangement the pixels are. At this writing not a disappointing DSLR camera is on the market. That means you can buy the DSLR that feels best to you and be assured you are getting a quality camera capable of making great 8 × 10 prints, at the minimum. They are all capable of making great photographs!

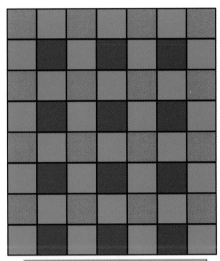

Bayer Array of Digital Sensor Pixel Colors

Figure 1-22: A Bayer Array.

8 bits in living color

You have seen how black and white is made of a grayscale image containing black, white, and 254 shades of gray for a total of 256 total steps. The question on the table is how that translates into a color photograph. When a digital photograph is made, the computer inside the camera calculates the color values for each pixel and maps them into three channels of color information. That becomes the image you see.

Figure 1-23 shows the three channels of colored grayscales: one each for Red, Green, and Blue (RGB). Every color digital photograph has the same three channels when captured. All color digital captures are in RGB.

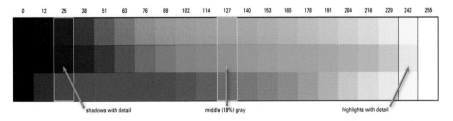

0 12 25 38 51 63 76 89 102 114 127 140 153 165 178 191 204 216 229 242 255

shadows with detail   middle (18%) gray   highlights with detail

Figure 1-23: Color is made of Red, Green, and Blue channels.

With three channels of color information, the 8-bit color file offers millions of color tones — way more than your eyes can perceive. How can three sets of 256 tones give that many choices? 256 red tones multiplied by 256 green ones multiplied by 265 blue ones gives 16,777,212 tones, including black and white. If you did the math you got 16,777,216. See Figure 1-24. I took away the black and whites for two of the channels because black and white don't carry any color information.

8-bit color

16,777,216 tones

Figure 1-24: Over 16-million colors are possible in an 8-bit color photograph.

The JPEG Format

ISO International Standard 10918-1:1994 is the original JPEG standard. JPEG uses a *lossy* compression routine that can achieve 10- and sometimes 20 to 1 savings in space. *Lossy compression* throws away some of the image data. The decompressed version is not exactly the same as the original. The compression system works to take advantage of the fact that humans cannot remember color accurately. Since JPEG files are meant to be viewed by humans, it works quite well.

A megabyte is roughly a million bytes of data. The true size of a megabyte is 1,000 kilobytes. A kilobyte is 1,024 bytes. The 24-byte part is dropped for the sake of easy conversion. A *megabyte* is, in casual terms, a thousand bytes.

Pegging the format

Work on the JPEG format began with a group of Europeans. In 1985, the working groups combined as the Joint Photographic Experts Group. The first letter of the name became the name of the standard they developed. It is abbreviated JPEG and the extension added to files in that format is .jpg.

An extension is part of the file name the computer uses to understand what the file is and how to open it. An image file in the JPEG format might be named img_0321.jpg. The .jpg is the extension. The format has been used in digital cameras for the last 10 years and will undoubtedly continue to play a role in future cameras. It works well with full-color natural photographs.

Weighing JPEG's pros

Portable digital cameras initially had very limited random access memory installed. RAM was expensive; 64MB cost around $1,100. This meant that a method of compressing those 1MB files was very desirable.

JPEG compression has two distinct advantages:

✔ It is fast. It does not take a lot of computing power to make a JPEG.

✔ Resulting files are small. You can store a lot of images on original 16MB CompactFlash cards. The small file size meant it could be sent to newspapers over telephone lines. (The Internet would not be born until 1995.)

Random Access Memory (RAM) is the set of chips in a computer or camera that temporarily store bytes of data. The more RAM a camera has, the more data it can handle before writing to a hard drive or flash media. In the case of digital cameras, more RAM means the camera can capture more images in its buffer before having to stop to write data to the flash card.

Seeing is understanding

Figure 1-25 is the original image. Figure 1-26 is a JPEG that's been opened and resaved several times with the same name.

Looking at them near each other shows little difference in quality. The sky shows some color distortion. JPEG compresses by throwing out color data, which explains the color shift. Now look at enlargements of the two in Figure 1-27. You can easily see the *artifacting,* visible squares of data and distortion, that has built up in the JPEG.

Figure 1-25: An original JPEG.

Figure 1-26: A JPEG opened, saved, and closed several times.

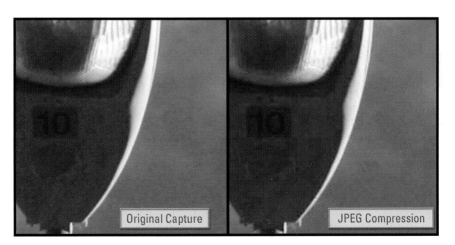

Original Capture

JPEG Compression

Figure 1-27: Sharpness and detail are lost in the photo on the right.

The back story

The first digital cameras were tethered to a computer by a cable that allowed the computer to shoot the camera and receive the captured image data. Digital cameras were freed from being tied to a computer around 10 years ago. CompactFlash cards, pioneered by SanDisk (www.sandisk.com) in 1994, offered a way to cut the cord. The capacity of the cards was small, starting at only 16MB. Image files were small then. The first digital cameras captured about 1MB of data that yielded a photograph 640 × 480 pixels. The images were most often used in newspapers, so the low resolution worked quite well. Image compression at that time was more important than any loss of quality. The JPEG standard already existed. The rest is history.

Capturing JPEG

JPEG files are 8 bits per channel. The sensor in most DSLR cameras sees and records 12 bits per channel, or 4,096 tones for each one of the Red, Green, and Blue channels. The camera sizes down the data to about ⅛ its original size by discarding data.

A DSLR camera set to capture JPEG has to do three things:

- First, it has to decide which 256 tones for each of the three colors to save, and throw away almost 3,900 tones.

- Secondly, the camera has to apply a curve to make the data look like a photograph.

- Finally, it applies compression to make it small.

The camera can do all of these things very quickly and produce a reasonable-quality image. An awful lot of data gets lost in the process.

Shooting RAW is faster than shooting JPEG in most cases. Although 16-bit RAW files are twice as big as 8-bit files, they're actually saved faster than the smaller JPEG. The reason is the camera has to do quite a lot of processing to make a JPEG from all of the data the sensor captured. The RAW file requires no additional processing after it's in the camera's buffer. The file's saved directly to the CompactFlash card immediately. Very few, very expensive professional digital camera backs capture in true 16-bit.

Rhetorical questions to consider about film

Imagine you are shooting film and there were a switch on the back of the camera that would divide each full 36 × 24mm frame of film into four 9 × 6mm frames. Can you imagine ever using it? Of course not!

Imagine you shot a roll of 35mm film and took it to the drugstore for processing. Here's the question: Would you run the negatives through a shredder before you even looked at the prints? Absolutely not! Shooting JPEG does both of the things you would never do, even if you could. The compression makes images smaller so more of them fit on a card. The process of conversion from 12 bit to 8 bit throws away the digital negative.

Serving It RAW

The RAW setting on a DSLR camera saves all the information the sensor in the camera was able to see. Most RAW captures are of 12-bit data. That means that each RAW file has three 12-bit channels, one each for Red, Green, and Blue.

Other than the bit-depth difference, data in RAW files is *linear.* That means the data flows in a straight line from the brightest point to the darkest. Your eyes see bright areas first; then the brain remembers that area and tells your pupils to dilate to look into the dark areas. This curve allows you to see highlights and shadows at the same time. A gamma of 2.2 is a curve that mimics what you see outside on a sunny day. It's how a computer monitor makes images look right.

A gamma of 1.0 is a straight line. *Gamma* is a technical function that engineers and color experts use to help control how images reproduce.

The top half of the chart in Figure 1-28 represents a linear RAW capture. Notice how almost half of the tones are very light gray to white. The greatest amount of the information the sensor has recorded is stored here. In a 12-bit image, 2,048 tones are contained in the first, or brightest, f/stop of exposure. (Book I, Chapter 2 talks about f/stop in detail.) Cut the exposure by one f/stop and half the remaining data (1,024 tones) are here. The third brightest f/stop has 512, the fourth 256, the fifth 128, and the sixth, deep in the shadows, has only 64 tones.

**Book III
Chapter 1**

Choosing the
Best Format:
JPEG or RAW

Early RAW

Digital camera manufacturers have been offering RAW capture from the very beginning. It is really the first format offered. The early suppliers of digital cameras and the photographers who used them realized that having a huge number of tones helped make up for the lower resolution of the sensors at the time. In my commercial work I used a digital back that had a 4-megapixel black and white sensor. Shooting three individual images of a subject made color. The first shot had a red filter over the lens, the second had a green filter, and the third had a blue filter. The software combined the images into a single high bit-depth file. Since the capture was in high bit depth, the files were 24MB.

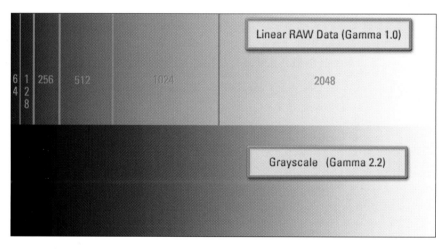

Figure 1-28: A linear RAW capture.

Non-RAW files have even tonal distribution. Compare the bottom of the two grayscale charts to the top one. Both show six stops of data. The RAW file on top has the largest distribution in the brightest steps and less data in each step as it moves to the left. The normal image has tones spread evenly from highlights on the right to the shadows on the left.

As long as the exposure is close to being correct you can easily get optimal results from RAW files using Adobe Camera Raw version 3 built into Photoshop CS2.

I'm not saying, "It's okay to be sloppy with your exposure." What I am saying is Camera Raw and the high bit-depth RAW digital negatives can take an exposure that's almost "there" and perfect it easily in post-production.

When a RAW file is manipulated with software like Adobe Camera Raw in Photoshop CS2, the original data is not touched. The settings you read about in Book III, Chapter 3 don't change the original data. They modify how a Photoshop editable file is developed. The settings in RAW files are almost infinitely adjustable and never cause the original file to degrade. That's why they are called *digital negatives*.

Eyeing the Bottom Line: RAW versus JPEG

The passions on which format to record your priceless, irreplaceable photographs run very high on both sides. JPEG proponents love

- The ease of storage because of the small file size
- The ability to view the photographs without special software
- And the simplicity of emailing them to family and loved ones

The photographers who shoot in RAW can't understand why anyone would throw away valuable image data. Quality to them is the holy grail of making photographs. No inconvenience is too great for them when it comes to having the best quality files containing the most information. They love

- The ability to tweak exposure, color, contrast, and brightness
- Making the photographs black and white without harming the original file

Personally, I never shoot JPEGs. I am a resolution fanatic. I want everything the sensor can capture available to bend to my whim in Photoshop. I admit to a huge RAW bias. And I come by it naturally. Back in the day when sensors were small, the RAW data allowed professional photographers to do things that were seemingly impossible. The first digital cameras weren't cameras at all. They were accessories that replaced the magazines that held film on existing cameras. They were called *digital backs* because that's where they went — on the back of the camera. The original digital backs only delivered RAW files. I grew up using them. JPEG simply wasn't an option. I'm a product of my upbringing when it comes to shooting RAW. I have no problem carrying extra CompactFlash cards when shooting. It's all right with me that processing out my working files takes a little bit of time. To me the results far exceed any inconvenience.

Consider the comparison between a typical RAW file and a compressed JPEG in Figure 1-29. The data contained in the JPEG is tiny against the huge amount of information carried in the RAW file.

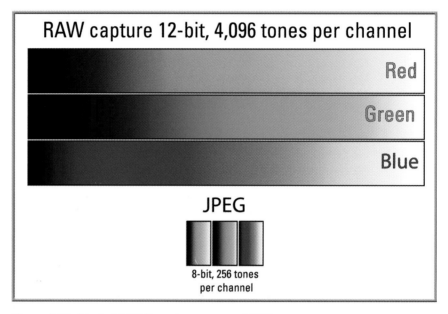

Figure 1-29: A typical RAW file and a compressed JPEG.

I encourage you to consider shooting RAW over JPEG. In Book III, Chapter 5, I show you how to use Camera Raw for setting white balance, color correction, and exposure control and how to make black and white and much more. The additional quality is worth it. As the RAW converters like Adobe Camera Raw improve, so do the photographs that come out of your digital negatives — even those shot years ago. My photographs are important to me, as I know yours are to you. And the most important photographs all are the ones of family and friends.

I'm reminded of what photographer and photographic educator Dan Burkholder said: "The most important photographs are the ones on the door of the refrigerator."

Chapter 2: Archiving Your Digital Negatives

In This Chapter

↙ **Renaming digital photographs**

↙ **Copying photographs from the DSLR camera's card**

↙ **Backing that thing up**

↙ **Burning hot and getting proofing down cold**

*I*f the photographs on your refrigerator are indeed the most important ones of all, then the files that created them are valuable beyond price. Making sure that you have permanent archives of these irreplaceable images is the purpose of this chapter.

This chapter is all about taking care of your newly minted digital negatives. Read how to rename your images so you can always find them. The archiving process covers copying the files from the CompactFlash card to the computer and backing up the copied files. Next you discover how to automatically enhance the files so they look great with a minimum effort. Then you burn your digital negatives to disc — either CD or DVD — and finally, proof the disc to make certain you have good copies of your precious memories.

Playing the Renaming Game

It might seem odd to start a chapter about archiving your photographs with the process of renaming them. When you think about it, the name that a digital camera assigns to an image file is remarkably devoid of anything even resembling useful. A naming convention wants to give you information and speed when looking for a specific image, no matter how long it's been since you actually took the photograph. Figure 2-1 shows examples of just such a convention.

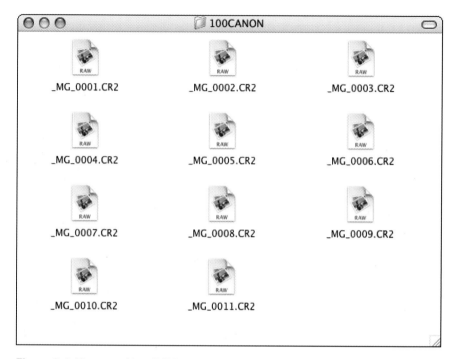

Figure 2-1: Files named by a DSLR.

Computing literally

Computers are really great at sorting and reporting information. They are really stupid when it comes to figuring out things that people think are obvious. When you are looking for something, you ask, "Have you seen that photo of Sara's third birthday party?" A person might reply, "Yes, I think it is in the shoe box of photos marked 2001-2002, in the closet." That answer comes from an image the brain stores of the last place it remembers seeing the photograph. (By the way, if you want to avoid having that shoe box, read Bonus Chapter 1.)

A computer wants as much specific information as possible. When asked, "Where is the photo of Sara's birthday party made on September 12, 2002, at 3:25:07pm?" the computer searches on the keywords *Sara, birthday, party, 09:12:2002:03:25:07pm.* With that amount of detailed information, the computer can zero right in on the file that was shot at 25 minutes, 7 seconds after 3:00 on the given date. Searching *Sara* brings back all of the photographs of Sara and would result in potentially thousands returned — especially if Sara had grown up, married, and had a daughter she named Sara. The computer must have enough specific information to sort the entire universe of photographs it's storing, down to the one you want.

Remembering significant events: The anniversary example

Your brain is great at remembering images. Having seen the photo of Sara's third birthday, where she is blowing out the candles with her cheeks puffed out and eyes closed, you can recall the image vividly in your mind. That vivid image allows you to pull more details about the day from your memory.

When a couple marries, the woman is much more likely to remember the minutest detail of her special day. Her husband is likely to forget or not remember the day — or even the date, for that matter. Why is this? It really has to do with the significance each one places on the wedding day. For the bride, her wedding is a day she has been dreaming of since she was a little girl. She has experienced her wedding in her mind countless times over many years. She is primed to remember everything that happens on the day her dream actually happens.

The groom is not so focused on the day because getting married is just not as compelling to little boys as being astronauts, firemen, soldiers, or pilots. He is there as a participant, not as the one who has planned for this day most of his life. The distinction is important. The groom knows he

married the woman of his dreams. He has the ring to prove it. It is likely that the date of the event will slip from his memory like sand through an hourglass. The bride not only will remember the date, she will recall specific details about everything that was important to her. When several years have elapsed after the ceremony, the wife can easily recall the date and details. Her husband relies on an entry in his Palm Pilot to remind him to celebrate the occasion.

Human brains just don't remember specific things, like exactly when a photograph was taken. We remember images, not specifics. That's why learning history by dates is so difficult. The numbers don't relate to images. It is also why we do remember dates like September 11, 2001. We have very specific images attached to the date. For example, do you remember the date that the space shuttle Columbia broke up on its return to earth? Do you even remember the year? The answer is February 1, 2003 at 9:00 am. Undoubtedly in your mind's eye you can see the picture of the burning parts of the shuttle scattered across the sky. That's because we remember in pictures.

Keywords are common descriptions of what is in an image. Some keywords are stored in the image file by the camera. Programs like Extensis Portfolio pick up these keywords when cataloging image files. You can add keywords after the photograph is made in Bridge and in cataloging programs like Portfolio.

Knowing how computers are great at remembering details tempts you to name an image file with all of the information you might use later. I have seen image files named "Sarasthirdbirthday91202001.jpg." While the information might be useful, the burden is heavy when someone has to order a print, make a web gallery, or create a slideshow. Every image file automatically stores information that can be used to find the file later.

Metadata is information about a digital image file. *Keywords* are a form of metadata. That information is stored inside the file or in *sidecar* files that have the same name and different file extensions (.xmp); Figure 2-2 shows a file and its sidecar. They carry any additional metadata that you add in Bridge or changes you make in Adobe Camera Raw. They are normally hidden from view in Bridge. When you move a RAW file within Bridge, the sidecar files are automatically moved, too. To see the .xmp files, choose View⇨Show Hidden Files from Bridge's menu bar. You can also navigate to the folder containing newly renamed and copied image files and see them in the Finder on Macintosh (My Computer in Windows).

3017-004.CR2
1/30 s at f/5, ISO 400
16

3017-004.xmp

Figure 2-2: A RAW file and its sidecar .xmp file.

Naming conventions

A good filename has a way to distinguish one image from another, is simple to use, and can be sorted down to a single image from thousands or tens of thousands of saved image files. A filename that meets these requirements might be worded like this:

event number-image number.file extension

Event or job number

The *event* or *job number* is a consecutive four-digit number followed by a dash. The event or job number is a serial number. Think of it like the number in the upper-right corner of a check. The check number is unique to every other check that you write. It also has the advantage of letting you know when one is missing, when you see a gap in the sequence.

Currently my event numbers are in the 2300s. The job number for this book is 2205. I assign job numbers to books because I also make all of the photographs for the illustrations. No matter what I am making photographs of, it is an event or job. I assign it the next number in order. An event could be Sara's Third Birthday or Our Family Trip to Disneyland.

You might want to get a notebook, ledger book, or blank check register (or create a spreadsheet) and keep your event numbers and their descriptions in it. A spreadsheet is a good choice because data can be searched electronically. Later you can import it to a database if you want to make the information even more useful. Figure 2-3 shows a sample spreadsheet event journal.

	Event Journal.xls		
	A	**B**	**C**
1	**Job Number**	**Description**	**Notes**
2	0001		
3	0002		
4	0003		
5	0004		
6	0005		
7	0006		
8	0007		
9	0008		
10	0009		
11	0010		
12	0011		
13	0012		
14	0013		
15	0014		
16	0015		
17	0016		
18	0017		
19	0018		

Sheet1 — Ready — Sum=0

Figure 2-3: A spreadsheet event journal.

A little dash'll do ya

When it comes to numbering images it takes a dash, not a village. The most critical component of the filename is the dash. Without the dash, a search for a low job number shows you every image with that number. Say you're shooting event number 17. Your image number without the dash is 00170025.jpg. When you sort for event number 0017, the computer shows you all of the images for event 17. It also shows you every 17th shot for every event that has at least 17 shots in it. Prevent this inconvenience. Put a dash between the event number and the image number. Event 17, image 25 is now named 0017-0025.jpg. Much better. To find event number 17, you search on 0017-.

Image number

The *image number* is a three- or four-digit consecutive number. Three-digit image numbers are good for 999 shots. Four-digit numbers go up to 9,999. If you need five digits, you are probably a professional photographer and I wonder why you are reading this book. (Just kidding.)

File extensions

The *file extension* is a three-letter file type designator preceded by a period. Computers assign file extensions to designate in which application to open a file (such as Photoshop or Paint Shop Pro). Typical image file extensions are .tif, .jpg, .psd, .crw, and so forth. Book III, Chapter 1 talks about the file extensions JPEG (aka .jpg) and RAW.

When renaming image files, be sure to include the file extension. Without the extension, the image does not appear in Bridge or other viewing applications. The camera automatically adds the proper extension when the shot is taken. Be certain to leave these three letters right where they are. Anything to the left of the period (dot) is fair game.

When you rename the next photos you've taken after today, the filename will look like this:

    0001-0001.RAW

Of course, this assumes you're shooting in RAW format (which is a good thing).

Making a folder

Put description information on the folder full of image files. The format is thus:

    event number-file type-disc number-event description

In the case of the birthday girl, you were excited and shot three CDs full of RAW files. Yes, I know she's cute and adorable and obviously worth close to 500 exposures. The folders would be labeled like what you see in Figure 2-4.

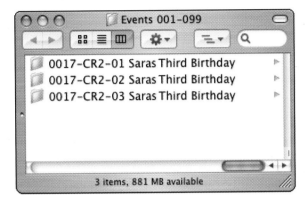

Figure 2-4: Three labeled folders of Sara's third birthday.

Computers don't like special characters like these and others: / ; : \ % '. When naming folders, don't use punctuation except for the dash (-) or the underscore (_).

The file type (in this case CR2 for files shot with a Canon 20D) and the disc number follow the event number. It is good practice to use dashes or underscores to separate the character groups. Some computers don't like spaces a whole lot either. If you are using another camera, look at one of the RAW files for its *extension,* the three letters following the dot.

Cataloging software and search programs like Apple's Spotlight automatically catalog the information in the title of the folder as keywords. Now the search can be made by event number, Sara, Birthday, or Third. You read more about keywords in Book III, Chapter 4.

Giving Your Digital Negative Files New Names

Let me show you how to actually rename files and copy them to the computer at the same time you're using the Bridge file-management and browsing program included with Adobe Photoshop CS2.

1. **Create a folder on your hard drive to hold the renamed image files.**

   Name it with the event number, file type, disc number, and event description. Use a spreadsheet like the one in Figure 2-3 to keep track of your events. You can download one from www.amesphoto.com/learning. Enter the code 4D59776 to go to the registration page.

2. **Make another new folder on your desktop and name it** 0 Automate Hot Folder.

3. **Click+Ctrl⇨Copy (right-click⇨Copy) the first folder.**

   This is the one with your event number on it.

4. **Open the 0 Automate Hot Folder by double-clicking it.**

   Figure 2-5: The 0 Automate Hot Folder.

   A copy of the folder you made to hold the image files is placed in the 0 Automate Hot Folder. You use it during the proofing part of the archiving process later in this chapter. See Figure 2-5.

   You can download the Excel Event Journal.xls from amesphoto.com/learning. It is in the folder for Book III, Chapter 2.

5. **Put a CompactFlash card with images on it into a card reader and connect it to your computer.**

6. **Open Bridge with one of these methods:**

   - Click the Bridge icon in Photoshop CS2, circled in red in Figure 2-6.
   - Choose File⇨Browse.
   - Type ⌘+Option+O (Ctrl+Alt+O).

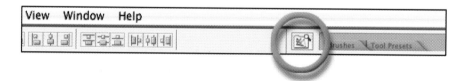

Figure 2-6: The Go to Bridge icon.

The ellipses (the three dots) following a menu item in Photoshop mean that a dialog will open, offering you more options.

7. **Click the Folders tab, then navigate to your CompactFlash card.**

Bridge populates with previews of the image files on the card. You see part of two image file thumbnails to the right of the highlighted folder; they're circled in red in Figure 2-7.

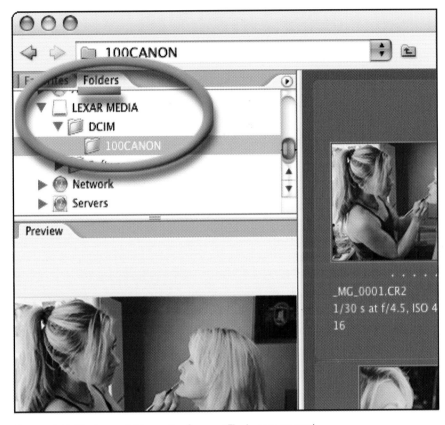

Figure 2-7: The image folder on the CompactFlash memory card.

8. Choose Tools⇨Batch Rename in Bridge, like you see in Figure 2-8.

The Batch Rename dialog opens so you can replace the camera-assigned name with yours. Figure 2-9 shows the dialog set up with these choices:

- **New Filenames section, Text window:** event number-.
- **New Filenames section, Sequence Number:** 1.
- **Drop-down menu: Three Digits.**
- **Preserve Current Filename in XMP Metadata: Checked.**

Figure 2-8: The Tools menu.

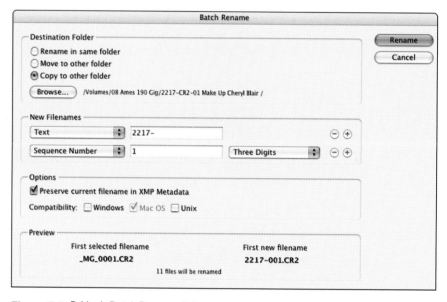

Figure 2-9: Bridge's Batch Rename dialog.

Choosing to preserve the original filename is useful if a copied file is corrupt. You can look at the corrupt file's metadata and get a fresh copy from the CompactFlash card carrying the original data. File corruption doesn't happen very often. It *does* happen. This archiving process is designed to catch any bad files before the CompactFlash card is reformatted, which permanently erases any files on it. Book II, Chapter 1 talks more about CompactFlash.

The first time you use Batch Rename, the dialog does not look like this. The first menu says Current Filename. Choose Current Filename⇨Text, then click the + button to the right of Text. A new line appears. Choose Sequence Number from the menu for that line. An entry window appears to the right of the words Sequence Number. Now your dialog looks like the one in Figure 2-9. You only have to do this the first time you use Batch Rename.

9. **Click Copy to Other Folder⇨Browse and navigate to the Desktop.**

10. **Click the new folder with your event number on it, then click Choose⇨Rename.**

Figure 2-10 shows the selected folder and my numbering system for images and folders. The files are *renamed as they are copied* from the CompactFlash card to a new folder on your hard drive. The data on the CompactFlash card is not changed.

**Book III
Chapter 2**

**Archiving Your
Digital Negatives**

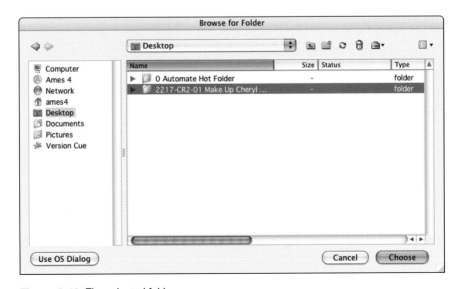

Figure 2-10: The selected folder.

If you are renaming RAW files, a Camera Raw dialog (see Figure 2-11) tells you that the metadata will not be written to the RAW file itself. Click OK. I recommend you check the Don't Show Again checkbox to keep this from appearing every time you rename something. Book III, Chapter 4 breaks down Camera Raw for you in further detail.

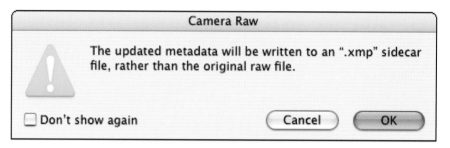

Figure 2-11: The sidecar notice.

Adobe has chosen not to allow modification to a RAW file from a DSLR camera other than renaming it — and for a couple of very good reasons. The first is that the process of writing data back to a RAW file carries the potential of corrupting the data needed to open the image. The second reason is to preserve the integrity of the image for forensic or court-of-law purposes.

Enhancing Digital Negatives

The digital negatives (RAW files) right out of your camera may not look very good when you first view them in Bridge. If you read Book III, Chapter 1 and followed those instructions, you turned off the Auto settings.

The Camera Raw Auto settings turned off is the only way you will know how to use your camera's exposure controls. It is impossible to see the effects of changing the exposure if the computer is fixing it behind your back.

1. **Open Bridge, then choose Favorites⇨Desktop⇨folder of renamed images.**

   The previews appear in the light box pane and most likely look dark.

2. **Choose Edit⇨Select All to highlight all of the previews; see Figure 2-12.**

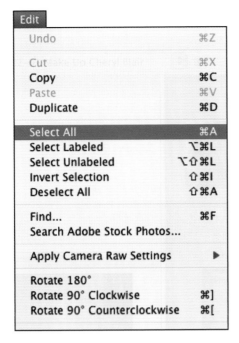

Figure 2-12: Select All from Bridge's Edit menu.

3. **Open them all in Camera Raw by typing ⌘+R (Ctrl+R).**

   The Camera Raw dialog opens. You can see the settings in Figure 2-13.

4. **Put a checkmark in each of the Auto checkboxes for Exposure, Shadows, Brightness, and Contrast.**

   This is labeled 1 in Figure 2-13.

5. **In the upper-left corner, click Select All; then Option+Synchronize (Alt+Synchronize).**

   Holding down the Option (Alt) key suppresses the Synchronize dialog. This is labeled 2 in Figure 2-13.

6. **Click Done.**

   This is labeled 3 in Figure 2-13. Look at the light box in Bridge in Figure 2-14. The previews brighten up and look much better as the Auto settings are updated.

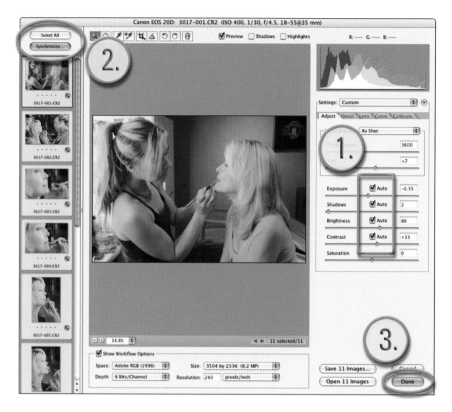

Figure 2-13: The Adobe Camera Raw 3 dialog.

7. Choose Tools⇨Cache⇨Export Cache, as shown in Figure 2-15.

This command puts a pair of hidden files named Adobe Bridge Cache.bc and Adobe Bridge Cache.bct in the folder with the RAW files and their .xmp sidecar files. You can see the pair in Figure 2-16.

The information carried in the two hidden *cache* files holds the last version of the image thumbnails, metadata you may have added, and file information from your camera and the settings made in Camera Raw. Exporting the cache allows Bridge to present previews and metadata much more quickly by reading the two files. Otherwise, Bridge has to regenerate the previews each time the folder is opened.

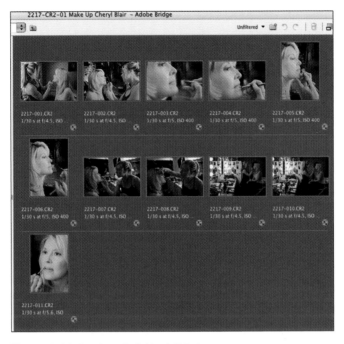

Figure 2-14: Previews in Bridge's light box.

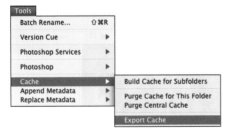

Figure 2-15: Export the cache.

Figure 2-16: Bridge's two cache files.

8. Check for the cache files before burning the folder to a CD.

If you don't see them (they're circled in Figure 2-17), go back to Bridge and export the cache. These two tiny files make opening a CD very fast (as opposed to extremely slow, when Bridge has to recreate the thumbnails for every image on the disc).

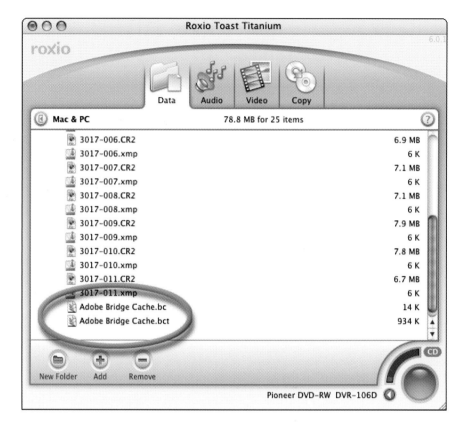

Figure 2-17: Checking for cache before burning a disc.

Backing Up Your Copied Files

NASA calls it *redundancy:* a backup system carried along on a space flight if the primary system fails. I call it common sense. Whenever you are working with digital negatives, make a backup. In this case the temporary backup is on hand just in case something goes wrong and corruption happens. You see a couple examples of corrupted files later in this chapter, in Figures 2-29 and 2-30.

When I am shooting on location, I carry my laptop, a card reader, and a backup FireWire hard drive. As soon as I have a break in shooting, I rename the RAW files while copying them onto the laptop. I let the previews update (using the Camera Raw Auto settings) and export the cache. Then I immediately copy the folder to the FireWire drive. That means I have my digital negatives in three places: on the CompactFlash card, on the laptop, and on the backup drive. See those things in Figure 2-18. The chance of all three being damaged beyond recovery is very slim. Call me paranoid when it comes to my digital negatives. If my team takes more than one vehicle to the location, I even hand off the backup drive to someone in the other car. You just can't be too cautious with your files, after all.

Figure 2-18: Lexar FireWire card reader, external hard drive, laptop, and camera, from closest to farthest.

Going with external hard drives

External hard drives plug into your computer through either the USB port or FireWire socket. They are a great way to keep your digital negative files from filling up the *internal* hard drive inside your desktop or laptop computer. The added benefit is that you can easily move your digital negatives from one computer to another.

This process is easy and cheap and is a very good habit to acquire. Get an external FireWire or USB 2.0 hard drive at your local computer store. Depending on how much you shoot, the size of the drive can vary. LaCie Mobile (www.lacie.com) and OWC Mercury On-The-Go hard drives are very good, very dependable, and come in sizes from 20–100GB in various drive speeds.

I use the On-The-Go drives from OWC (www.macsales.com); because they have transparent cases, I can put a label inside with my name, address, drive number, and size it will hold. This is what you see in Figure 2-19. This makes it easy to identify. The FireWire cable on Apple PowerBooks also provides power to the external hard drive. It saves carrying a power cord and is very handy when you're on location and want to run off of the computer's battery.

Figure 2-19: One of my external hard drives.

FireWire is a very fast means of connecting hard drives, digital video cameras, and digital still cameras to computers. It was developed by Apple and is known as IEEE-1394 on some Windows computers. Sony calls FireWire i.Link.

Backing up other ways

I prefer taking a laptop because I want to review the images in Photoshop's Camera Raw. That way I am certain I have the digital negatives that I mean to capture. Did I mention that I am paranoid? The Epson P-2000, the JOBO GIGA Vu PRO, and GIGA Mini are battery-powered card readers with built-in hard drives for on-location backup. Some of these devices offer support for selected RAW files for their built-in LCD monitor.

Be sure to check that the portable storage device you choose works with your flavor of RAW files from your DSLR camera. These solutions are a good choice for the photographer on a budget of either dollars or weight.

This is not the time to reformat your CompactFlash card. There is a remote possibility that during the initial copying of files from the card to the computer that one or more files were corrupted. You can retrieve the original and replace the damaged one. If you reformat the card before doing the steps in the next section and corruption happens, the corrupted file will surely be the ultimate prize-winning-so-stunning-it-shakes-the-very-core-of the-art-world-and-the-foundations-of-nature-itself photograph in the universe. It never happens to the one where you are pointing the camera at your feet and accidentally trip the shutter.

Weighing CD against DVD

The choice of media for archiving your digital negatives really boils down to *compact disc (CD)* or *digital versatile disc (DVD)*. Lots of opinions differ on how to store your digital negatives. Some suggest using hard drives or tapes. The problem is that you really want storage media that will allow your grandchildren to enjoy the photographs you make today. Saying that this is a challenge is something of an understatement.

That digital files can last forever sounds like a preposterous claim when we don't know for certain how long a CD recorded in a computer will last. The digital advantage is that the files can be perfectly copied. So no matter what the file is stored on, it can be copied from one form of storage to another. Whether the software that reads them will be available is anyone's guess. The problem boils down to how digital negatives are going to be archived.

The current market has two types of what I consider *nonvolatile* media in multiple flavors. CDs and DVDs have no moving parts, can be played back in almost any computer made today, and CDs are compatible for both recording and playback in the latest DVD recorders. CD players and recorders are so widespread that the players will be available for years to come. That's not to say forever. New storage technologies will be invented and popularized like the CD was. When that happens, you make copies to the new media.

Any storage media that has moving parts is *volatile* to my way of thinking. That means it can (and will) fail at some point going forward. Types of volatile media include hard disk drives, tape cartridges, and removable storage like Zip disks. Another problem is that the technology itself becomes obsolete. Try finding a working 8-track tape player or a turntable for 78s, for example.

Film versus digital negatives

I have some black and white negatives that my grandfather made in the early 1900s. They survive to this day. I can either print them or scan them (my favorite option). I also have black and white prints that he made around the same time. On the other hand, I have color slides and negatives that were made in the 1970s that have degraded so much they are unusable. Black and white negatives and prints have a better chance of enduring the ravages of time than color ones. The problem was that up until the time of digital, there was no way to make perfect copies of a negative.

CD or DVD? That is the question

No, I am not going to parody *Hamlet.* It really is the question. Which one do you choose? CDs hold up to 700MB and single-layer DVDs hold 4.7GB. That's almost 7 times the amount of data as on a CD. If a DVD-R gets misplaced or damaged, an entire vacation, graduation, or (in my case, and maybe yours if you decide to turn pro) job can be irretrievably lost. When archiving to DVD-R, I make a copy and store it in another location.

The market offers six types of recordable DVD. For archiving purposes, you should only have to decide between DVD-R and DVD+R, both of which can record data only once. DVD+Ws can be rewritten. (The folks who make DVD-R refer to them as DVD-dash-R, not DVD-minus-R.) DVD-R is the most accepted and you can see why in Table 2-1. A new flavor called Blue Ray promises to offer even greater storage capacities.

Table 2-1: Plusses and Minuses of Recordable DVD Formats

DVD-R	*DVD+R*
Plays in DVD+R	Plays in DVD-R
Writable in DVD+R	Not writable in DVD-R

I have CDs recorded in 1994 that I recently made perfect copies of to new discs. So I know that CDs last at least 10 years when stored in paper envelopes, on their edges, in the dark. My choice of media, either CD or DVD-R hinges on two factors: capacity and longevity. I have recorded DVD-Rs that are three years old and work just fine. For small events I archive to CD, and for those big events I use DVD.

Burn Baby, Burn

Logically it makes sense to put as many events as possible on a disc. Please resist the temptation. When the discs get filed away, they go in an event envelope and are filed numerically. The envelope is a great place to store event-related stuff like invitations, programs, and brochures.

Burning the CD or DVD

Okay. You'd think that you would call it recording a CD or DVD. This is hotter stuff than that. These recorders use lasers to literally burn data into the grooves on the disc, hence the term *burning a disc*.

1. **Insert a blank CD or DVD into your computer's disc burner.**

   Some computers can read DVDs and not burn them. Check your computer's manual for details.

2. **Name the digital negatives folder using the following convention:**

   event number-file type-disc number-event description

   The image filename contains the event number, followed by a dash, then the image sequence number, followed by a dash, then the extension. Notice that the name is the same for the .CR2 file and its .xmp sidecar file; see Figure 2-20. There is no reason to duplicate the information in the folder in every image name.

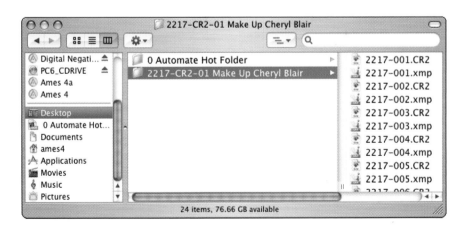

Figure 2-20: A folder of digital negatives ready to burn to disc.

3. Navigate to the area that tells you the CD size.

On Macintosh go to the Finder and type ⌘+I to open the information pane for that folder. The file size in Figure 2-21 is 78.7MB; it will fit nicely on a CD.

In Windows, either choose Start⇨My Computer or right-click Start, choose Explore, and right-click Properties. The file size in Figure 2-22 is 78.7MB and will fit nicely on a CD.

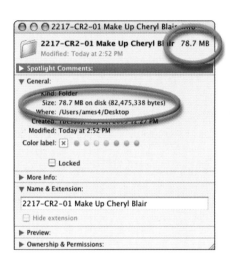

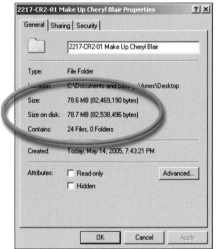

Figure 2-21: The Info dialog on a Mac.

Figure 2-22: The Properties window in Windows.

4. Open up your favorite disc-burning utility.

I use Roxio's Toast Titanium on my Macs and Roxio's EZ CD Creator on the Windows machines.

5. Follow the utility's instructions for burning the image folder to disc.

6. Make sure you exported the cache from Bridge by looking for the two Adobe Bridge Cache.bc and Adobe Bridge Cache.bct files in the burn window.

Figure 2-23 has the cache circled in red. If they are not there, remove the folder from the Burn window and export the cache. Then drag the folder with the cache files back to the Burn window.

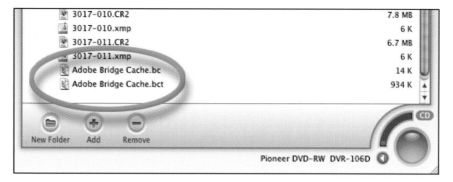

Figure 2-23: Check for Bridge's cache files.

7. **Take a quick break.**

   This won't take long.

8. **When the disc is finished, take it out and label it with the information on the folder name.**

   Only use Sanford Sharpie brand markers to write directly on CDs and DVDs. Never use ballpoint pens. They will indent the surface of the disc. The layer that is burned is right below the surface layer. The indentations from a ballpoint will destroy it.

Printing the label

Photoshop is not a page layout program and yet lots of professional designers use it for quick projects. Follow along step-by-step to set up the dialog and send the label to your printer.

1. **Download the file Disc Label Template.psd from www.amesphoto.com/ learning.**

   If you haven't already registered, you are asked to do so and provide the code 4D59776.

2. **Open the file in Photoshop and follow the instructions (in the file) for completing it.**

3. **Load a sheet of standard CD adhesive labels into your printer.**

   Follow your printer's instruction manual to know in which direction to load the labels for proper printing. Your label is open in Photoshop and all of the information is filled in and ready to go.

4. Press ⌘+Option+P (Ctrl+Alt+P) to open the Print preview dialog.

5. Fill in the dialog with these settings:

- **Scale:** 100%.
- **Scale to Fit Media checkbox: Unchecked.**
- **Document (Profile: Adobe RGB (1998)) radio button: Selected.**
- **Color Handling: Let Printer Determine Colors.**
- **Rendering Intent: Relative Colorimetric.**

Figure 2-24 shows these settings.

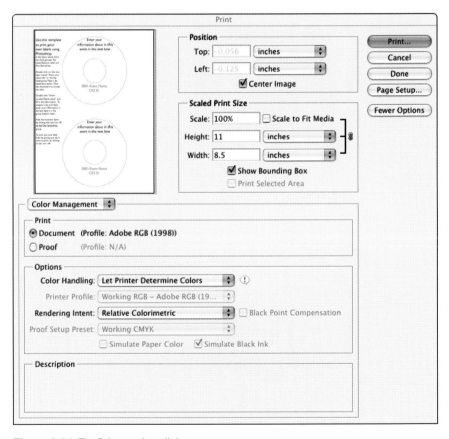

Figure 2-24: The Print preview dialog.

6. Click Print.

A warning dialog (see Figure 2-25) tells you that the image is larger than the paper's printable area. This happens if you leave the instruction layer's eye icon on. It doesn't matter if the instructions get clipped. You've already followed them in Photoshop.

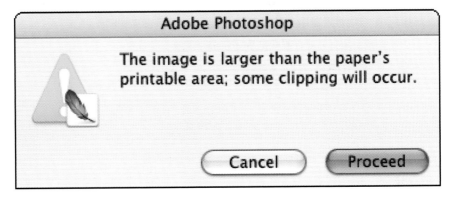

Figure 2-25: The "This-might-be-too-big" warning.

7. Click Proceed.

The Print dialog opens.

8. Choose your printer from the Printer drop-down menu.

The default settings shown in Figure 2-26 are fine.

Print
Printer: Stylus Photo 1270
Presets: Standard
Copies & Pages
Copies: 1 ☑ Collated
Pages: ○ All ⦿ From: 1 to: 1
? PDF ▼ Preview Supplies... Cancel Print

Figure 2-26: The Mac's Print dialog.

9. Click Print.

A PostScript warning comes up (see Figure 2-27), telling you that your printer can't handle some instructions that relate to PostScript-enabled printers. There are very few instances where this affects output from Photoshop. It mainly concerns page layout programs like InDesign.

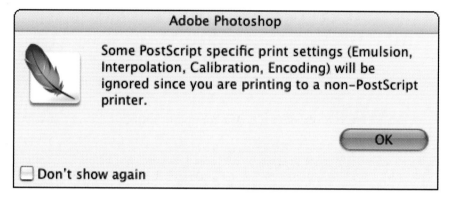

Figure 2-27: Another "Adobe-warning-you-can-safely-ignore" dialog.

10. Click OK.

Your label prints out.

11. Peel it off and use a CD alignment tool to place it perfectly on your burned disc.

CD alignment tools use the hole in the center of the CD to help center the bigger hole of the CD label.

Shopping around

Memorex, which you can find online at www.memorex.com, makes a complete line of labels, alignment tools, and software. They can usually be found at stores like Office Depot, Office Max, or Staples. Avery makes blank CD/DVD labels. Look for product number 5825 online at www.avery.com.

Goof-Proofing the Discs

You'd think that after burning and labeling the discs, the process would be complete. And it more than likely is. Sort of. . . . There is a possibility — albeit a remote one — that during copying a file might have been corrupted. As I mentioned earlier, the photo that's out of focus is never the one that goes bad. It is a very good practice to proof the discs by making JPEG files from them. This section shows you how step-by-step.

The first inkling that a file is bad is an innocent little dialog that pops up in Photoshop; see Figure 2-28. Click OK and pray.

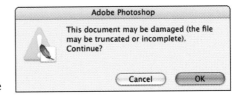

Figure 2-28: This Adobe warning is serious!

Figures 2-29 and 2-30 show a couple of examples of what corruption looks like. The first one is easily fixed by cropping. At first glance you might miss it. Look at the bottom of the image. It is a repeat of a slice of the bottom third. The second is damaged beyond hope unless, of course, you are shooting just the boots.

Figure 2-29: A corrupted file that can be cropped.

Figure 2-30: A totally useless corrupted file.

No one would proof a disc if it had to be done one file at a time. All right. I admit it. There is one person. I'm paranoid about my files, remember? And it was a very long time ago, before Photoshop had actions. In this section, you create an action that sharpens the file a little bit, takes care of color aliasing, and adds your copyright notice. Then you use Photoshop's image processor to make a set of JPEG files that have a lot of uses in Book III, Chapter 4 and in Bonus Chapter 2.

Making a copyright notice file

Copyright notices are important, even for amateurs. When you post your work on the web, you want people to know it is your work. And if you register your work with the Copyright Office once every 90 days, you have legal recourse if your photographs are used without your permission.

For more information on copyrights, how they work and how to register your images, check out www.copyright.gov. and the Professional Photographers of America web site at www.ppa.com.

1. Choose File➪New from the Photoshop menu.

2. Choose 2 × 3 in the Preset drop-down menu, as shown in Figure 2-31.

3. Click OK.

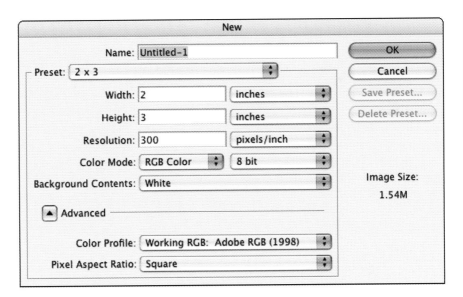

Figure 2-31: The New dialog in Photoshop.

4. **Select File⇨File Info, as shown in Figure 2-32.**

   The File Info dialog opens.

5. **Choose Copyright Status⇨ Copyrighted.**

6. **Enter your copyright information in the Copyright Notice section.**

 If you have a web site, enter it in the Copyright Info URL window.

The copyright symbol keystroke is Option+G (Alt+0169). Figure 2-33 shows my copyright information entered.

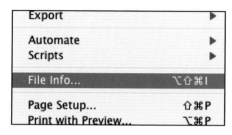

Figure 2-32: Choose File Info from the drop-down menu.

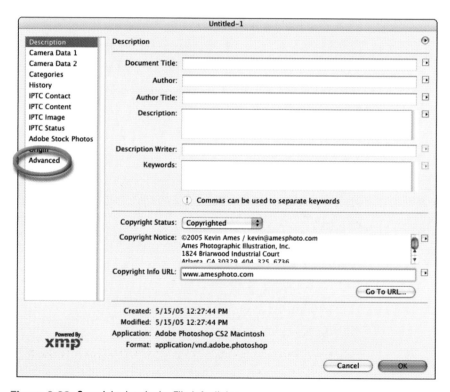

Figure 2-33: Copyright data in the File Info dialog.

7. Click the word Advanced.

It's at the bottom of the column on the left of the dialog and circled in red in Figure 2-33. A new section of the File Info dialog opens. Advanced is highlighted; see Figure 2-34.

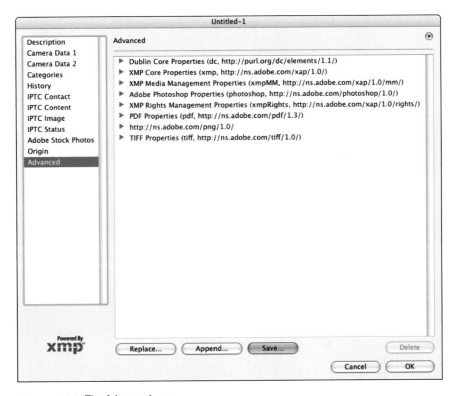

Figure 2-34: The Advanced pane.

8. Click the Save button to save the file.

The Save dialog opens.

9. Name your file ©2006.xmp **(then make a new one next year and name it** ©2007.xmp**).**

I saved mine to the documents folder. The copyright symbol moves the file close to the top of the files, making it easy to find.

10. Click OK in the File Info window.

A copyright symbol (©) appears in the header bar of the document window, indicating that File Info has been applied and the copyright status is copyrighted. The symbol is circled in red in Figure 2-35.

Figure 2-35: The copyright notice in the document window header.

11. Choose File⇨Close.

12. When the Save dialog appears, choose Don't Save.

Writing the action to proof your disc

Actions record a series of steps you do in Photoshop. You can play them back and have them do the work you did when the action was made. The best part of actions is that once they are written and saved, you have them forever. This is a simple action to write. Follow the steps in this section.

Digital images, whether captured as pixels originally or scanned from film, are slightly soft. A gentle application of the Unsharp Mask filter snaps the photograph's sharpness up and makes it look much better. Figure 2-36 compares photographs with and without the filter.

1. **Choose File⇨New from the Photoshop menu.**

2. **Choose 2 × 3 from the preset menu.**

   Make sure the file's Color Mode is RGB.

3. **Click OK.**

4. **Click the Actions tab, which is nested under the History palette.**

   If your Actions palette is not visible, select Window⇨Actions from the menu bar.

5. **Click the Create New Set icon at the bottom of the Actions palette.**

   The icon looks like a folder.

6. **Name the set** File Finishing **in the New Set dialog; click OK.**

   A new set named File Finishing appears in the Actions stack; see Figure 2-37.

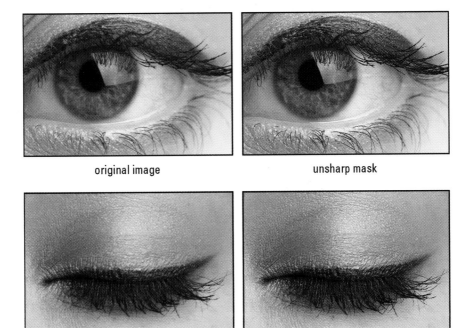

original image   unsharp mask

Figure 2-36: The eyes have it! Sharper is better.

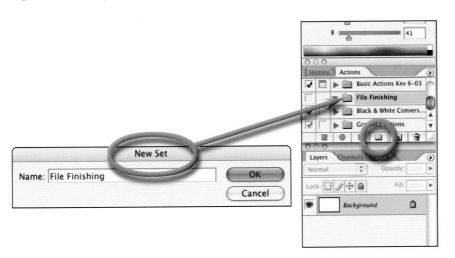

Figure 2-37: The New Set dialog and New Set icon.

7. Click the Create New Action icon.

It's the one to the right of the Create New Set icon and labeled 1 in Figure 2-38.

8. Name the action USM > Alias > © **in the New Action dialog.**

This is labeled 2 in Figure 2-38.

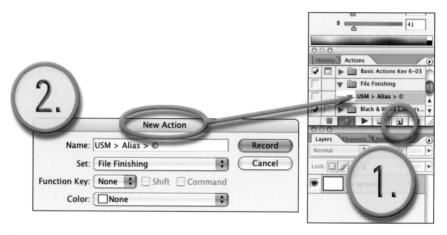

Figure 2-38: Making and naming a new action.

9. Click Record to start recording.

You're off!

10. Select Filter⇨Sharpen⇨Unsharp Mask to open the filter's dialog, as is done in Figure 2-39.

11. Enter these settings:

- **Amount:** 100
- **Radius:** 1
- **Threshold:** 0

Figure 2-40 shows these settings.

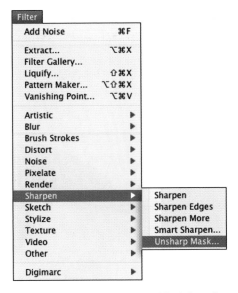

Figure 2-39: Choose Unsharp Mask from the menu.

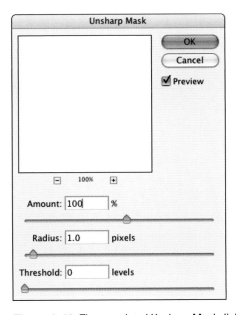

Figure 2-40: The completed Unsharp Mask dialog.

12. **Click OK.**

13. **Choose Edit⇨Fade Unsharp Mask, as shown in Figure 2-41.**

14. **In the dialog, choose Mode⇨ Luminosity, as shown in Figure 2-42.**

15. **Click OK.**

Luminosity in an RGB image is the black, white, and gray tones that make up the photograph's detail. Fading the Unsharp Mask to Luminosity applies the sharpening only to the details. How perfect, don't you think?

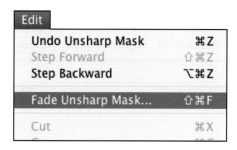

Figure 2-41: Choose Fade Unsharp Mask.

Figure 2-42: Choose Luminosity.

16. Choose Filter⇨Blur⇨Gaussian Blur, as shown in Figure 2-43.

17. Enter 1.3 **in the Radius textbox and click OK, as shown in Figure 2-44.**

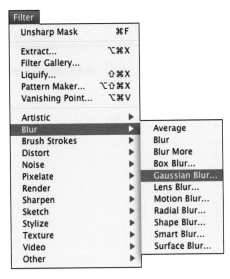

Figure 2-43: Choose Gaussian Blur from the Filter menu.

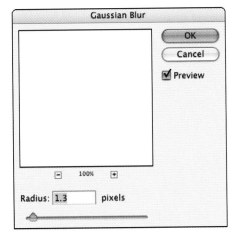

Figure 2-44: The Gaussian Blur dialog.

18. **Choose Edit⇨Fade Gaussian Blur⇨Mode⇨Color, as shown in Figure 2-45.**

Color aliasing is caused by the camera computer as it integrates the data in the highlights into RGB (Red, Green, and Blue) colors. In the bright highlights, the computer sometimes has to guess what color the pixels are. The Before photograph in Figure 2-46 shows the color pixels out of place on the edges. The After photograph shows the result of running Gaussian Blur and fading it to Color. The aliasing is almost completely gone.

19. **Choose File⇨File Info⇨ Advanced⇨Append, labeled as 1 in Figure 2-47.**

20. **Navigate to the ©2005.xmp file in the Open dialog and choose Load⇨OK.**

The Open dialog is labeled 2 in Figure 2-47. Load and OK are shown chosen (labeled 3 and 4, respectively).

Append adds the information to the metadata that is already in the file. Replace wipes out all of the metadata, leaving only the copyright notice. Replace is probably a very bad choice.

Figure 2-45: Choose Color from the Edit Fade Gaussian Blur dialog.

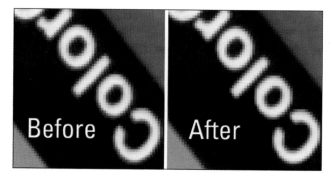

Figure 2-46: Color aliasing.

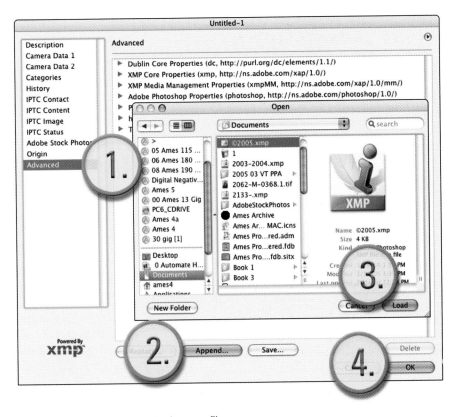

Figure 2-47: Adding copyright data to a file.

21. Click the square next to the red recording button at the bottom of the Actions palette.

The icon you should click is circled in red in Figure 2-48. You've stopped recording.

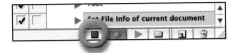

Figure 2-48: The Actions palette Stop button.

Now is a very good time to save the action set you've just created. You can do this two ways:

✒ The first is simply quitting Photoshop and starting it again. The Action Set is saved in the preferences. This is fine until you upgrade Photoshop. At that point the preferences are replaced with new ones and the Action Set is deleted.

✒ The permanent way to save is to

1. Highlight the set, File Finishing, in the Actions palette.

2. Click the flyout menu triangle.

3. Choose Save Actions.

4. Save your actions and other presets in your own folder in either the applications folder (Mac) or My Documents (Windows).

Checking your action

Action writing is a form of programming. Instead of having to write code, you do the steps and Photoshop records them. Spin down the disclosure triangle (circled in red in Figure 2-49) on the USM⇨Alias⇨© action. It is interesting to note that the steps in the action are exactly the same as those in the History palette for the file after the action was run on it. See Figures 2-50 and 2-51.

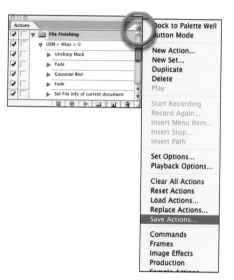

Figure 2-49: The disclosure button in red and the Save Actions menu item.

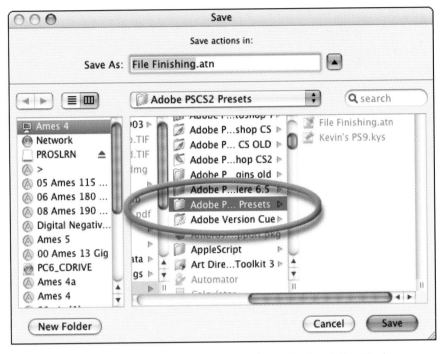

Figure 2-50: The save destination folder created in the applications folder (Mac).

**Book III
Chapter 2**

**Archiving Your
Digital Negatives**

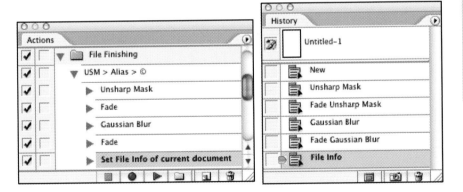

Figure 2-51: The action proofed in the History palette.

Reviewing your disc

This is a critical step, and you will only appreciate it when Photoshop hangs because it can't open a truncated file right after you click OK on the warning shown in Figure 2-11. When you go back to your CompactFlash card and find the image that was copied badly, restore it, burn a new disc, proof it, and everything is beautiful — then you get behind disc proofing. Until then, trust me.

1. **Put the disc into your computer's drive.**

2. **Navigate to the Desktop to the folder of RAW files.**

3. **Highlight the name and press ⌘+C (Ctrl+C).**

   You copied it to the Clipboard.

4. **Open 0 Automate Hot Folder.**

5. **Create a new folder; press ⌘+V (Ctrl+V) to paste the name of the original RAW folder into the Name field.**

   The duplicate filename appears in Figure 2-52.

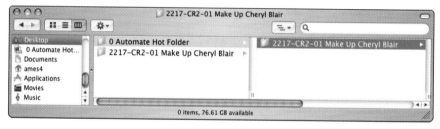

Figure 2-52: The new folder inside the 0 Automate Hot folder.

6. **Click the Disc icon under the Folders tab in Bridge.**

   The thumbnails populate the light box pane.

7. **Choose Tools⇨Photoshop⇨ Image Processor as shown in Figure 2-53.**

   The Image Processor dialog opens. There are four sections to set up. The first one knows that you want to proof files from Bridge because it was launched there.

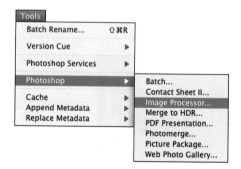

Figure 2-53: Choose Image Processor from the Tools menu in Bridge.

8. **Choose these settings (shown in Figure 2-54) in the Image Processor dialog:**

   - **Open First Image to Apply Settings checkbox: Selected.**

   - **Select Folder radio button: Selected.**

   The Select Folder section tells the image processor where to put the proofs.

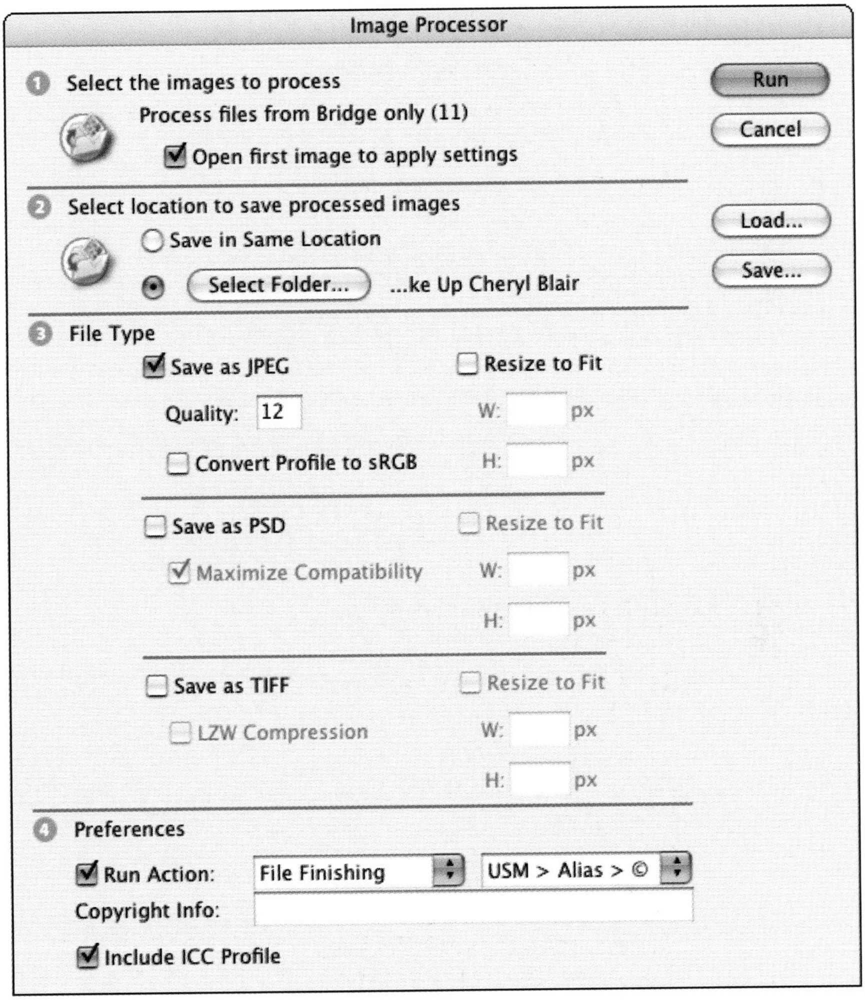

Image Processor

① Select the images to process

   Process files from Bridge only (11)

   ☑ Open first image to apply settings

② Select location to save processed images

   ○ Save in Same Location

   ◉ (Select Folder...) ...ke Up Cheryl Blair

③ File Type

   ☑ Save as JPEG   ☐ Resize to Fit

      Quality: 12   W: px

      ☐ Convert Profile to sRGB   H: px

   ☐ Save as PSD   ☐ Resize to Fit

      ☑ Maximize Compatibility   W: px

                                        H: px

   ☐ Save as TIFF   ☐ Resize to Fit

      ☐ LZW Compression   W: px

                                          H: px

④ Preferences

   ☑ Run Action: [File Finishing ▲▼] [USM > Alias > © ▲▼]

   Copyright Info: [   ]

   ☑ Include ICC Profile

Run

Cancel

Load...

Save...

Book III
Chapter 2

Archiving Your
Digital Negatives

Figure 2-54: The Image Processor settings.

9. **Go to the Desktop, open 0 Automate Hot Folder, and click the folder you created in Step 5.**

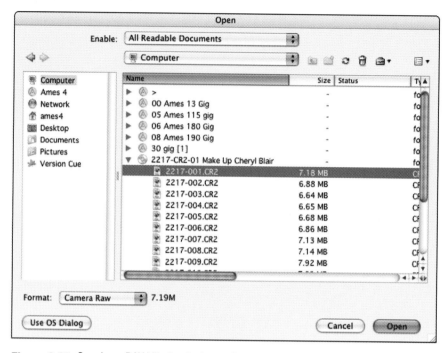

Figure 2-55: Opening a RAW file for the Image Processor.

The third section sets the file type.

10. **Continue choosing settings in the Image Processor dialog:**

   • **Save as JPEG: Selected.**

   • **Quality:** 12.

   • **Run Action: Selected. (Area four, Preferences, is where the action is applied.)**

   • **From the Run Action drop-down menu: File Finishing (for the set).**

   • **From the Run Action drop-down menu: USM > Alias > © (for the action).**

   Leave the Copyright Info window blank. The action handles that for you. Allow Include ICC Profile to remain checked.

11. Click Run.

The image processor allows you to make several different file types at once. Check the ones you want, then click Run. When you open the destination folder you find folders named with the file types you selected; see Figure 2-56.

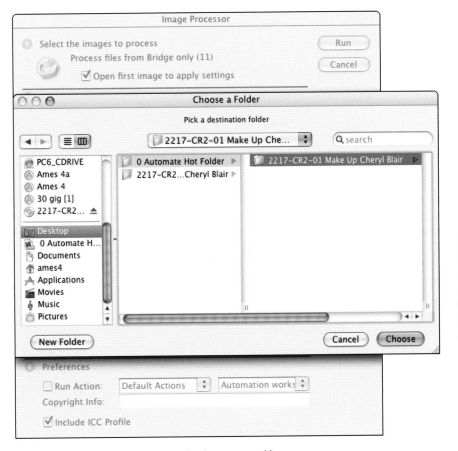

Figure 2-56: The destination folder for the processed images.

12. Navigate to the disc, open it, and click Open to see the first image.

In this case the first image is 2217-001.CR2. The Camera Raw dialog appears so you can make sure it is set up correctly.

Figure 2-57: The native resolution is selected.

13. **Choose the native resolution for your camera from the Size menu; set Depth at 8 Bits/Channel.**

    Native resolution is the one that does not have a minus or a plus next to it. You can see it's chosen in Figure 2-57.

14. **The Auto settings want to be on. Check them if they aren't.**

15. **Click Open.**

    When you click Open, the Image Processor takes over in Photoshop, making a high-resolution JPEG from each RAW file on your disc. They are saved inside the folder you created in another folder. It is named JPEG, as shown in Figure 2-58.

16. **Double-click the JPEG folder. The previews appear in the light box.**

17. **⌘+A (Ctrl+A) to select all.**

18. **Click inside one of the image thumbnails and drag them to the folder holding the folder JPEG.**

    This is shown in Figure 2-59.

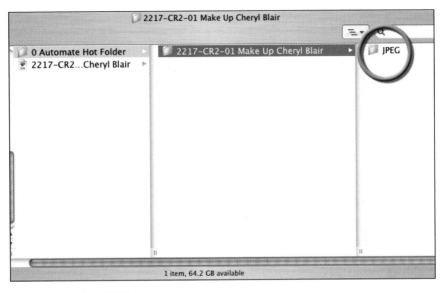

Figure 2-58: The JPEG folder.

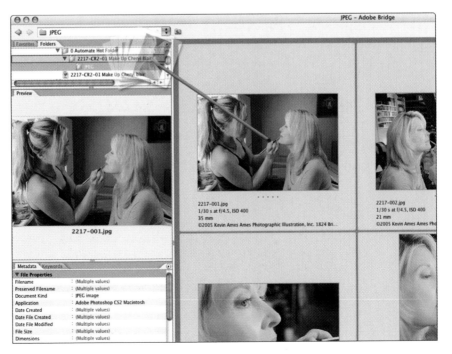

Figure 2-59: Drag all of the images out of the folder JPEG.

19. Double-click the folder you dragged the images into.

The previews open in Bridge.

20. Scroll down to and click the folder JPEG; click the Trash icon.

The Trash icon is circled in red in Figure 2-60.

Figure 2-60: Delete the JPEG folder.

All of the JPEG files made by the Image Processor are now in the folder you made inside the 0 Automate Hot Folder. These JPEGs are at your camera's native resolution and saved at the highest quality. You use them in Bonus Chapter 1 for cataloging, and in Book III, Chapter 3 on presenting your work. These highest-quality JPEGs are yet another backup. Paranoia runs deep.

Chapter 3: Presenting Proofs to Friends, Family, and the World

*Y*ou have all of these fabulous photographs. It's time to show them off to your friends and family and the world in general. (Why not; your photos are fabulous, don't you know?) You use Bridge and Adobe Photoshop CS2 to do a quick sort of your files, then make proof sheets in the mold of the photographic contact sheets of days gone by. Pick a style or two to snazzy them up a bit and send them off to your printer.

Who wants to look at plain old photographs when edges can be stroked, beveled, embossed, and made thoroughly stylin'? Finally, if all of this is not enough, the world at large is waiting to see your work. You discover and explore the power of Photoshop's Web Photo Gallery automations to build galleries of your photographs for posting to your own web site.

Proof Sheets: Showing Your Work the Classic Way

Photographers have been making *contact sheets* (or *proof sheets*) of their negatives from the very beginning of the black and white print. As a matter of fact, before photographic enlargers were invented, contact printing was the only way to make a print. The process involved laying a negative over a light-sensitive piece of paper and exposing for a predetermined time to light. The paper was then processed in trays of chemicals, and the image appeared.

After the invention of roll film and enlargers, contact printing was relegated to making ganged-up groups of negatives on a single sheet. Figure 3-1 shows contact sheets from The Paralympic Portrait Project I did during the games in 1996. Each page represents a single roll of film. Each roll was individually processed by hand, the edges numbered again by hand; then the film was cut into strips, which were slipped into plastic pages. Each contact sheet was exposed under the enlarger, then processed by hand. This photograph represents a lot of work after the shoot was finished.

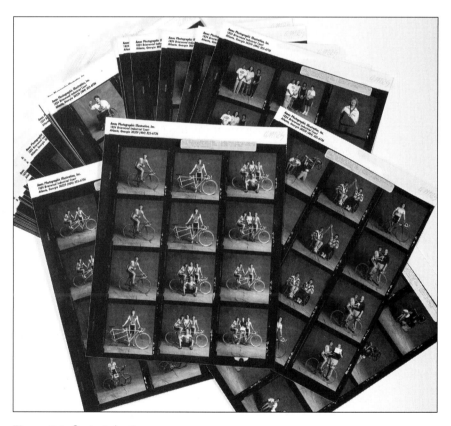

Figure 3-1: Contact sheets.

Using Contact Sheet II

Even though digital capture has almost completely replaced film, people still like looking at prints. The Contact Sheet II feature in Adobe Photoshop CS2 captures the spirit of the past — only without chemicals, darkrooms, or nasty-smelling fingers — and in full color to boot. Hooray!

Making your contact sheet

Here's how to make your own contact sheet for your printer:

1. **Open a folder of JPEG or RAW files in Bridge.**

   I am using some photographs (that I made during Music Midtown in Atlanta) of legendary rock and rollers Joan Jett and the Blackhearts.

2. **⌘+click (Ctrl+click) the 16 photographs you want to have on your proof sheet.**

   Figure 3-2 shows the RAW files I have chosen.

Book III
Chapter 3

Presenting Proofs to
Friends, Family, and
the World

Figure 3-2: RAW files.

Once you have selected the photographs you can type ⌘+8 (Ctrl+8) to label their ranking in green. ⌘+1–5 (Ctrl+1–5) puts the respective number of stars in the ranking field. For more, see Kevin's Essential Bridge Keyboard Shortcuts on the Cheat Sheet in the front of the book.

3. **Choose Tools⇨Photoshop⇨Contact Sheet II.**

   Figure 3-3 has the menus highlighted. The Contact II dialog opens. Refer to Figure 3-4 for where each section in the following steps lives.

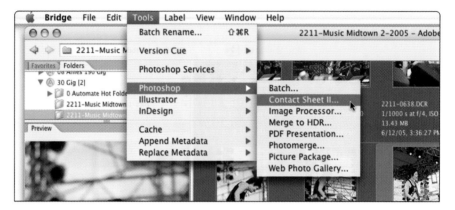

Figure 3-3: Select Contact Sheet II.

4. **In the Source Images section, under the Use menu, choose Selected Images from Bridge.**

5. **In the Document section, set Units to Inches, Width at 8.5, Height at 11.**

6. **Enter 240 for the Resolution, then choose pixels/inch from the menu.**

7. **For Mode, choose RGB Color.**

8. **Check the Flatten All Layers checkbox.**

9. **In the Thumbnails section, in the Place menu, choose Across First. Check Use Auto-Spacing.**

10. **Enter 4 in both the Columns and Rows fields.**

11. **Make sure Rotate for Best Fit and Use Filename as Caption are checked.**

12. **Choose from the very limited Font drop-down menu.**

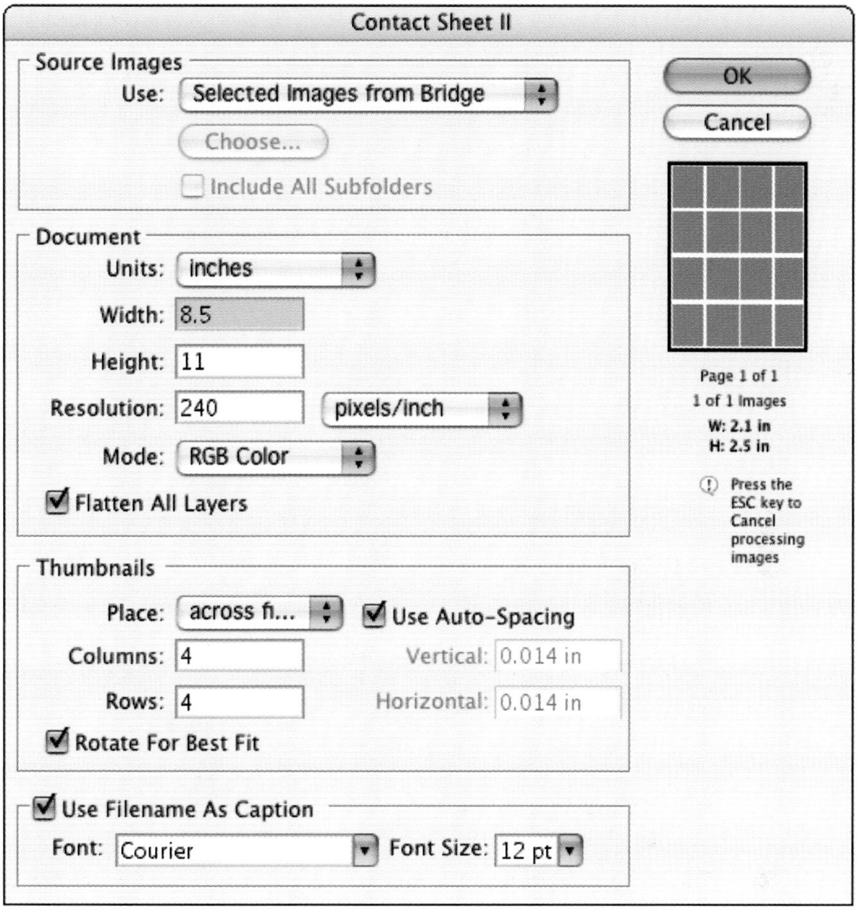

Contact Sheet II

Source Images

Use: [Selected Images from Bridge ⬍]

(Choose...)

☐ Include All Subfolders

Document

Units: [inches ⬍]

Width: 8.5

Height: 11

Resolution: 240 [pixels/inch ⬍]

Mode: [RGB Color ⬍]

☑ Flatten All Layers

Thumbnails

Place: [across fi... ⬍] ☑ Use Auto-Spacing

Columns: 4 Vertical: 0.014 in

Rows: 4 Horizontal: 0.014 in

☑ Rotate For Best Fit

☑ Use Filename As Caption

Font: [Courier ▾] Font Size: [12 pt ▾]

(OK)

(Cancel)

Page 1 of 1
1 of 1 Images
W: 2.1 in
H: 2.5 in

⓵ Press the ESC key to Cancel processing images

Figure 3-4: Set up these sections.

13. Choose a font size.

The default, 12 pt, is easy to read.

14. Click OK.

Photoshop opens each of the files you chose and resizes them to fit 4 across in 4 rows, for a total of 16 2.1 × 2.5-inch full-color photographs with captions, all on a single file ready for printing. You can see in Figure 3-5 the file is named ContactSheet-001. The name of the first image is displayed in the header in parentheses: (2211-0635).

Figure 3-5: ContactSheet-001.

Adding embellishments

The proof sheet you have just created is ready to go to your printer. You can jazz it up and make it look ultra cool by adding a drop shadow and a beveled and embossed edge. Here's the dish:

1. **Click the Add a Layer Style icon at the bottom of the Layers palette, shown circled in red in Figure 3-6.**

   The layer with your proofs on it is the one just above the Background layer in the Layers palette.

2. **Choose Drop Shadow from the contextual menu in Figure 3-7.**

   This opens up the Layer Style dialog.

3. **Click in your file and drag the shadow out from one of the thumbnails on the contact sheet.**

   Don't pull it too far. Look at Figure 3-8 for an example.

4. **Enter numbers in the Drop Shadow dialog to make yours look exactly like Figure 3-8:**

   - **Blend Mode: Multiply.**
   - **Opacity:** 42%.
   - **Angle:** 120.
   - **Distance:** 7 px.
   - **Spread:** 0%.
   - **Size:** 5 px.
   - **Noise:** 0%.

5. **Click the Bevel and Emboss checkbox in the Styles section on the left.**

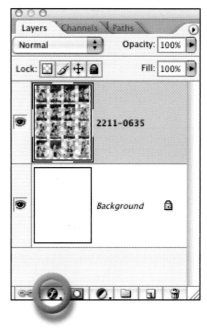

Figure 3-6: Add a layer style.

Figure 3-7: Choosing Drop Shadow.

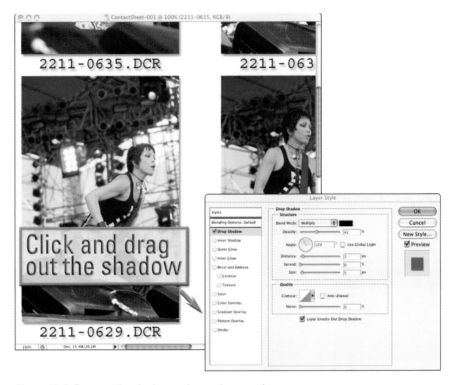

Figure 3-8: Drag out the shadow and copy these settings.

6. **Click the words Bevel and Emboss to open that section of the Layer Style dialog.**

7. **Enter the settings you see in Figure 3-9.**

   • **Style: Inner Bevel.**

   • **Technique: Smooth.**

   • **Depth:** 291%.

   • **Up radio button: Selected.**

   • **Size:** 5 px.

   • **Soften:** 2 px.

   • **Angle:** 120.

   • **Altitude:** 30.

Figure 3-9: Enter these settings.

- **Highlight Mode: Screen.**
- **Opacity:** 92%.
- **Shadow Mode: Multiply.**
- **Opacity:** 54%.

That sets the beveled edge and embosses each photograph and the type too. Very fancy!

8. **Click OK.**

The dialog closes and the Add a Layer Style icon appears at the right edge of the layer. It's circled in Figure 3-10.

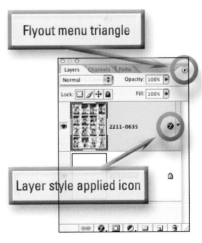

Figure 3-10: Click the flyout triangle to access the submenu.

Printing your contact sheet

All that's left to do is to send your contact sheet to your printer.

1. **Click the Layers flyout triangle in the upper-right corner of the palette, shown circled in Figure 3-10.**

2. **Choose Flatten Image from the menu you see in Figure 3-11.**

   Flattening the image means making all of the layers in the file into one layer, leaving only a Background layer.

Figure 3-11: Choosing Flatten Image.

3. **Load letter-size photo paper into your inkjet printer.**

4. **Choose File⇨Print with Preview from the Photoshop menu.**

   You see a preview of the final print in the preview pane of the Print dialog. The setup appears in Figure 3-12.

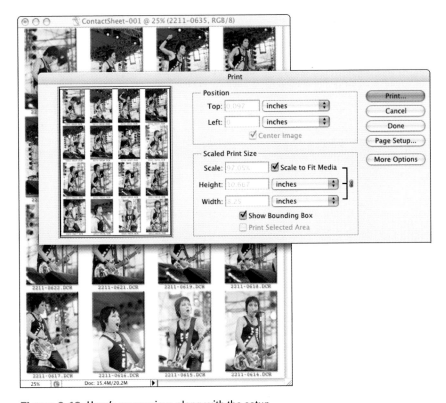

Figure 3-12: Here's my preview, along with the setup.

5. Make sure that the Scale to Fit Media checkbox is selected.

If you leave it unchecked you see the warning box in Figure 3-13. In that case, follow these steps:

a. Click Cancel to return to the Print dialog.

b. Click the Scale to Fit Media checkbox. Think of the warning as an "Oops! Forgot that silly checkbox," reminder.

6. Click Print.

The Print dialog disappears and another info box (see Figure 3-14) pops up. All this tells you is that your printer doesn't print PostScript. Don't worry about it.

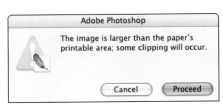

Figure 3-13: Click Cancel to get back to the Print dialog.

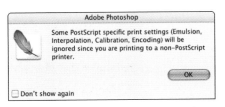

Figure 3-14: No need to worry about this — click OK.

7. Click the Don't Show Again checkbox, then click OK.

Your print is finished in a minute.

The contact sheet you have just made is proof positive that you are a photographer. You have made photographs with your DSLR camera, processed your digital negatives, chosen your favorites, and made a contact sheet. Go show your results to a friend. Bask in the glow. You deserve it. Check out Figure 3-15.

Figure 3-15: The final product.

Going Once more onto the Bridge: Web Photo Galleries

Okay. You have taken care of friends and family with proof sheets (in full color no less). What about the world? Well, that would be the World Wide Web. This section shows you how to create web sites of your photographs chosen my favorite way from Bridge — automatically!

Make Web Photo Galleries using different templates to see what they do. Create a folder for each new gallery. Then you will have a catalog of galleries to choose from. These galleries are small, so they won't use much disk space.

Making your own photography web site automatically

Get used to using Bridge for what it does best: helping you select your best work.

Entering basic information

This example features photographs of Brandon Flowers of The Killers, a great alternative band from Las Vegas. Check 'em out at www.thekillers music.com. The site gives you a preview of their music and opens their main site too.

1. **Choose a new set of photographs.**

   If you create an electronic presentation after reading Bonus Chapter 1, you can use those photographs.

2. **Choose Tools⇨Photoshop⇨Web Photo Gallery from the Bridge menu.**

   See Figure 3-16. Most of the steps coming up are only filled in once.

3. **Select the Banner dialog.**

   The default opening dialog is the general one. These settings are fine.

4. **Choose Banner from the Options drop-down menu to get the box in Figure 3-17.**

5. **Enter your e-mail address in the Email window.**

   In the Source Images section, Use automatically chooses Selected Images from Bridge when you call Web Photo Gallery from the Bridge Tools menu. The other option is Folder, which you can choose if you want to make a gallery of every photo in a folder. Selecting Folder activates the Choose button beneath it, which you use to navigate to the folder you want.

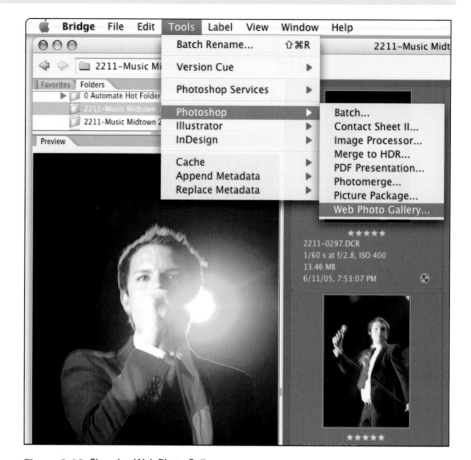

Figure 3-16: Choosing Web Photo Gallery.

6. **Click the Destination button.**

A Select a Destination Location dialog appears.

7. **Click the Desktop and create a folder called** WPG_Simple.

8. **Click Choose.**

9. **Enter a description of the web site in the Site Name window.**

10. **Enter your name in the Photographer field.**

Add the copyright symbol before you enter your name in the Photographer field (for example ©2005 Kevin Ames). The keyboard shortcut for the copyright symbol is Option+G (Alt+0169).

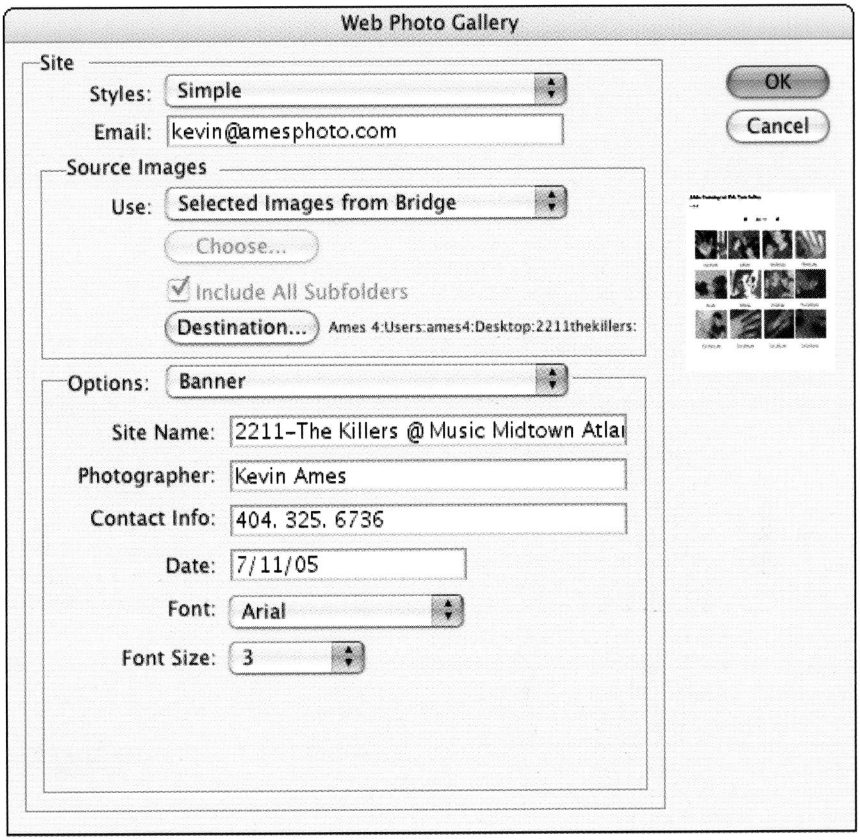

Figure 3-17: Setting up the Web Photo Gallery.

11. **Type your phone number in the Contact Info window.**

    Photoshop automatically fills in the date for you.

12. **Choose your favorite font from the limited selection in the drop-down menu.**

    In this web site, 3 is a good size for your text.

13. **Choose your style from the Style menu, then continue with the next section of steps.**

Adobe has added even more Web Photo Gallery templates to Photoshop CS2. Look through them by clicking the Styles menu to display the choices, which appear in Figure 3-18. The thumbnail on the right shows you a tiny preview for any style you select. You can see examples of three templates at the end of this chapter.

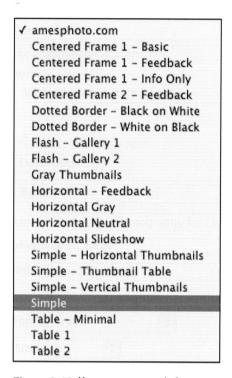

✓ amesphoto.com
Centered Frame 1 – Basic
Centered Frame 1 – Feedback
Centered Frame 1 – Info Only
Centered Frame 2 – Feedback
Dotted Border – Black on White
Dotted Border – White on Black
Flash – Gallery 1
Flash – Gallery 2
Gray Thumbnails
Horizontal – Feedback
Horizontal Gray
Horizontal Neutral
Horizontal Slideshow
Simple – Horizontal Thumbnails
Simple – Thumbnail Table
Simple – Vertical Thumbnails
Simple
Table – Minimal
Table 1
Table 2

Figure 3-18: You can see your choices.

Setting up the large images

Now you decide how you want to set up your images.

14. **Choose Options⇨Large Images to see the dialog in Figure 3-19.**

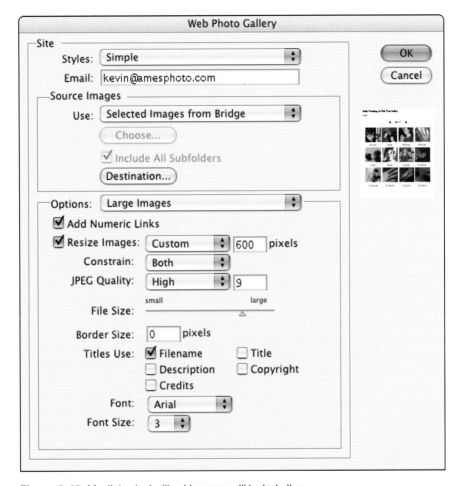

Figure 3-19: My dialog looks like this; yours will look similar.

15. Select or deselect Add Numeric Links (in the Options section) based on the number of images.

If you have fewer than 20 images selected, leave Add Numeric Links checked. When you are making galleries of hundreds of images, uncheck it. (On big galleries, the numeric links can take up several pages. Not useful.) Leave the Resize Images box checked.

16. 600 pixels in the long direction is a good size to type into the Resize Images text box.

I like to look at big images when I click a thumbnail.

17. From Constrain, choose Both.

This resizes your images so that the longest side is 600 pixels, whether that's the height or width. Computers purchased in recent years have monitors that display pages 1,024 × 768 pixels. If your audience is using older displays that show only 640 × 480 pixels, choose a smaller size, like 350 pixels. Leave JPEG Quality on High.

18. Choose a border for your image by entering a number in the Border Size window.

I prefer no border. The choice is yours.

19. Pick the kind of data you can display on your web site with the Titles Use checkboxes.

My preference is Filename. Using more than one can create a cluttered page.

20. If you want, change fonts and size.

I use Arial and 3.

Biting your thumbnails

Figure 3-20 shows the dialog you get when you set up thumbnails.

1. Choose Options⇨Thumbnails.

2. If your viewing audience is using newer monitors, enter 200 **pixels for Size,** 5 **for Columns, and** 3 **for Rows.**

3. Click OK.

Photoshop goes into action and automatically builds your web site of photographs. Photoshop then opens the completed web site in your computer's default web browser for your viewing pleasure. You can view the Killers gallery on my web site by going to www.amesphoto.com/2211thekillers. It displays in my custom-tailored version of the Simple gallery style.

If you have your own web site, load the whole folder of your newly built Web Photo Gallery onto your server using a *file transfer protocol (FTP)* program like CuteFTP on Windows or Fetch on Macintosh.

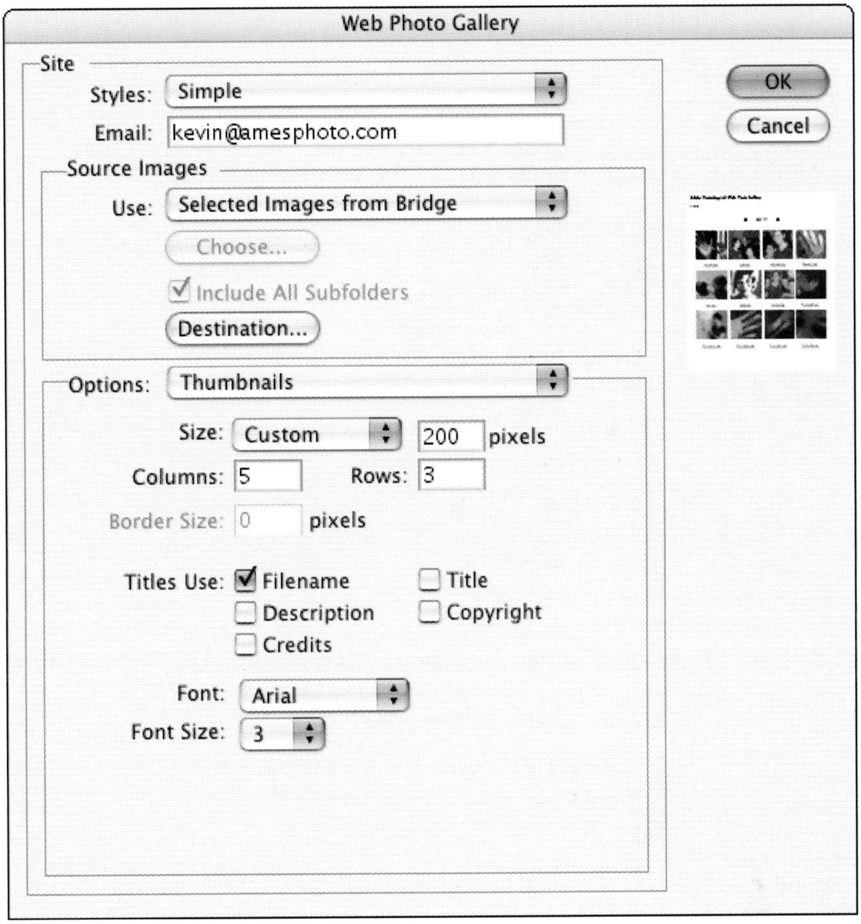

Figure 3-20: Setting up thumbnails.

Web Photo Gallery styles

Figure 3-21 through 3-23 show 3 of the 20 styles built into Photoshop CS2. The first one, in Figure 3-21, is a very cool Flash-based site that enlarges the thumbnails when you move the mouse over the mini version. Figure 3-22 is the Simple–Horizontal Thumbnails with thumbnails that run across the bottom. The style closest to a photographic proof sheet is Simple, shown in Figure 3-23.

Figure 3-21: This is the Flash-based site's offering.

Figure 3-22: The thumbnails run across the bottom of the page.

Figure 3-23: Similar to a proof sheet.

Chapter 4: Introducing Adobe Camera Raw 3

In This Chapter

↙ **Getting around in Adobe Camera Raw**

↙ **Setting the white balance**

↙ **Fine-tuning your exposures**

↙ **Making black and white in Adobe Camera Raw**

↙ **Setting up the workflow options**

*A*dobe Camera Raw 3 is an absolutely amazing tool for making the most of the data captured by your DSLR camera set to shoot in RAW. Here you explore the different sections of the Adobe Camera Raw 3 (ACR3) dialog. You read how to color balance your digital negatives. Exposure tweaking is next on your journey through ACR3, followed by a quick tour of how your work will look in black and white. Finally, you go through the steps of setting up ACR3's workflow options for making the files you use in Adobe Photoshop CS2.

Book III, Chapter 1 explains the differences in the quality and quantity of information contained in JPEG and RAW files. This chapter shows you how to use all of the information you get shooting in RAW.

Cooking with Adobe Camera Raw 3

Adobe has packed a huge amount of power into ACR3. As a matter of fact, the original author of Photoshop, Thomas Knoll, wrote ACR3. His name is the first one you see on the splash screen when Photoshop starts. See Figure 4-1. You don't get more powerful than that.

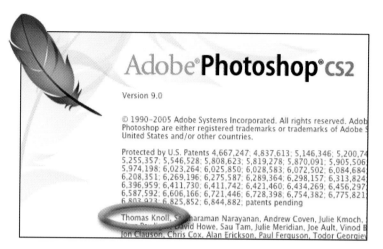

Figure 4-1: Thomas Knoll is the father of Photoshop and Adobe Camera Raw 3.

Thomas has packed an entire photo processing lab into a single dialog. Everything you need to get the phenomenal results out of a RAW file is in one place. I've labeled each of the features and pulled out the menus for you in Figure 4-2. All of the labels make it look intimidating at first, so let me go through each section.

Tooling around ACR3's Bar

Along the top of the ACR3 dialog is the toolbar. Each tool is shown and named in Figure 4-2. The Zoom Tool is selected by default when you launch Camera Raw. Here's a quick look at each tool from left to right, along with its keyboard shortcut.

Zoom Tool (Z)

Click to zoom in. Click and drag diagonally across an area in the preview window and the image enlarges to that size. Hold down the Option (Alt) key and click to zoom out.

Hand Tool (H or Spacebar)

Click and drag to scroll the window. Rather than clicking the hand icon or typing an H to select the tool, you can access the Hand tool by holding down the spacebar. The Hand tool reverts to the previously selected tool when you release the spacebar.

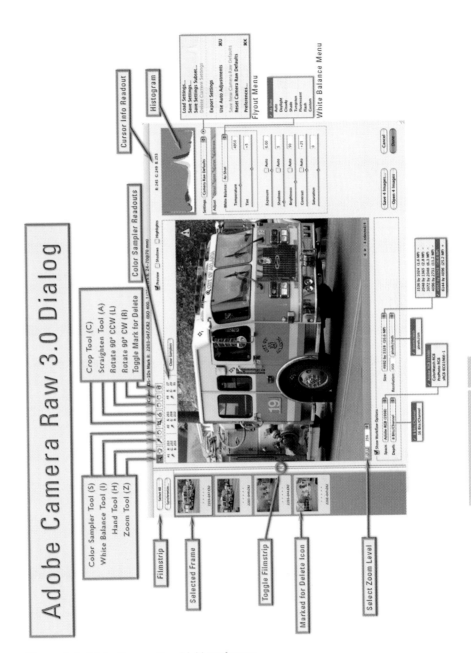

Adobe Camera Raw 3.0 Dialog

Color Sampler Tool (S)
White Balance Tool (I)
Hand Tool (H)
Zoom Tool (Z)

Crop Tool (C)
Straighten Tool (A)
Rotate 90° CCW (L)
Rotate 90° CW (R)
Toggle Mark for Delete

Color Sampler Readouts

Cursor Info Readout

Histogram

Flyout Menu

Load Settings...
Save Settings...
Save Settings Subset...
Delete Current Settings

Export Settings

Use Auto Adjustments
Save New Camera Raw Defaults
Reset Camera Raw Defaults

Preferences...

White Balance Menu

Filmstrip

Selected Frame

Toggle Filmstrip

Marked for Delete Icon

Select Zoom Level

Figure 4-2: Adobe Camera Raw 3 laid out for you.

White Balance Tool (1)

Click a neutral value — white, gray, or black — and the White Balance Tool corrects the color temperature to a neutral tone. It makes the highlight, midtone, or shadow RGB (Red, Green, and Blue) values equal each other. Color temperature is how the color of light is measured. An incandescent lightbulb and light from the sun right at sunset have the same orange color. The color temperature of both is around 2800° Kelvin. This is interesting stuff. Book II, Chapter 3 talks more about color temperature.

Color Sampler Tool (S)

New to ACR3, the Color Sampler Tool places up to nine color samplers in your image preview so you can monitor exposure, shadow, and brightness changes at specific points. Hold the cursor over a placed color sampler and the icon changes. Click+drag to move it to another place. Click Clear Samplers to remove the color samplers from the preview. Look for the color samplers in the preview in Figure 4-3 and their readouts in the Color Sampler Readout area. The samplers are circled in red. The readouts are boxed in red.

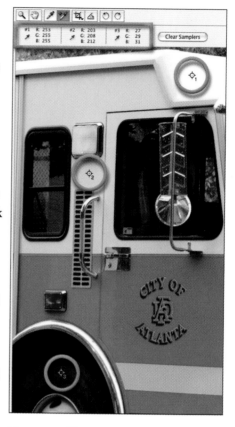

Figure 4-3: Two color samplers and their readouts in ACR3.

Crop Tool (C)

Another new ACR3 feature is the Crop Tool. This versatile tool allows you to crop your RAW file to a small size, then reopen ACR3 and change the crop to a larger size later — something that's impossible in Photoshop. Here's how to use the Crop Tool:

1. **Select a RAW preview in Bridge by clicking it (as shown boxed in red in Figure 4-4).**

Figure 4-4: Select an image by clicking its thumbnail. The border changes to show it's selected.

2. **Type ⌘+R (Ctrl+R) to open the file in ACR3.**

   TIP

   You may choose several files to open at once by ⌘+clicking (Ctrl+clicking) the files. Choosing more than one file automatically opens the filmstrip view in ACR3.

3. **Click Crop Tool icon⇨Custom, shown in Figure 4-5.**

   The Custom Crop dialog appears.

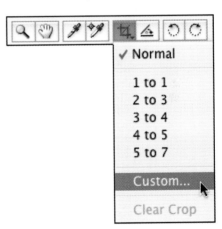

Figure 4-5: The Crop menu.

4. **Enter a** 4 **and then a** 6 **in the two ratio fields, as shown in Figure 4-6.**

5. **Choose Crop➪Inches➪OK.**

Figure 4-7 shows how to select inches.

The Crop Tool in ACR3 remembers the last setting. If you always make 4 × 6-inch prints, you can click several RAW files in Bridge, open them in ACR3, and crop to your heart's content.

6. **Crop your photograph by click+dragging a box around the subject.**

By default, the first number in the chosen crop size or ratio is width and the second is height. When you first draw a crop, it is framed vertically. You see this in Figure 4-8.

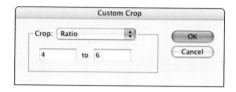

Figure 4-6: A 4 × 6 crop.

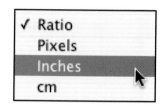

Figure 4-7: Choosing inches makes it perfect for printing.

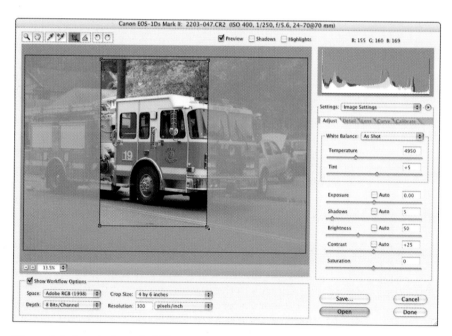

Figure 4-8: A vertical crop in ACR3.

Drag one of the handles to the side and the crop automatically flips to a horizontal frame. The area of the crop is still 4 × 6 inches, only now 4 is the height and 6 is the width. See Figure 4-9. Do this yourself. It is so much cooler than the Crop Tool in Photoshop.

Figure 4-9: The crop flips to horizontal by dragging a corner.

7. Open the cropped file in Photoshop by clicking Open.

It's in the lower-right corner of the dialog. Your newly cropped file opens in Photoshop.

Take a look at the thumbnail of the RAW file in Bridge, Photoshop's image viewing program. (Book IV, Chapter 1 details Bridge.) Notice that the preview is cropped to the size you chose in ACR3. A cropped icon, circled in red in Figure 4-10, appears in the lower-right corner of the frame. The icon to its right tells you that the settings in the RAW file have been changed from the way the photograph was saved in the camera. Open the file in ACR3 and select Crop Tool icon⇨Clear Crop to clear the crop settings.

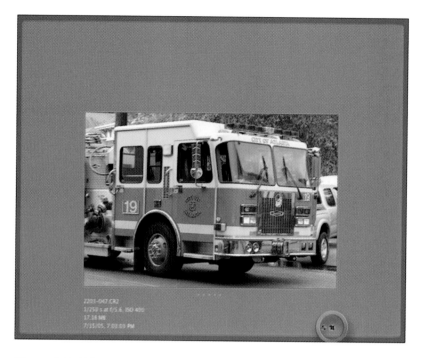

Figure 4-10: This is a cropped RAW file.

Straighten Tool (A)

Sometimes the lines in your photographs are just a little bit off from horizontal or vertical. A new tool in ACR3 helps. It tells the Crop Tool exactly how much to rotate the file to make an image level.

1. **In Bridge, choose a photograph that is not quite level. Click its thumbnail to select it.**

2. **Type ⌘+R (Ctrl+R) to open it in ACR3.**

3. **Choose the Straighten Tool by typing the letter A.**

4. **Click one end of a line that should be horizontal or vertical and drag the dotted line out along it.**

   In Figure 4-11 the dotted line is along the edge of a shelf under a shuttered window I photographed in Orvieto, Italy.

Figure 4-11: The Straighten Tool in action.

5. Release the mouse button.

The Straighten Tool icon changes to the Crop Tool. The Crop Tool's *bounding box,* or outline, appears in the preview window, as shown in Figure 4-12.

6. Click Open.

The cropped photograph opens in Photoshop with the windows perfectly level.

The Straighten Tool is especially handy when shooting ocean scenes. The horizon line in water scenes really has to be level.

Rotate Tools: CCW (L) and CW (R)

The next two tools in ACR3 are the Rotate Tools. The first one rotates the preview 90° counter clockwise (CCW). Its keyboard shortcut is L. The next one rotates the image preview 90° clockwise using the keystroke R. This is handy if your DSLR camera does not provide orientation information to Camera Raw through the EXIF metadata.

Figure 4-12: The straightened crop is shown by the rotated box.

You'll know if your DSLR adds orientation information to an image. If the metadata is added, vertical photographs preview as verticals. If the info is not provided, verticals are horizontal. You can rotate them to the correct position in ACR3. Seeing how an abstract photograph would look upside down is also useful. A good composition works no matter how it is rotated.

I often shoot editorial product photographs turned upside down on the set, as in Figure 4-13. The image gets rotated in Camera Raw before delivery to the client. The right-side up, upside down photograph in Figure 4-14 has an edge that one shot "correctly" is missing.

Figure 4-13: This is how the purse was shot in my studio.

Figure 4-14: The purse is rotated in ACR3 to look right-side up.

Toggle Mark for Delete icon

This icon appears when more than one RAW file is selected in Bridge and opened in ACR3. If you truly don't want to keep a RAW file, select it in the filmstrip column and click the Toggle Mark for Delete icon. The red X in the upper-left corner of the thumbnail tells you that the file and its .xmp sidecar file will be moved to the Trash (Recycle Bin in Windows) when you click the Done, Save, or Open button. .xmp sidecar files are how Camera Raw stores information about the changes you have made. Read more about them in Book III, Chapter 2.

The Toggle Mark for Delete icon moves digital negatives to the Trash (Recycle Bin). When you empty the Trash or Recycle Bin, the file is permanently deleted from your hard drive. In my book, this is a never-use-this-tool tool.

Setting the White Balance in ACR3

Sometimes setting the *white balance* (light's color temperature) in the camera doesn't work as you might like. It is a great idea to always include a reference card in the first photograph you make in a given lighting situation;

it has known values of white, gray, and black that when photographed can be used in ACR3. That allows you to tweak the settings to perfection in Camera Raw. Reference cards are covered in Book II, Chapter 3. When a known white is available, getting rid of unwanted color cast is handled with a single click of your mouse. *Color cast* is an off-color tone in a photograph. Late afternoon sunlight has an orange color cast. A white, gray, or black object would appear to have an orangish tone.

Set the white balance with these steps:

1. **Select a set of files, including one that features a white reference, in ACR3.**

   A *white reference* is a known neutral white.

2. **Type ⌘+R (Ctrl+R) to open the digital negatives in Camera Raw.**

   If the scene has a white, you can use that to white balance in Camera Raw. Figure 4-3 is a good example of a photograph with all of the reference points. The fire truck has a white, a gray, and a black.

3. **Click the White Balance Tool icon or type I.**

   The icon is circled in red in Figure 4-15 in ACR3's toolbar.

4. **Move the White Balance Tool over the white reference.**

   Look at the color readouts above the histogram in Figure 4-15. The values are Red 244, Green 235, and Blue 221. Readings of more red and green than blue means the color will have an orange cast. Compare the white of the page this book is printed on to the white in the reference card, and the orange is easy to see.

5. **Click the white reference area in your photograph to neutralize the color to white.**

   Camera Raw instantly adjusts the Color Temperature and the Tint sliders to make the red, green, and blue readings in the info window the same. Compare the color and readings in Figure 4-16 to those of Figure 4-15.

When the RGB values of a white, gray, or black are the same, the color cast is neutralized. For more on color temperature see Book II, Chapter 3.

Figure 4-15: Tucker and the reference card have an orange color cast.

Figure 4-16: Tucker and the reference card with no color cast at all.

Fine-Tuning Exposure

Exposure is the amount of light the sensor in a DSLR records. One of the great advantages of shooting in the RAW format is the ability to adjust the exposure values after the shoot is over. The photograph of my friend, magazine editor Tucker Berta, in the previous exercise is a great example. The info readouts in Figure 4-17 show neutral RGB values of 233 each. White with detail wants RGB values of around 245. A space to the right of the histogram has no pixels in it. That too indicates underexposure.

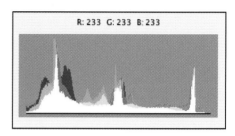

Figure 4-17: A slightly underexposed histogram.

These steps help you fine-tune exposure:

1. **Click the Color Sampler Tool icon or type S to choose the Color Sampler Tool.**

2. **Place an info sampler in the white reference.**

   Click in the same place you clicked with the White Balance Tool to place a color sampler there (as shown in Figure 4-18). The image preview shrinks a bit and an info readout appears for sampler #1 below the toolbar.

3. **Click the Exposure slider.**

4. **Drag it to the right while you watch the RGB values.**

   Stop when they reach 245 as you see in Figure 4-19. Notice that the pixels in the histogram have moved to the right, filling up the space shown in Figure 4-17.

If the Auto checkboxes in the Adjust tab are checked as you see in Figure 4-20, turn them off by typing ⌘+U (Ctrl+U). Change the default by choosing Settings⇨Save New Camera Raw Defaults, as shown in Figure 4-2. The Auto settings change to make a "proper" histogram. They override changes you make in your camera. Turning them off permanently will help you see what happens when you over- or underexpose on purpose. For more on Auto settings, see Book I, Chapter 3.

Figure 4-18: Color Sampler #1 and its readouts in ACR3.

Figure 4-19: Proper exposure by the numbers and the histogram.

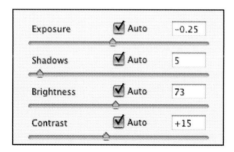

Figure 4-20: The Auto settings are on by default.

Applying the new settings

It would be a real pain in the anatomy to have to apply new settings to each file individually. Fortunately, you can apply the settings you have already made to all of the files in the filmstrip view — in this case 24 of them.

1. Click Select All⇨Synchronize.

TIP

Both buttons are at the top of the filmstrip. Select All chooses all of the files. The first image is selected, as indicated by the blue border in Figure 4-21. The Settings dialog appears when you choose Synchronize. You see the dialog in Figure 4-22. Pressing Option+Synchronize (Alt+Synchronize) bypasses the Synchronize dialog.

Figure 4-21: The Synchronize button.

2. Click OK, then watch the filmstrip column.

The previews briefly display a yellow warning symbol, then they update to reflect the changes you have applied.

Figure 4-22: The Synchronize dialog.

3. Click Done in the lower-right corner of ACR3.

Done (see Figure 4-23) updates the changes in the .xmp sidecar files without opening the photographs. Or you can choose to save all of the color-corrected, exposure-enhanced files as Photoshop documents by clicking the Save button. Clicking Open does just that; it opens all 24 files in Photoshop CS2.

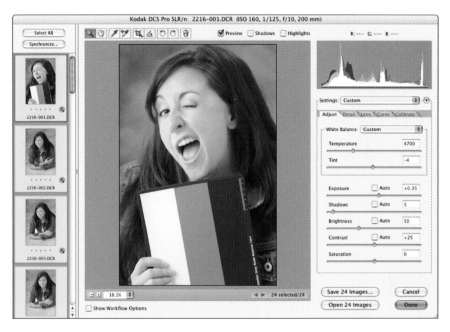

Figure 4-23: The Done button in ACR3.

Look at the thumbnails in Bridge in Figure 4-24. All of them have been updated with the tweaked exposure and proper white balance. A slider icon in the lower-right corner of each one (one is circled in red in the figure) tells you its settings have been modified in Camera Raw.

Sliding into perfect exposure

Four additional controls are available for enhancing exposure in ACR3.

Shadows slider

Shadows increase the density of the dark areas of an image. The Shadows slider is best left at the default setting or less. Moving the Shadows slider to the right can result in parts of the image printing as total black.

Brightness slider

Brightness/contrast adjustments in Photoshop are to be avoided at all costs. The opposite is true in Camera Raw. The Brightness slider makes the values in between the highlights and the shadows brighter or darker. It does not do much at all to the highlights or shadows themselves. Once you have set the white point at around RGB 245 (as you did in the previous exercise), brighten the rest of the photograph by moving the Brightness slider to the right.

Figure 4-24: The modified-in-ACR3 icon.

Contrast slider

Move the Contrast slider to the right to brighten the tones above middle gray and darken those below middle gray with minimal change to the highlights or shadows. Drag it to the left to darken the tones brighter than middle gray and lighten the tones darker than middle gray.

Saturation slider

Moving this slider to the right increases the color values. Moving it to the left removes color. You get a hand-colored look when this slider is set between –50 and –75. You can choose each Adjustment field in turn by pressing Tab. Once the field is selected, you can use your up- and down arrow keys to change the information.

What's Black and White and Raw All Over?

RAW files, like all color digital images, are made of three channels of black, white, and gray. One channel is shot through a Red filter, one through a

Green filter, and one through a Blue filter. What this means is that color digital files — especially the high-bit depth, data-rich RAW files — have everything you need to make amazing black-and-white photographs. For more on bit depth, read Book II, Chapter 1.

1. **Go to www.amesphoto.com/learning and register if you haven't already.**

   The code to go to the login/registration page is 4D59776.

2. **Go to the Downloads section for this book and click the files for Book III, Chapter 4.**

   Please note that the files provided on the download site are copyrighted and only for use in doing the exercises.

3. **Highlight the 2124-018.X3F file in Bridge and type ⌘+R (Ctrl+R).**

4. **Make sure the Auto checkboxes are unchecked.**

   To uncheck all of the Auto checkboxes, type ⌘+U (Ctrl+U).

5. **Move the Saturation slider all the way to the left.**

   The reading is –100 and the photograph is black and white. The image in Figure 4-25 looks a little flat. The sky is too light. Overall it looks kind of blah.

6. **Click the Calibrate tab in the Settings section and make these settings.**

   - **Green Hue slider: –75**

   - **Green Saturation slider: –75**

   - **Blue Hue slider: +100**

   - **Blue Saturation slider: +100**

   These sliders control the hue and saturation of the individual channels. Figure 4-26 is looking much better.

7. **Click the Adjust tab.**

   - **Move the Brightness slider to 95.**

   - **Move the Shadows slider to 15.**

   The results are shown in Figure 4-27. This black and white image is much better than the one in Figure 4-25. There is great contrast in it. The sky is much darker and the highlights are bright and still have detail. Keep the file open and work through the next section.

Do you want to see what those calibration sliders did? Move the Saturation slider back to 0. The result is color from a really bad dream, as you can see in Figure 4-28. And when it's desaturated, it works very well indeed.

**Book III
Chapter 4**

Introducing Adobe
Camera Raw 3

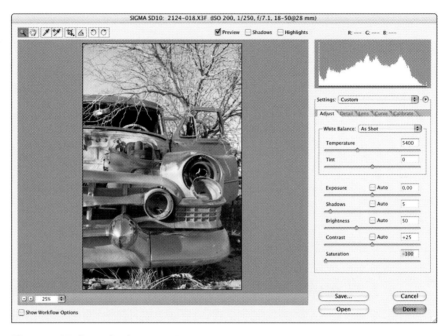

Figure 4-25: Saturation is set at –100.

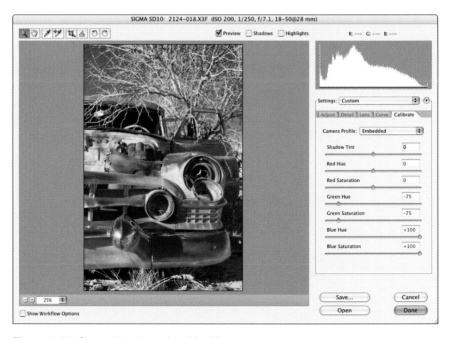

Figure 4-26: Channel tweaks make a big difference.

Figure 4-27: Black and white Camera Raw style! Nice.

Figure 4-28: Psychedelic colors.

Setting Workflow Options

The last part of Adobe Camera Raw 3 you want to know about is the Workflow Options. Use the file of the car from the preceding project.

1. **With the file from the previous steps open, click the Show Workflow Options checkbox.**

   It's at the bottom right under the Select Zoom Level drop-down menu. A panel opens up and reveals the four settings shown in Figure 4-29.

Figure 4-29: ACR3's workflow options.

2. **Choose Adobe RGB (1998) in the Space drop-down menu.**

   This menu has four choices, as you can see in Figure 4-30: Adobe RGB (1998), ColorMatch RGB, ProPhoto RGB, and sRGB IEC61966-1. The default is sRGB IEC61966-1. It is used primarily for images shown on the Internet. My favorite is Adobe RGB (1998).

Figure 4-30: Select Adobe RGB (1998).

3. **Choose the output size in the Size drop-down menu.**

   Camera Raw has the ability to resize the number of pixels to larger or smaller sizes. The smaller sizes are ideal for use on the Internet. The larger sizes are great when making a big print. The default size is the one for the *native,* or original, number of actual pixels captured by your DSLR camera. See Figure 4-31.

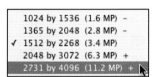

Figure 4-31: Upsizing the output of the black and white car.

4. **Set the resolution.**

   This is pixels per inch (or pixels per centimeter for the metrically inclined) setting. 240 is a great choice for inkjet prints; 72 is ideal for the Internet; 300 is the standard for the printing press.

5. **Click OK.**

   The file opens in Photoshop and is ready to edit. See Figure 4-32.

Figure 4-32: The finished black and white photograph.

Book IV

Working with Photographs in Photoshop CS2

The 5th Wave — By Rich Tennant

"...and through computer simulation, we're able to recreate the awesome spectacle known as Tyrannosaurus Gwen."

*A*dobe Photoshop CS2 is your color darkroom without the dark, chemicals, film, water, or processing. This remarkable software is also your digital light box, allowing you to sort, rename, rank, and label your images. You read about how to control color in Photoshop and refine your exposures there, too. You command color using Photoshop features that create the color and allow you to apply it creatively, wherever you want.

Chapter 1: Building Bridges: Working with Adobe Bridge

In This Chapter

- ✓ Using a digital light box
- ✓ Selecting thumbnails
- ✓ Sorting, rating, and labeling your photographs
- ✓ Opening RAW files in Adobe Camera Raw 3 from Bridge
- ✓ Opening JPEGs in Photoshop CS2

*A*dobe has made Bridge your access point to Photoshop CS2, as well as to the other programs in the Creative Suite. Bridge is a digital light box that you set up for the way you work. You select and sort your photographs, apply a one- to five-star rating, then label them in color so you know, at a glance, your favorite images. Finally, here you can tell Bridge how to show your best work and open it in Adobe Camera Raw 3 (if you shoot the RAW format) or in Photoshop (if you are shooting JPEGs).

Bridge is truly a remarkable piece of software. It is the gateway for working on all kinds of digital graphics files in addition to JPEGs, TIFFS, PDFs, and Photoshop documents (PSD).

Tripping the Digital Light Box . . . Fantastic!

The old-fashioned way of sorting photographs meant bending over the backlit table with a loupe to make sure the image was well composed, properly exposed, and sharp. Photo editors marked slide mounts with colored China markers. Images were sorted into pages holding 20 slides. The *hero,* or best, photograph was ultimately chosen. And it had to be handled with extreme caution. The hero, like all the other pieces of film, were originals. There were no backups. Bridge uses the metaphor of the light box, loupe, China markers, and slide pages.

Bridge is the digital version of the *light tables* or *light boxes* you have seen in classic movies and television shows. And if you shot film in the last millennium you've probably used one yourself.

Bridge's work area is shown in Figure 1-1. The main areas include the content or light box panel, Folder and Favorites panels, Preview panel, Metadata and Keyword panels, as well as Thumbnail Size slider and display option buttons. The toolbar along the top of the dialog includes a drop-down menu that controls sorting by rating and label, and New Folder, Rotate, Delete Item, and Switch to Compact Mode buttons.

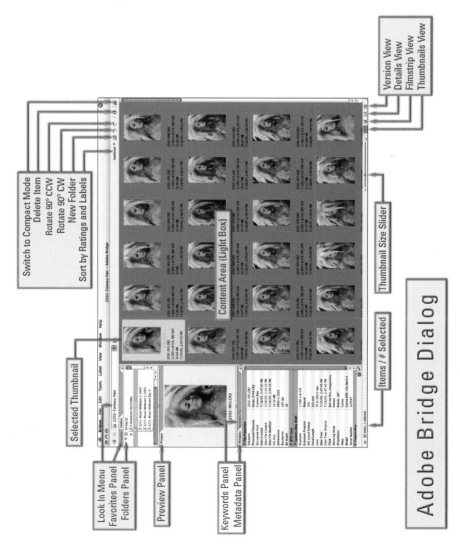

Figure 1-1: The Adobe Bridge dialog.

Getting Choosy about Images

The basic skill required in working in Bridge is selecting *thumbnails* (smaller versions of photos). Here's how:

1. **Open your hard drive by clicking the triangle next to its icon.**

   The icon is circled in Figure 1-2 in the Folders panel.

Figure 1-2: Working in the Folders panel.

2. **Click the folder of images you want to work with.**

   I've chosen a folder named 2202-Fantasy Hair shot for Toni & Guy Hair Salons. Thumbnails of each photograph appear in the content area, or light box panel.

3. **Click a thumbnail to select it.**

4. **Click another image to select it.**

   The previously selected image is deselected and the newly clicked thumbnail is highlighted. Clicking alone selects only the last clicked thumbnail.

5. **Click the first thumbnail in a series you wish to select. Shift+click the last image in the series.**

   A portion of the series is selected, as shown in Figure 1-3.

**Book IV
Chapter 1**

Building Bridges:
Working with
Adobe Bridge

Figure 1-3: Selected images highlighted in a consecutive series.

6. **⌘+click (Ctrl+click) the second image before the first one in the series; then ⌘+click (Ctrl+click) the third image after the series.**

You've added two more thumbnails to the selected series. The example in Figure 1-4 shows that image number 2202-003.CR2 and 2202-013.CR2 have been added to the series, which begins with 2202-005.CR2 and ends with 2202-010.CR2.

Clicking selects a single thumbnail. Clicking the first thumbnail in a series, then Shift+clicking the last thumbnail of a series selects the whole series. Pressing ⌘ (Ctrl) and clicking selects each thumbnail clicked. Select all thumbnails in the light box by typing ⌘+A (Ctrl+A). Deselect by typing ⌘+Shift+A (Ctrl+Shift+A).

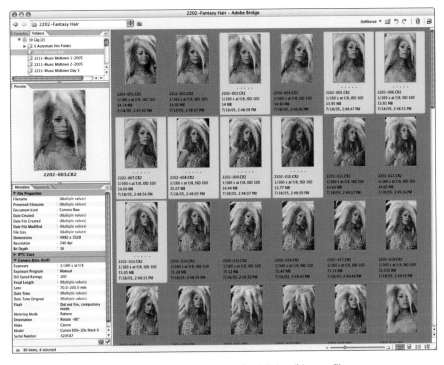

Figure 1-4: A nonconsecutive series of selected (highlighted) image files.

Resorting to Sorting Photographs

Choosing the best photographs from the hundreds or thousands you shoot is easy using the tools in Bridge. Often a first impression is lasting and right on the money when it comes to finding the one (photograph) you love. Bridge is your little black book of favorite and not-so-favorite images.

Sorting manually

Bridge allows you to move your photographs around in the light box by simply clicking and dragging. Say I want to move image number 16 to the front of the line. I click and drag it until the blue insert line appears, as shown in Figure 1-5; then I release the mouse button. The thumbnail of 2202-016.CR2 is the first in line. See Figure 1-6.

Figure 1-5: Release the mouse button to drop a thumbnail in front of the blue line.

Figure 1-6: 2202-016.CR2 moved to the front of the line.

The thumbnails can be reset to their original order by choosing View➪ Sort➪By Filename from the Bridge menu bar. Figure 1-7 illustrates this path.

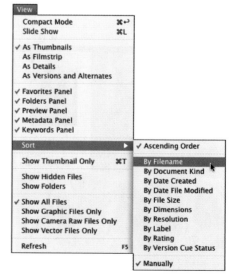

Figure 1-7: Ordering the sort by filename.

Shooting them a star

Bridge lets you rate your photographs with one to five stars. The keyboard shortcut is ⌘+★ (Ctrl+★★), with you typing the number of stars you wish to grant to a thumbnail. You can use the mouse to rate a thumbnail. Move the cursor under the image portion of a selected thumbnail. Five dots appear in a line. Click the dot that represents the rating you want. The photograph in Figure 1-8 displays four stars (★★★★). Click the circle with the slash to the left of the first star to clear the rating. You can select a group of images and press the keyboard shortcut for the rating.

2202-016.CR2
1/160 s at f/8, ISO 100
15.47 MB
7/18/05, 2:49:43 PM

Figure 1-8: A four-star thumbnail.

You can eliminate having to hold down the ⌘ (Ctrl) key by unchecking the Require the ⌘ (Ctrl) Key to Apply Labels and Ratings checkbox in Bridge's preferences. This is shown in Figure 1-9. You can also change the label's name from the color to anything you want. I think the best photo should be labeled HOT!!! Access preferences by choosing Bridge➪Preferences➪Labels (Edit➪ Preferences➪Labels).

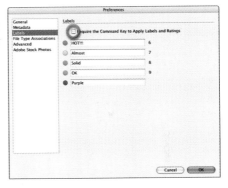

Figure 1-9: Save a keystroke. Uncheck this box.

Labeling in color

Labels are the color equivalent of a China marker in Bridge. You can apply labels to already rated photographs by selecting a thumbnail and using the keyboard shortcut or choosing Label➪HOT!!! from the menu in Figure 1-10. This menu reflects whatever custom ratings you typed in the Label Preferences dialog; look back at Figure 1-9.

Red is the default label for your highest rating. (Again, mine is HOT!!! Yours might be DANGER.) The shortcut keys appear to the left of each color. Figure 1-10 is from the Macintosh OS. If you use Windows, press the Ctrl key.

Filtering

Filtering is what database engineers call "looking at your data (photographs in this case) according to labels and ratings you have applied." Bridge has a menu in the toolbar that lets you choose exactly which thumbnails appear in the light box. Figure 1-11 shows you how I display all thumbnails of Ava with a ★★★★ or higher rating.

I think that the red-label images are the best. That's why they're labeled HOT!!!, after all. I can either ⌘+click (Ctrl+click) the individual thumbnails with red labels or choose Filter⇨Show HOT!!! Label. See the menu in Figure 1-12.

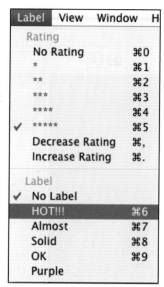

Figure 1-10: Labeling selected thumbnails using the menu.

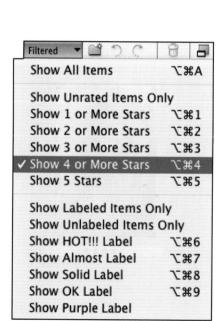

Figure 1-11: Sorting by star rating.

Figure 1-12: Sorting by color labels.

Opening the chosen ones in Adobe Camera Raw 3

The choice of hero photographs of Ava has been narrowed down to five. The final selection is done best in Adobe Camera Raw 3 (ACR3). Here you can zoom in to the actual file to check focus and use the adjust controls to tweak the photograph's look. I open all of the files in ACR3 by pressing ⌘+A (Ctrl+A) to select all and then, still pressing ⌘ (Ctrl), type R. All five RAW files appear in the filmstrip view on the left side of the dialog. I zoom in to each one and look at it closely for composition and sharpness. See Figure 1-13. When I have found the ultimate hero, I add the fifth star by either clicking it in the color label at the bottom of the thumbnail or pressing ⌘+R (Ctrl+R). Click Open to retouch it in Photoshop. See Book V, Chapter 3 for retouching tips.

Figure 1-13: Reviewing photographs in ACR3's filmstrip view.

JPEGs, Bridge, and Photoshop

Sorting, rating, and labeling JPEG files work exactly the same in Bridge as do their RAW counterparts. The only difference is that the JPEG files can't be opened in ACR3 for final examination. Click the Filmstrip View icon (third icon from the lower-right corner at the bottom of the Bridge window; see it labeled in Figure 1-1) to use the Filmstrip view in Bridge.

The default Filmstrip view is a horizontal row of thumbnails. To change the view to a vertical column like you see in Figure 1-14, click the Switch Filmstrip Orientation button, which is shown circled in red.

The ratings and labels show on the thumbnails. The vertical view gives a bigger thumbnail. See the frog sitting on the lily pad? Bigger *is* better. Select the best JPEG or JPEGs, then double-click one of the thumbnails to open the file in Photoshop. (In Photoshop CS2, double-clicking a RAW file opens it in ACR3, not in Bridge.)

The JPEG format is a lossy compression routine. Every time a JPEG file is opened and resaved, more data is lost. It is a very good idea to save opened JPEG files as TIFF or PSD files. This prevents additional data corruption. Book III, Chapter 1 talks more about JPEGs.

Figure 1-14: Click the icon to switch to the vertical filmstrip view.

Chapter 2: Controlling Colors and Balancing White

In This Chapter

✓ **Knowing about neutral colors**

✓ **Understanding the Info palette**

✓ **Using the Color Sampler Tool**

✓ **Getting into the Layers palette**

✓ **Adjusting color with levels**

*W*elcome to the magic known as Photoshop CS2! Here you read about what makes a color neutral and how to use the Info palette's numbers. You set up the Color Sampler Tool options to give the most accurate readings of the colors that make up your photograph in the Info palette. You place color samplers on highlights and shadows then, using a Levels Adjustment Layer, fine-tune their individual colors until they are neutral.

This chapter begins your journey into the wonders of Photoshop. I start you out with good photographic habits. You discover at least one other way to do the things you read about here. There are many, many ways to get the same or similar results in this amazing program. My methods are a jumping-off point for you to explore your creativity and your technique. The steps are designed to always let you go back and have "do overs," even if you have saved and closed your Photoshop document.

You might have used Photoshop before and have your own way of achieving the effects I describe. Give these steps a work through. They build on each other. By the time you have finished all the projects, you will be proficient at nondestructive Photoshop editing. You can create digital photographic files with unlimited undos — forever!

This chapter builds on the information in Book II, Chapter 1. The projects work best with a color-calibrated monitor. See Book V, Chapter 4 for more on color calibration.

Photoshop Color, Neutral Color, and All Those Numbers

Before I go into how to neutralize off-color photographs, it is useful to understand how Photoshop makes 256 *steps,* or tones, of Red, Green, and Blue *(RGB)* into different colors. When looking at the Info palette numbers, 0 (zero) is always black; 255 is always the purest form of a color. When all three color channels — Red, Green, and Blue — each read 255, the result is white.

When the amount of Red, Green, and Blue are equal, the tone is *neutral,* or gray, with the exception of black (0) or white (255). White added to pure color creates a pastel.

If you want to follow along with this, "How Photoshop Makes Color," go to www.amesphoto.com/learning, enter the code **4D59776**, and find the files for projects in this chapter. (If you have already registered, type in your user name [your e-mail address] and password.) Click the link for Book IV, Chapter 2. Open Making Orange.tif. Click and hold the Eyedropper Tool, then choose the Color Sampler Tool. Click the Info palette tab to open it. (Book III, Chapter 1 details the Info palette.)

Digital photographs are made of differing quantities of Red, Green, and Blue *pixels,* the picture elements that make up a digital photograph. Orange, for example, has twice as many red pixels than green ones and no blue pixels at all. Take a look at Figure 2-1. Solid Red is overlapped by half as much Green. There is no Blue. The Info palette displays the RGB values for each of the three color samplers: #1 (Red), #2 (Orange), and #3 (Green).

- Sampler #1 shows R: 255, G: 0, B: 0. The Red is pure Red reading 255 with zero amounts of Green and Blue.

- Sampler #2 shows R: 255, G: 128, B: 0. So far so good. 128 is exactly half of the 256 values available to Green. So 50% Green over 100% Red makes an orange color.

- Sampler #3 gets strange. It reads R: 127, G: 255, B: 127. What gives? Sampler #2 shows Green is 128.

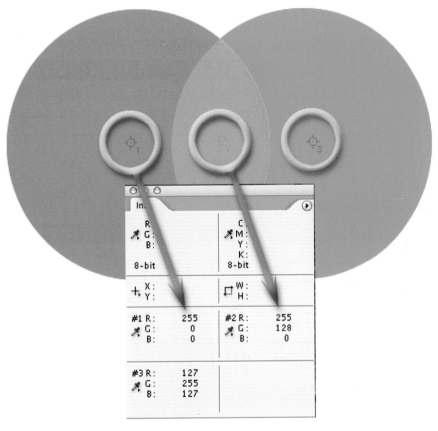

Figure 2-1: Orange a la Photoshop CS2.

 Okay, here's what's happening: Equal amounts of all three colors are neutral. If the recipe calls for 50% Green against a white background, the Green will be a pastel. That means the Green has to be mixed with 50% neutral color. The image has 254 tones plus black and white. 127 is half, or 50%, of the tonality. Sampler #3 now makes sense: 127 Red, 127 Blue, and 127 Green comprise the neutral value — the white added to create the pastel. 128 Green is left after the neutrals are subtracted from it. That 128 is the tone of Green that mixes with the pure Red in Sampler #2 to create the orange color.

Playing the Correcting Color Numbers Game

A photograph that has equal numbers in the highlights and shadows will have practically no *color cast,* or tint of color, in the middle tones. If you read Book III, Chapter 1 you already know how easy it is to white balance (color correct) a RAW file. Here's how to white balance a JPEG capture. (Book III, Chapter 1 compares RAW and JPEG formats for you.)

The Info palette tells you the RGB values of the pixels under the cursor or placed color samplers. *Color samplers* are eye-droppers you place in a photograph to monitor the changes made to the pixels under them. This project gives you a working understanding of how to use the Info palette to neutralize and color correct a photograph.

Setting up

Start from the beginning by settings things up:

1. **Go to www.amesphoto.com/learning, enter** 4D59776, **and find the files for projects in Book IV, Chapter 2.**

   If you have already registered, type in your user name (your e-mail address) and password. Click the link for Book IV, Chapter 2.

2. **Navigate to and open the downloaded and unzipped folder using Adobe Bridge.**

   The 2203-047.jpg file of the fire truck appears in the Bridge light box. Book IV, Chapter 1 details Adobe Bridge.

3. **Click the Full Screen Mode with Menu Bar icon in the Photoshop toolbox.**

   The icon is circled in Figure 2-2. When you move the cursor over the icon, it turns blue.

4. **Hold down the spacebar to change the cursor to the Hand Tool; click+drag the fire truck until you see the whole thing.**

   Your desktop will look like Figure 2-3.

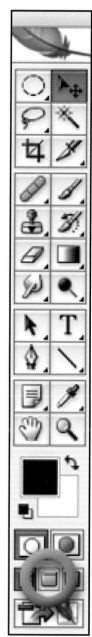

Figure 2-2: The Full Screen with Menu Bar icon in the toolbox.

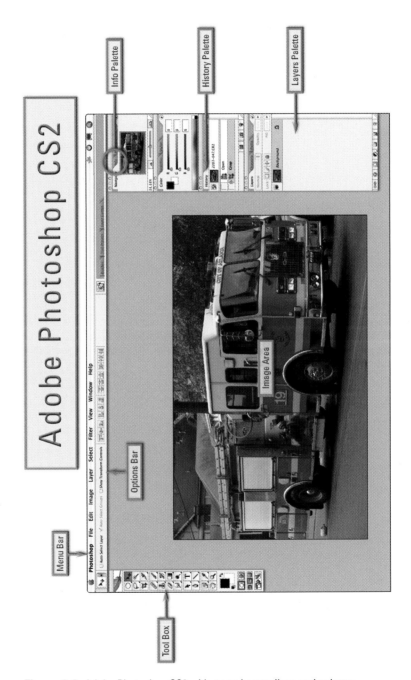

Figure 2-3: Adobe Photoshop CS2 with menu bar, toolbox, and palettes.

5. **Click the Info palette tab. In the toolbox, click and hold the Eyedropper Tool icon, then choose the Color Sampler Tool.**

Figure 2-4 shows the Eyedropper Tool, circled in red, and the Color Sampler. Now set up the Color Sampler Tool's options. The option bar (under the Photoshop main menu) displays the Color Sampler Tool icon in Figure 2-5.

6. **Click the drop-down arrow and choose 5 by 5 Average.**

The 5 by 5 Average setting tells Photoshop to average an area 5 pixels by 5 pixels, giving a more accurate overall reading. The Point Sample setting measures a single pixel.

7. **Click the frame to the right of the fire truck's visibar.**

Color Sampler #1 appears there in the highlight.

8. **Click the rail on the side of the truck, directly at the gold stripe, to place Color Sampler #2.**

That is a midtone.

9. **Click the front tire (below the tread in alignment with the front edge of the chrome rim).**

And that is the shadow. The three color samplers are shown circled in red in Figure 2-6.

10. **Click the Add New Adjustment Layer icon⇨Levels; continue to the next section.**

If you don't see the Layers palette, click its tab (nested with Channels and Paths) or choose Window⇨Layers from the Photoshop menu. The icon, at the bottom of the Layers palette, is divided in half diagonally, with black on top and white on the bottom. It's the exact middle icon and is circled in red in Figure 2-7. When you choose Levels, a Levels Adjustment Layer appears in the layer stack and the Levels dialog opens.

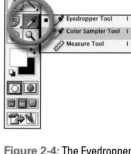

Figure 2-4: The Eyedropper Tools.

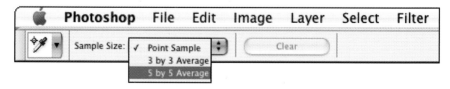

Figure 2-5: The Eyedropper Tool's option bar with Sample Size menu.

The refinements that adjustment layers make are also available at Image⇨ Adjustment. These settings are permanently applied to the photograph and cannot be undone once the file has been saved and closed. It is a very good idea to always use Adjustment Layers instead of Adjustments from the Image menu. Adjustment layers can always be modified at any time. Someday you might change your mind about how you want your photograph to look. Change and the ability to change are good.

Figure 2-6: Color samplers #1, #2, and #3 in place.

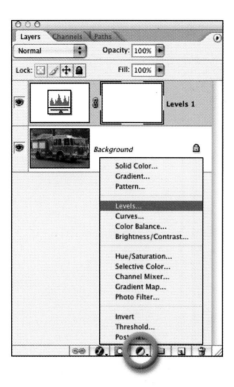

Figure 2-7: The Layers palette and new adjustment layers menu.

Balancing the highlights

Always start a color correction with the brightest part of the photograph. The bright areas are known as the *highlights*. These areas are bright and still have detail. Run your cursor over the spotlight you see in Figure 2-8. Look at the numbers in the Info palette: R: 254, G: 254, B: 255. There is no detail. Color correction is impossible when the numbers are too close to pure white (R: 255, G: 255, B: 255).

Highlights that reflect the photograph's light source are called *specular highlights. Specular* means mirror. The chrome-covered spotlight in Figure 2-8 shows a reflection of the sky and the sun behind the clouds. This area is too bright to use as a source of information for color correction.

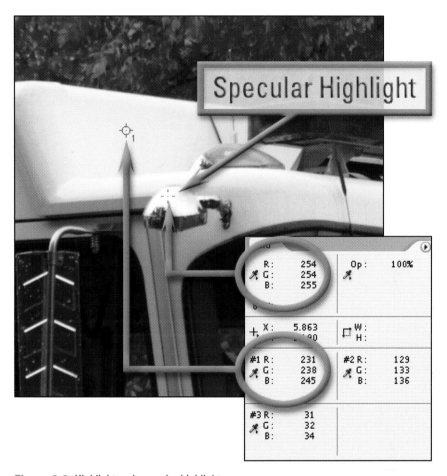

Figure 2-8: Highlight and specular highlight.

Look at the Info palette reading for Color Sampler #1 in Figure 2-9. The Blue channel is the brightest. It reads 245. Look at the photograph. The whites have a bluish cast to them. This is because there is more Blue than Red and Green. The Red is 231 and the Green channel is 238. Again, these numbers have to be equal to be completely neutral.

When color correcting the highlights, you make the channels with the lower numbers brighter until they equal, or come as close as possible to, the channel with the highest number. Here's how:

Figure 2-9: The #1 Color Sampler readout in the Info palette.

1. **Open the file 2203-047with_samplers.psd.**

   It's in the sample folder you downloaded from the preceding steps.

2. **Choose the Red channel in the drop-down menu in the Levels dialog shown in Figure 2-10.**

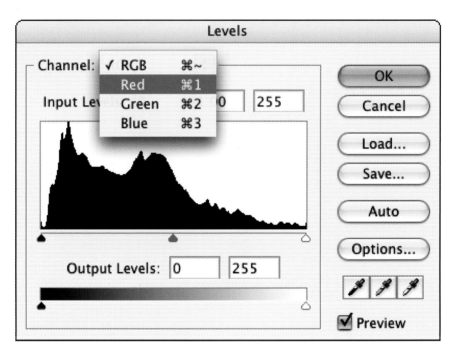

Figure 2-10: The Levels dialog, Highlight slider, and Info palette.

3. **Click+drag the Highlight slider slowly to the left until the Red reading in the Info palette equals the Blue reading.**

   The Highlight slider is circled in red in Figure 2-11. Watch the Red readings in the Info palette change. The numbers to the left of the / are the original color values. The ones to the right of the / are the new values.

   Ignore the changing numbers in the Input Level section of the Levels dialog. Look only at the Info palette when making color corrections.

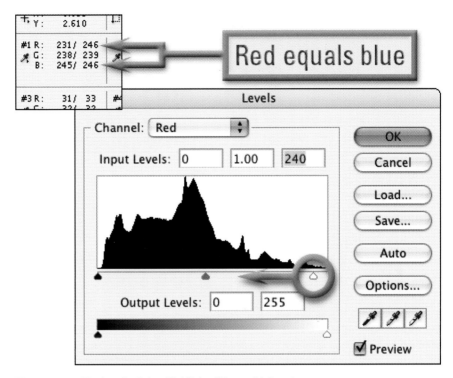

Figure 2-11: The Levels dialog, Highlight slider, and Info palette.

4. Choose Channel⇨Green in the Levels dialog.

5. Click+drag the Highlight slider to the left until the Green reading in the Info palette equals the Red and Blue values (in this case 246).

The highlights are neutral when all three numbers are equal. Look at the reading for the midtones (Color Sampler #2). They are neutral too, as you can see in Figure 2-12. Keep this image open and continue to the next section.

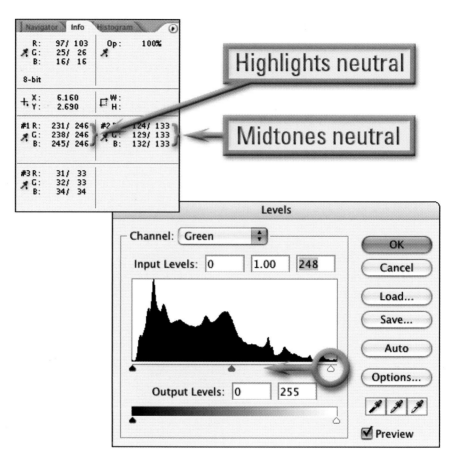

Figure 2-12: Neutralizing the Green channel.

Neutralizing the shadows

The fire truck image is technically neutral. There is a one-point difference between the Red, Green, and Blue channels in the shadow readings represented by Color Sampler #3. Neutralizing the shadows is similar to what you have done in the highlights. The exception is you make the brighter channels darker until they display the lowest value. The example shows readings of 33 for both the Red and the Green channels and 34 for the Blue.

1. **Choose Channel⇨Blue in the Levels dialog**.

2. **Click to activate the Shadow slider.**

   The first window in the Input Levels section of the Levels dialog high-lights the 0.

3. **Press the ↑ key until the Info palette readings match what you see in Figure 2-13: 33.**

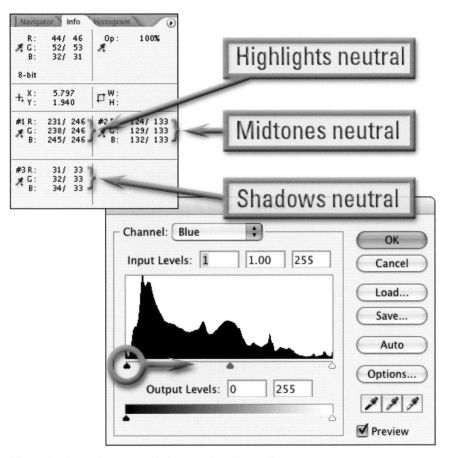

Figure 2-13: A color-corrected photograph and its readings.

4. Click OK.

5. Choose File⇨Save As from the Photoshop menu.

6. In the filename, place the cursor just before the period and type a dash and your initials.

I have done this for myself in Figure 2-14.

7. Choose Format⇨Photoshop⇨Save.

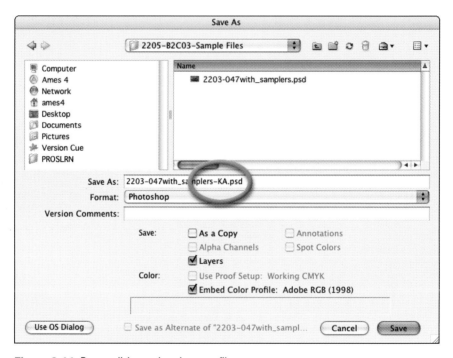

Figure 2-14: Personalizing and saving your file.

TIP

Sliding is fine

Fine-tune the slider by using the ↑ and ↓ keys on the keyboard. Once you have moved a slider, the arrow keys are active. Sometimes the brightest value to the right of the / change from the original brightness of the color shown to the left. This is normal. Always balance the numbers in the column to the right of the /.

Daring to compare

Now you can see the difference color correction makes. Compare the before and after photos:

1. **Find the layer named Levels 1 in the Layers palette.**

2. **Click the eye icon (circled in Figure 2-15) to hide and reveal the changes you made to the color.**

   Notice how much more blue the white areas of the fire truck are.

   When the eye icon is gone the Levels Adjustment Layer is hidden. Its effects are turned off, and the original colors of the photograph are showing.

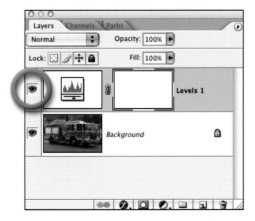

Figure 2-15: The eye icon hides and shows the Levels Adjustment Layer's effect.

**Book IV
Chapter 2**

**Controlling
Colors and
Balancing White**

3. Click the eye icon on Levels 1 to reapply the corrections.

Compare how much difference there is in Figure 2-16. The photograph is now color correct.

Figure 2-16: Color corrections make a big difference!

Chapter 3: Refining Exposure

In This Chapter

✔ **Exploring the histogram**

✔ **Getting familiar with Levels adjustment layers**

✔ **Understanding white points**

✔ **Setting shadow values**

*I*t would be ideal if all exposures were perfect. Mine certainly aren't and I'm willing to bet yours won't be either. This chapter deals with how to identify a good exposure and how to adjust a file whose exposure is not so good. In Book III, Chapter 4 you see how versatile Adobe Camera Raw 3 is when it comes to getting the most out of files shot in the RAW format. And if you are like a lot of digital photographers, you didn't know what RAW was so you stayed away from it. (If you still think RAW has to do with your dinner, see Book III, Chapter 1.) Now you have photographs captured in the JPEG format or you have saved them as TIFFs or PSDs.

What to do? Fear not! Adobe Photoshop CS2 tools can tweak exposure. In this chapter you use the Info palette and see what its numbers mean regarding exposure. You explore the histogram and discover how it can tell you when a normal scene is over- or underexposed. You discover how to use Levels to set the brightest and darkest parts of the photograph and how to brighten or darken the overall image. And you use a Levels adjustment layer to make the corrections.

This chapter builds on the information in Book II, Chapter 2. This chapter works best with a color-calibrated monitor. See Book V, Chapter 4 for more.

Exposing Yourself Well

Before you can make a good exposure you have to know what one looks like. Look at Figure 3-1. Not bad. It's a close-up of the fire truck shown in Book IV, Chapter 2. The color is good because it has been white balanced.

Figure 3-1: The white-balanced fire truck.

Going by the numbers

A good digital exposure has highlight with detail whose values in the Info palette read high 240s. Highlights with numbers higher will probably print as pure white. Shadows with detail have numbers that fall in the 30s or higher. Figure 3-2 shows the high and low numbers on a grayscale step chart. Values below 30 print a solid black and those above 247–249 print as white. The first indication of poor exposure is numbers that fall outside these ranges. A photograph whose highlights read in the 220s is *underexposed*. One whose highlights read 255 in the Red, Green, and Blue channels is *overexposed*.

The numbers are read in the Info palette. Move your cursor over a highlight or a shadow to see its values. You can also use color samplers as shown in Figure 3-3. For more on color samplers, see Book IV, Chapter 2.

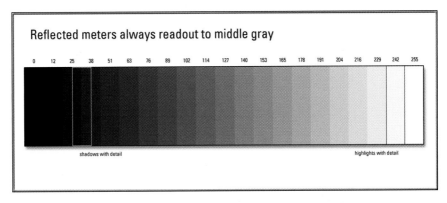

Figure 3-2: Shadows and highlights with detail on a grayscale.

The reality is that the photograph of the fire truck is underexposed by about a full f/stop. (Book I, Chapter 2 details f/stop information.) The Info palette in Figure 3-3 tells the story. The white band on the top of the truck reads R: 217, G: 217, B: 217. It wants to read R: 249, G: 249, B: 249. The tire reads R: 20, G: 20, B: 19. It wants to read R: 32, G: 32, B: 32.

Figure 3-3: The underexposed fire truck by the numbers.

TIP

Learn to read the numbers of a photograph. You will always be able to tell that it is properly exposed. The numbers also tell you the predominant color if they are not neutral.

Going by the histogram

Another indicator of exposure problems is the histogram. *Histograms* plot the distribution of *pixels* by brightness in your photograph across the full range of exposure (or 256 steps). Figure 3-4 shows the histogram of the underexposed fire truck and a grayscale so you can see how the pixels fall. The red box I inserted at the far right shows the area of the histogram that has no pixel distribution. There are no pixels above 217. Look to the left. The shadows have a lot of pixels — especially in areas of the grayscale that are black. Underexposure is

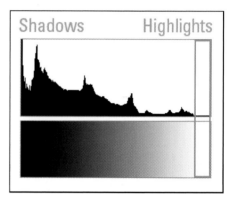

Figure 3-4: Missing pixels in the highlights mean an underexposed photograph.

indicated by a histogram with no pixels on the far right portion and lots of pixels at the far left. Photoshop has a Histogram palette. Choose it from the Window menu.

Overexposure

An overexposed photograph is easier to spot than an underexposed photo. It tends to look washed out and low in contrast, like the fire truck in Figure 3-5. Check out the numbers in the Info palette. RGB: 255 for the highlights and R: 74, G: 69, B: 67 in the shadows. Those shadow numbers are quite high. The sidewalls of the tires look more gray than black.

REMEMBER

GIGO

Boosting exposure in Photoshop is perfectly fine to do for minor adjustments. The best solution is to get the photograph's exposure right when you take it with your DSLR camera. The next best solution is to correct it in ACR3 if you shoot in the RAW format. Fixing an underexposed JPEG in Photoshop is the least desirable. Photoshop is not a solution for poor technique behind the camera. The old adage, "Garbage in, garbage out," was never truer. Think of it positively. Great Photoshop starts with great photography!

Figure 3-5: By the numbers: the overexposed fire truck.

The histogram with grayscale for this photograph is in Figure 3-6. It shows a heavy distribution of pixels in the highlights (where I inserted the red box) and many fewer in the shadows and midtones. The black spike on the very left of the histogram shows the pixels representing the tire tread and the asphalt under the truck. These pixels are completely black.

Overexposure when shooting in the JPEG format is unrecoverable. Once the pixels reach a 255 value, there is no information to work with.

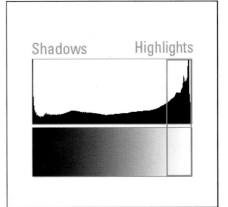

Figure 3-6: Pixels all the way to the right in an overexposed histogram.

**Book IV
Chapter 3**

Refining Exposure

Figure 3-7 shows the underexposed photograph with a properly exposed version. The whites are white. Color is bright and vibrant. Detail shows in the shadows.

Figure 3-7: Underexposure and correct exposure compared.

Boosting Exposure Values

What do you do when you have an underexposed file? There are solutions available in Photoshop. This project takes you through the steps.

Setting up

You've got to start with the basics: Getting things set up correctly is always first.

1. **Go to www.amesphoto.com/learning and register if you haven't already.**

   The code to go to the login/registration page is 4D59776.

2. **Go to the downloads section for this book and click the files for Book IV, Chapter 3.**

3. **Double-click 2203-049.psd to open the file in Adobe Photoshop CS2.**

   If you did the color correction in the previous chapter, you may use that file instead. The preview appears in the Bridge light box. Steps 3–7 are detailed with illustrations in Book IV, Chapter 2.

4. **Type F to enter Full Frame mode.**

   The photograph is centered on the screen and surrounded by gray.

5. **Press the spacebar to change the cursor to the Hand Tool.**

6. **Click+drag the fire truck until you see the whole thing.**

7. **Click the Info palette tab.**

8. **Click Eyedropper Tool⇨Color Sampler Tool.**

9. **Make sure the Color Sampler Tool's options bar shows 5 by 5 average.**

10. **Click the frame to the right of the fire truck's visibar to tell Photoshop where you want Color Sampler #1.**

    Color Sampler #1, in a highlight, is placed there.

11. **Put Color Sampler #2 on the sidewall of the tire.**

    This is placed in a shadow for reference. The placements and Info palette readings are shown in Figure 3-8. Keep this file open, continuing on through the next section.

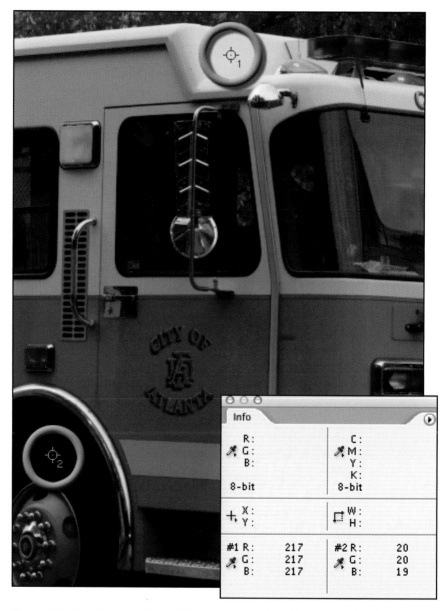

Figure 3-8: Color Samplers # 1 and #2 in place and their readings in the Info palette.

Adding a Levels adjustment layer

Now you add a new Levels adjustment layer. The previous chapter shows how to color correct using a Levels adjustment layer. Another use for a Levels adjustment layer is to fix underexposure.

1. **Click Add New Adjustment Layer icon⇨Levels.**

   The Add New Adjustment Layer icon is at the bottom of the Layers palette. When you choose Levels, a Levels adjustment layer appears in the layer stack and the Levels dialog opens. See Figure 2-7 in Book IV, Chapter 2 for the location of the New Adjustment Layer icon.

2. **Move the Highlight slider (indicated by a red arrow in Figure 3-9) to the left.**

   Watch the numbers on the Info palette as you move the slider. The numbers in Color Sampler #1 to the left of the / begin to climb.

3. **Stop when RGB reads 249.**

   You see the before and after numbers in Figure 3-10. The numbers to the left of the / are before adjustment. Those to the right of the slash show the effect of the adjustment. Stay the course and continue in the next section.

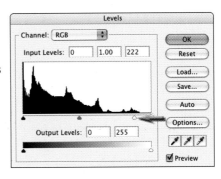

Figure 3-9: Move the Highlight slider left to brighten the photograph.

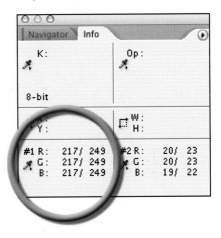

Figure 3-10: The numbers before and after moving the Highlight slider to the left.

Working up dark shadows

The shadow numbers in Figure 3-10 (at the bottom right of the Info palette) are still in the low 20s. They have to be boosted as well.

**Book IV
Chapter 3**

Refining Exposure

1. **Move the Gamma slider in the Levels adjustment layer to the left.**

   The Gamma slider is the middle one, pointed out with a red arrow, in Figure 3-11. Watch Color Sampler #2 in the Info palette.

2. **Stop when the numbers for Color Sampler #2 read as follows:**

   - **R: 32**
   - **G: 32**
   - **B: 31**

   See Figure 3-12.

3. **Click OK.**

   Now compare the result.

4. **Click the eye icon of the Levels adjustment layer on and off.**

   The eye icon is circled in red in Figure 3-13.

You can compare the correction to the underexposed version. The result looks much better than the under-exposed version. As a matter of fact, it looks quite good in comparison.

Now look at all three in Figure 3-14. The adjusted version in the middle does look better than the under-exposed version. It does not look as good as the correct exposure version on the bottom. And it is now a useful photograph.

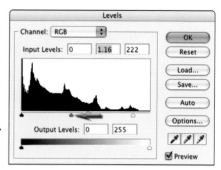

Figure 3-11: Move the Gamma slider left to brighten the middle values and shadows.

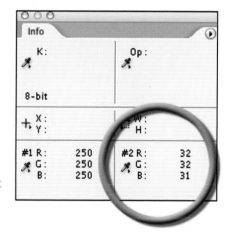

Figure 3-12: Shadows with detail have numbers like these.

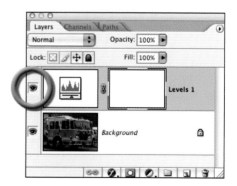

Figure 3-13: Hide the Levels adjustment layer by clicking the eye icon.

1 f/stop Underexposed

Exposure Adjustment

Correct Exposure

Figure 3-14: Comparing underexposure, boosted exposure, and a correct exposure from the camera.

TANSTAAFL: There Ain't No Such Thing as a Free Lunch

Any correction made in Photoshop to cover shortcomings at the camera come at a cost of time and twisted pixels. Corrections take a lot more time than getting a correct light reading in the first place. And corrections and adjustments damage, maim, and destroy pixels.

Seeing missing pixels

For this demonstration use the file from the previous exercise in which you boosted the exposure with the Levels adjustment layer.

1. **Click the Levels adjustment layer's eye icon to hide it.**

2. **Click the Histogram tab.**

   It's next to the Info palette in Figure 3-15 or at Window⇨ Histogram.

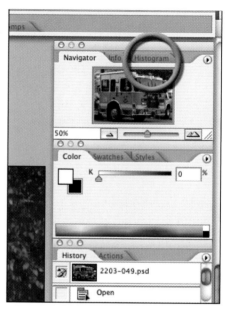

Figure 3-15: The Histogram tab.

3. **Click the triangle in the upper-right corner of the Histogram palette.**

4. **Select Expanded View from the menu, as shown in Figure 3-16.**

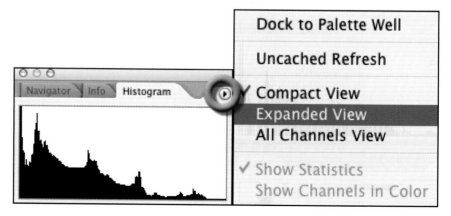

Figure 3-16: Choosing the expanded view.

5. **Click the Refresh icon or the triangle with the exclamation point to update the view.**

   You can see these icons circled in red in Figure 3-17. The histogram in Figure 3-17 shows a solid distribution of pixels.

6. **Click the eye icon for the Levels adjustment layer.**

7. **Refresh the Histogram palette by clicking the Refresh icon or the triangle.**

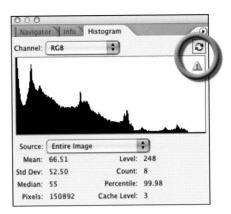

Figure 3-17: Click either one to refresh the histogram.

Combing

Look at the histogram in Figure 3-18. It is broken by gaps. This effect is called *combing* because the histogram resembles a comb. Every gap you see is where there are missing pixels caused by the Levels adjustment layer. The levels adjustment stretches the available pixels over the histogram to increase the exposure.

Extreme corrections, or lots of them, can degrade the image to the point where you see banding or posterization when it is printed. *Banding* and *posterization* are abrupt transitions in a continuous tone. Figures 1-2 and 1-3 in Book III, Chapter 1 illustrate these effects.

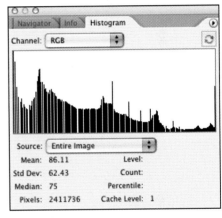

Figure 3-18: The combing effect in a histogram.

Chapter 4: Commanding Colors and Using Layer Masks

In This Chapter

 ✔ Coloring for mood

 ✔ Understanding how layer masks work

 ✔ Working with layer masks

 ✔ Using nik multimedia Color Efex Pro 2.0

Colors really influence how you feel. The orange light of late afternoon sun or the light of a blazing fireplace is warm and romantic. The blue of an overcast day is dreary and cold. Adobe Photoshop CS2 offers the Photo Filter adjustment layer so you can color for mood. Other third-party plug-ins for Photoshop are amazing mood-altering tools. My favorite is nik multimedia's Color Efex Pro 2.0.

Filtering Photos

Now it's time to play. One of Photoshop's great values is altering photographic reality to fit what you imagine it to be. Changing the colors of a photograph subtly or dramatically is an example. This project is about selectively warming up the skin in a portrait and cooling the model's dress and the background. You use *Photo Filter adjustment layers* to add the color, and *layer masks* to control what gets colored. The icons in the bar at the bottom of the Layers palette are identified in Figure 4-1.

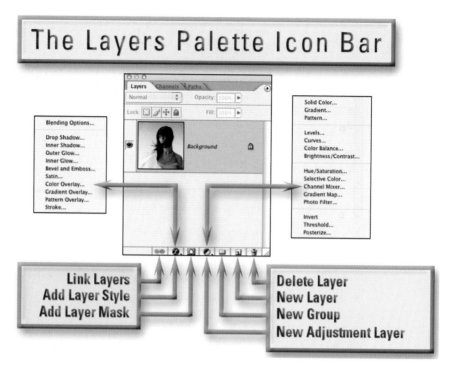

Figure 4-1: The Layers palette icons.

1. **Go to www.amesphoto.com/learning and click the link for projects in Book IV, Chapter 4.**

   The code to go to the login/registration page is 4D59776. If you have already registered, type in your user name (your e-mail address) and password.

2. **Open Christina.tif from the sample folder.**

   The photograph is shown in Figure 4-2.

Figure 4-2: Elite model Christina Parfene.

3. **Click the Create New Adjustment Layer icon⇨Photo Filter (at the bottom of the Layers palette).**

Now you set the warmth. Both Photoshop and Bridge have menu choices followed by three periods. This means a dialog offering you choice opens when you select the item.

4. **Drag the Density slider to the right until the Density window displays 50%, as seen in Figure 4-3.**

5. **Choose Warming Filter (85) from the Filter drop-down menu.**

   The Warming Filter (85) is a good choice. Its color shows in the box below the menu. Leave Preserve Luminosity checked.

6. **Click OK.**

   The adjustment layer named Photo Filter 1 is added to the layer stack above the Background layer.

7. **Double-click the words Photo Filter 1 to get a rename window.**

8. **Type in** Warming Filter, **then press Enter.**

   See Figure 4-4. The overall photograph becomes *warmer,* or more orange. Christina's face has a beautiful warm glow. The background and her dress are warm, too. That is a problem considering the project wants them to be more blue than in the original.

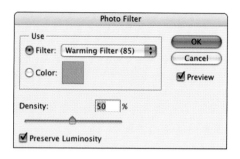

Figure 4-3: The Photo Filter adjustment layer dialog.

Figure 4-4: The renamed Photo Filter adjustment layer in the Layers palette.

Keep your file open to continue working through the remainder of this chapter.

Introducing Layer Masks: Black Conceals, White Reveals

Each adjustment layer comes with a layer mask ready to go. The parts of an adjustment layer are shown in Figure 4-5. The layer mask either reveals the effect of the layer mask or hides it. A white layer mask allows the effect to be seen. A black layer mask conceals the effect of the adjustment layer. This is really easy once you wrap your mind around it.

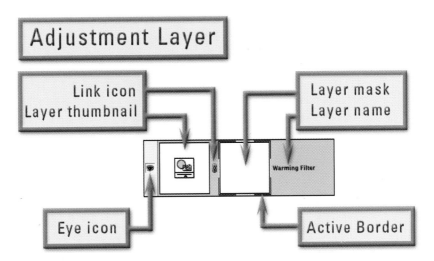

Figure 4-5: An adjustment layer and its parts.

1. **Choose the Rectangular Marquee Tool from the toolbox.**

   Its icon is circled in red and the tool is highlighted in Figure 4-6.

2. **Click in the upper-left corner of the photograph and drag in the direction of the red arrow shown in Figure 4-7.**

   The selection cuts through Christina, dividing her in half. The selection looks like marching ants. Lots of people call a selection in Photoshop *marching ants*.

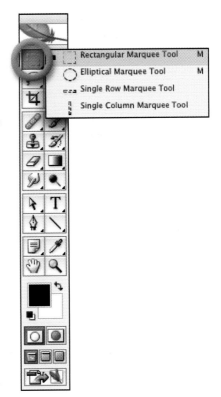

Figure 4-6: The Rectangular Marquee Tool.

**Book IV
Chapter 4**

Commanding Colors and Using Layer Masks

Figure 4-7: Selecting the left half of Christina's photograph.

3. **Click inside the layer mask of the adjustment layer Warming Filter to make it active.**

   The active border shown in Figure 4-8 appears around the layer mask to tell you it is active. Activating a layer's layer mask automatically highlights the layer.

4. **Choose Edit⇨Fill.**

Figure 4-8: An active layer mask.

5. In the Contents section, select Black from the Use drop-down menu and click OK.

Leave the Blending Opacity at 100%. The dialog is shown in Figure 4-9.

Take a look at Figure 4-10 (or your photo onscreen). The left half of the Warming Filter layer mask is black. The right half is white. (Shift+click the layer mask to turn it off. A red X appears over the mask, telling you it is disabled. Shift+click it again to enable it.)

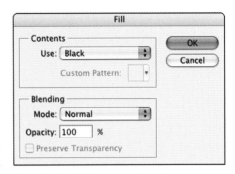

Figure 4-9: The Fill dialog.

Now check out Figure 4-11. The left side (black layer mask) of Christina.tif is the same color as the original. The right side (white layer mask) is very warm. Keep the file open and follow along in the following sections.

Filling the layer mask with black

The stated project is to warm up Christina's skin and make her dress and the background a lot more blue. The first part of the exercise is warming the color of the skin.

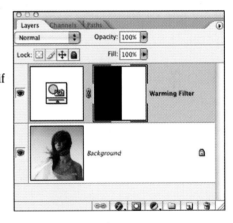

Figure 4-10: A half black, half white layer mask.

The Warming Filter is already in place. The layer mask wants to be white over the skin and black everywhere else. Remember, black conceals the warming effect and white reveals it.

There is less skin than dress and background. It is less work to fill the layer mask with black and then put white over the skin. Get started.

Figure 4-11: Black on the layer mask conceals the effect from the left side. White reveals it on the right side.

The Warming Filter layer mask is still active. You fill it with black in the following steps:

1. **Choose Select⇨All⇨Edit⇨Fill from the Photoshop menu bar.**

   This is a good keyboard shortcut to know by heart: Press ⌘+A (Ctrl+A) to select all. Deselect with ⌘+D (Ctrl+D).

2. **Choose Black as the contents color and 100% as the opacity.**

3. **Click OK.**

4. **Clear the selection by choosing Select⇨Deselect or using the keyboard shortcut.**

   The layer mask is now filled with black. The whole photograph is the original color, as you see in Figure 4-12.

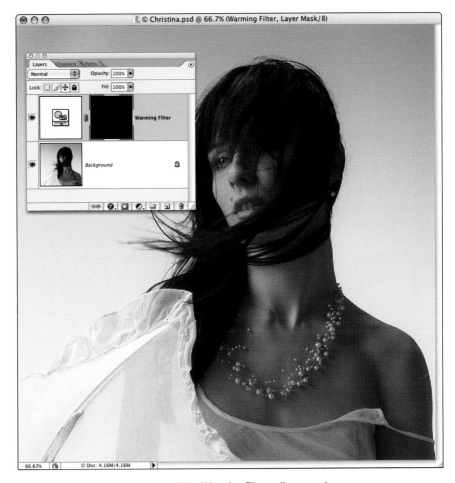

Figure 4-12: Black conceals all of the Warming Filter adjustment layer.

Setting up your brush

You have a lot of setting up to do the first time you use Photoshop. Once all these setups are finished, you won't have to do them again until you upgrade. First set up the Brush's preferences:

1. **Open Photoshop preferences with ⌘+K (Ctrl+K).**

    From the menu you will find it at Photoshop⇨Preferences⇨General. The general Preferences pane opens.

**Book IV
Chapter 4**

**Commanding Colors
and Using Layer
Masks**

2. **Choose Displays & Cursors from the menu in the upper left, as shown in Figure 4-13.**

3. **Choose the options shown selected in Figure 4-14:**

   - **Full Size Brush Tip radio button: Selected.**

   - **Show Crosshair in Brush Tip checkbox: Checked.**

   - **Precise radio button: Selected.**

The full-size brush tip shows the edge of the brush even when it's soft. The *crosshair* indicates the exact center of the brush. The Precise setting for the other cursors shows a crosshair instead of the icon. This gives you much more control.

4. **Click OK.**

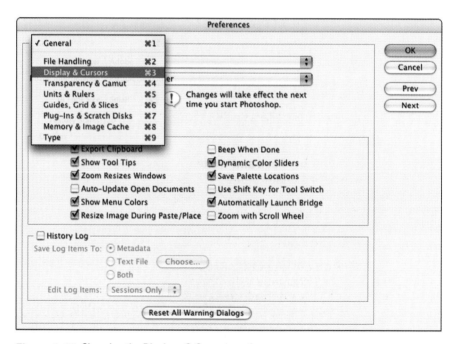

Figure 4-13: Choosing the Displays & Cursors preference pane.

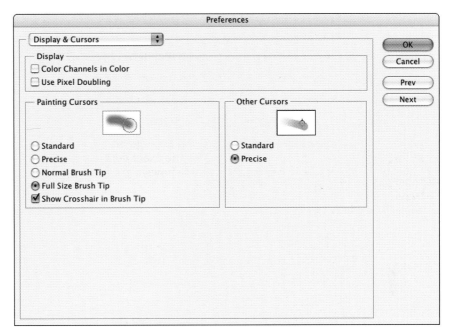

Figure 4-14: The settings for Displays & Cursors.

5. **Click the black and white Default Colors icon.**

   The icon, in the lower-left corner of the toolbox's colors section, is shown in Figure 4-15. Its keyboard shortcut is D.

6. **If it's not already, make white the foreground color by clicking the Exchange Colors icon.**

   This icon is in the upper-right corner of the colors section. Its shortcut is X for X-change. Clever, huh?

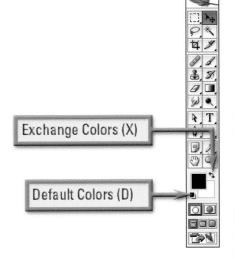

Figure 4-15: The foreground and background colors in the toolbox.

7. **Click the Brush Tool icon in the tool-box, as shown in Figure 4-16.**

8. **Click the arrow in the Brush Size icon to open some options.**

9. **Enter** 20 **in the Master Diameter window or adjust the slider.**

    This makes your brush 20 pixels wide. Figure 4-17 labels this result 1.

10. **Click+drag the Hardness slider to the left until the window reads 0%.**

    Figure 4-17 labels this 2.

11. **Click anywhere in the menu again to close the brush options.**

12. **Make sure that the Opacity and Flow windows read 100%.**

    Figure 4-17 labels this 3. Your brush is set.

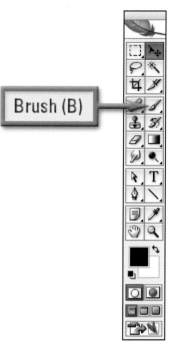

Figure 4-16: The Brush Tool icon in the toolbox.

Moving sliders with the mouse is a very slow way of changing the brush. These shortcuts are worth memorizing. The bracket keys ([ ]) control brush size. You can see the Brush icon in the options bar change with each stroke size, softness, or hardness:

  ✔ Left bracket [makes the brush smaller.

  ✔ Right bracket] makes it larger.

  ✔ Shift+[softens the brush in 25% steps.

  ✔ Shift+] hardens the brush in 25% steps.

A *hard* brush paints with a sharp, distinct edge. A *soft* brush paints with a feathered edge.

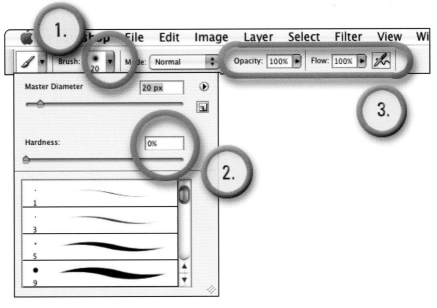

Figure 4-17: The Brushes options bar.

Zooming a zoom zoom

Choose View⇨Actual Pixels when editing a photograph in Photoshop. Sometime you will want to work at a larger size: Choose View⇨Zoom In. The keyboard shortcuts are: Hold down the ⌘ and Option keys (Ctrl and Alt keys) and press the 0 (zero) key to view actual pixels. This move is normally written this way: ⌘+Option+0 (Ctrl+Alt+0). See the following table. Makes sense doesn't it? These and other great timesaving keyboard shortcuts are in Appendix B.

Task	*Mac*	*Windows*
View actual pixels	⌘+Option+0	Ctrl+Alt+0
Zoom in	⌘++	Ctrl++
Zoom out	⌘+ –	Ctrl+ –
Fit in window	⌘+0	Ctrl+0

Painting on the layer mask

Filling the layer mask with black hides the Photo Filter adjustment layer's effect. Now you use your newly set-up brush to paint with white over Christina's skin to make it a warmer color.

1. **Using the Brush Tool, click an area of Christina's skin.**

2. **Click+drag over the skin.**

   When you release the button, an area of white appears on the layer mask. Figure 4-18 shows the completed layer mask. Keep painting until your layer mask looks like Figure 4-18.

3. **Click the eye icon on the layer Warming Filter to see the change.**

   As you paint, more and more of Christina's skin becomes warmer.

Figure 4-18: The areas of white are over Christina's skin.

Follow these steps when you make a mistake like painting over the strap on the dress:

1. **Press X to exchange white for black in the color portion of the toolbar.**

2. **Get a smaller brush.**

   Remember, the left bracket key makes the brush smaller.

3. **Paint over the mistake.**

4. **Press X to switch back to white and continue painting.**

   Master this technique of correcting the Adjustment layer mask. Major cool factor: It works exactly the same on all of Photoshop's layer masks.

Cooling the dress and background

The layer Warming Filter is still active. The next layer you create appears above the active layer.

1. **Choose the Create New Adjustment Layer icon⇨Photo Filter⇨Filter⇨Cooling Filter (82).**

   Refer back to Figure 4-2 for a visual. When left at the default density setting of 25%, you cancel out the effects of the layer Warming Filter.

2. **Make the color cooler (more blue) still by moving the slider to 35%.**

Notice that now Christina's face has a blue tint to it. I know what you're thinking: "Now I have to paint black over her skin to conceal it from the effects of the Cooling Filter layer." And you are right. That's exactly what you want to have — a black mask on the layer Cooling Filter to bring back the effect of the layer Warming Filter underneath.

3. **Click OK and name the new Adjustment layer** Cooling Filter.

4. **Make black the foreground color.**

   Remember the shortcut? Typing X on the keyboard exchanges the foreground and background colors.

5. **Press the] key to make the brush 40 pixels.**

6. **Brush across Christina's shoulder.**

   Figure 4-19 shows the warm filter showing as the brushstroke. Notice that the brushstroke is repeated in black on the layer mask. Stay the course in the next section.

Figure 4-19: The warm skin revealed.

I've got my icon you

Here's how to make your layer and layer mask icons larger so they look like the ones in the book:

1. Click the flyout menu triangle circled in red in the figure on the left.

2. Choose Palette Options from the menu.

3. Click the big thumbnail icon button, which has a red circle around it in the figure on the right.

4. Click OK.

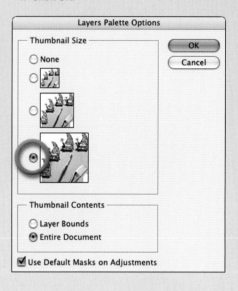

Working smarter

It is good practice to paint in layer masks accurately. And over the course of your Photoshop career you will paint in a whole lot of them. So there is no reason to do the work twice. You've already made a great layer mask. Here's how to put it to use:

1. **Click+drag the layer mask Cooling Filter to the Trash icon at the bottom of the Layers palette.**

2. **Click Delete when the Delete layer mask? dialog appears.**

   You can see the dialog in Figure 4-20.

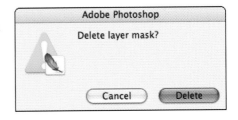

Figure 4-20: Click Delete to remove the layer mask.

3. **Option+click (Alt+click) the layer mask in Warming Filter and drag it to the Cooling Filter layer.**

   You copied the layer mask from Warming Filter to Cooling Filter.

4. **As soon as you see the outline shown in Figure 4-21, release the mouse button.**

   The newly copied layer mask appears on Cooling Filter. The colors remain the same. Remember that you want to hide the effects of the layer Cooling Filter where they are showing through white onto Christina's skin. White reveals the effect of

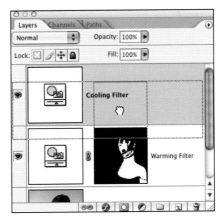

Figure 4-21: Copy the layer mask on Warming Filter to the Cooling Filter adjustment layer.

the layer. You want the white areas of the layer mask to be black and the black areas to be white. This is called *inverting*.

5. Make sure the layer mask on Cooling Filter is active.

It has a border around it like you see in Figure 4-8 when it is active.

6. Choose Image⇨Adjustments⇨ Invert.

That's it. What was once white is now black. What was black is white. You've done it! Cool move huh? Enjoy what you have accomplished in Figure 4-22. One last tweak: Christina's lips don't look good blue.

7. Paint over her lips on layer mask Cooling Filter with a black brush.

Touch up any other spots you may have missed. That's better! The final result is shown in Figure 4-23.

Figure 4-22: The inverted layer mask on the Cooling Filter adjustment layer.

Figure 4-23: Great job!

Getting Special Effects with nik Color Efex Pro 2.0

Play . . . yes I said play. It's okay. So many things in this book have a specific number or absolute technique attached. Explore, experiment, and discover your very own style of digital creativity. You can make a total mess and no one is going to holler at you for paint on the walls, trash cans full of gooey mess, or crayons strewn about on the carpet. Your creative mess is nicely contained inside Photoshop, thank you very much. And since you marked the Keep as Layer checkbox (in the preceding section), you can always go back and have a do over or two.

Lots of plug-ins on the market add functionality and creativity to Photoshop. My personal favorite for adding moody or even outlandish color to a photograph is, hands down, nik multimedia's Color Efex Pro 2.0. I want to show you how to use just one of the 75 filters that come with the complete package to continue helping you understand layers and layer masks.

Download a free trial version of nik Color Efex Pro 2.0 from www.nikmultimedia. com. The trial version of Color Efex Pro 2.0 applies a watermark with the word DEMO on your image. If you like the demo you can purchase a serial number directly from nik or a packaged version from many camera stores. Check nik's web site for dealer information.

Beginnings

After you install nik Color Efex Pro 2.0, launch Photoshop CS2. The Color Efex Selective palette appears inside the workspace. You must do a little bit of setup.

1. **Open Christina.tif or one of your own photographs.**

2. **Click Settings.**

   Settings is labeled 1 in Figure 4-24. The nik Settings dialog opens.

3. **Click the Keep as Layer checkbox, then click OK.**

   If you are going to use these filters a lot, leave the Launch When Photoshop Is Started checkbox selected.

4. **Click the S-Z tab in the nik Selective palette.**

   This tab is labeled 2 in Figure 4-24.

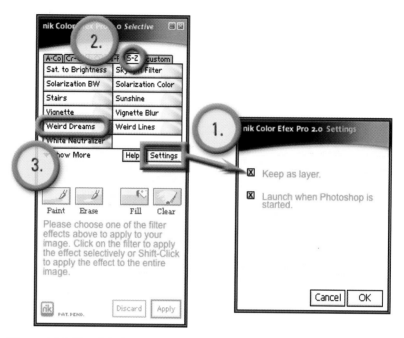

Figure 4-24: The nik Selective and Settings palette.

5. **Close the Selective palette by clicking the X in the upper-right corner and continue with the following section.**

   Get it back by choosing File⇨Automate⇨nik Color Efex Pro 2.0 Selective from the Photoshop menu seen in Figure 4-25.

All of the Color Efex filters work by creating a layer and a layer mask that allow you to paint the effect in selectively. The following project is an example of a tiny part of the creative work you can do with these tools.

Having weird dreams

You've installed nik Color Efex Pro 2.0, started Photoshop CS2, and opened a photograph. Now get to the fun stuff, which you see in Figure 4-26.

1. **Choose Weird Dreams.**

   See label 3 in Figure 4-24.

2. **Play with the Weird Dreams dialog shown in Figure 4-26.**

   Experiment with the settings in the dialog. Move each slider. See what it does. In short, play with everything. When you see something happen that makes you say, "Oooohhhhh!" that's the setting you want.

3. **Drag the Size slider all the way to the right.**

Don't like the result? Drag it all the way to the left. Stop when it looks good to you. (This is all about you.) I stopped at 3% for the size because when I'm doing it it's all about what I like. That number feels good to me right now. Stay tuned because it's pretty certain to change over time. Or not. We are different, you and I. That is a very good way to be.

4. **Click the color set and choose each one in turn.**

   Some of the results are very 60s pop art-ish. After a careful intuitive review of about four or five seconds, I'm going to stick with Color Set 1. The preview is shown in Figure 4-26.

5. **Click OK in the Weird Dreams dialog.**

   Click the size ratio (circled in red in Figure 4-26) to see the preview at 100%. Enlarge the preview by clicking +. Zoom out by clicking –.

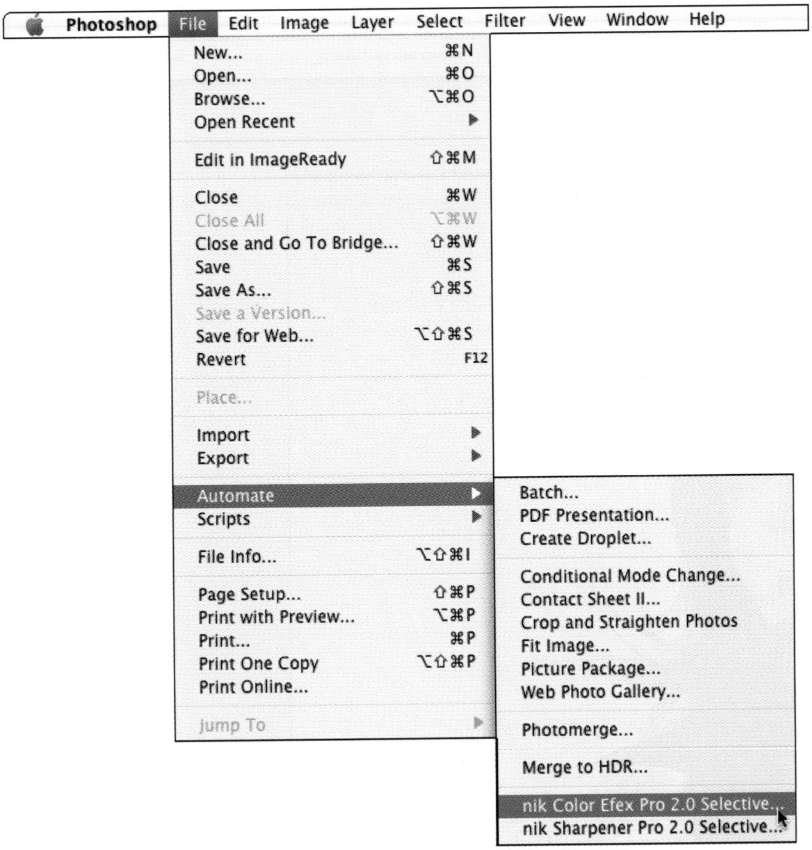

Figure 4-25: Get the Selective palette back using File➪Automate➪nik Color Efex Pro 2.0 Selective.

Book IV
Chapter 4

Commanding Colors and Using Layer Masks

Figure 4-26: nik's Weird Dreams dialog.

6. **Click Apply in the Selective palette.**

   The Weird Dreams layer is placed in the layer stack.

7. **Double-click the name Weird Dreams and add the word** Skin.

   Your layer stack looks like Figure 4-27. Keep going to the next section to create a background.

Color Efex Selective allows you to paint and still modify the effect at the same time. Explore this feature and the rest of nik Color Efex 2.0 on your own with the most excellent online guide that comes with the download. Access it by clicking Help on any dialog.

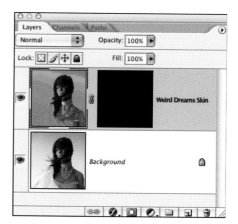

Figure 4-27: Weird Dreams Skin in the layer stack.

More weird dreams

The project on mood, earlier in this chapter, warms Christina's skin and cools her dress and background. So far in this exercise you have created skin (if you're following along with Christina's photograph). Now you build the background.

1. **Click Weird Dreams on the Selective palette.**

2. **Pick a new color set, set the size, and click OK in the Weird Dreams dialog.**

    I like Color Set 4. It is cool in tone and has fun patterns. I like more detail in the effect so my size setting is 4%, as shown in Figure 4-28.

Figure 4-28: Weird Dreams background settings.

3. Click Apply in the nik Selective palette.

The cool-colored Weird Dreams layer appears in the Photoshop layer stack.

4. Double-click the new layer name and rename it Weird Dreams Background.

Your layers stack resembles Figure 4-29.

5. Choose X in the upper-right corner of the nik Selective palette.

The X is in the top-right corner and clicking it closes the dialog. The rest of the work is done in Photoshop CS2.

6. Choose File⇨Save as.

7. Name the file ChristinaWD, **set the format to Photoshop, and click Save.**

The new name for the file is ChristinaWD.psd.

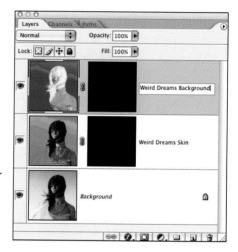

Figure 4-29: The layers stack with both Weird Dreams layers.

Seeing weird dreams

Now look at the effects created on the two layers, Weird Dreams Skin and Weird Dreams Background.

1. Click the Full Screen Mode with Menu Bar icon in the toolbox.

The icon is circled in red and highlighted blue in Figure 4-30. This mode displays the image against a neutral gray background.

The display modes in order of their icons on the toolbar are: Standard Display Mode, Full Screen with Menu Bar Mode, and Full Screen Mode. Toggle through them by typing F.

2. Press the spacebar to change the cursor to the Hand Tool.

3. Click+drag the image into the center of the workspace.

Figure 4-30: The full screen with menu bar icon in the toolbox.

Spacebar+click+drag to quickly scroll around an image in Photoshop. This technique is much faster than using the scrollbars on the bottom and right side of the Standard Display Mode and the only way to go in the other two modes since they hide the scrollbars.

4. Shift+click in the layer mask of the layer Weird Dreams Skin.

A red X appears on the black layer mask. The entire effect is revealed in the photograph. It covers the Background layer of the original image. Look at the tattoo quality of the pattern in Christina's skin in Figure 4-31.

5. Shift+click the layer mask of Weird Dreams Background.

A red X appears in that layer mask and the image in the layer covers both Weird Dreams Skin and the Background layer, as you see in Figure 4-32. The background has an electric feel, while the dress takes on an interesting pattern.

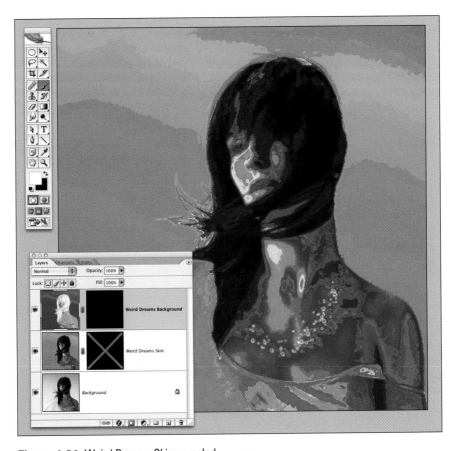

**Book IV
Chapter 4**

**Commanding Colors
and Using Layer
Masks**

Figure 4-31: Weird Dreams Skin revealed.

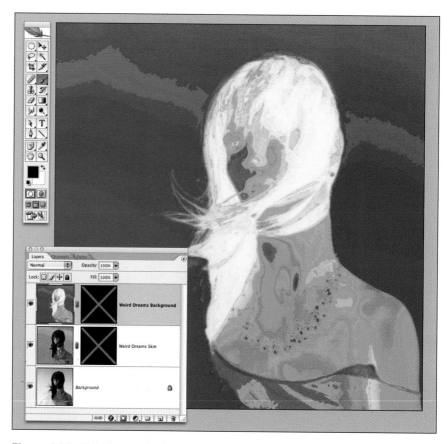

Figure 4-32: Weird Dreams Background revealed.

Shift+clicking a layer mask disables and places a red X in it. Shift+clicking the layer mask again enables it. You can also choose to enable or disable a layer mask from the Photoshop menu bar by selecting Layer⇨Layer Mask⇨Enable or Layer⇨Layer Mask⇨Disable. Note: If a layer mask is enabled, Photoshop offers only the choice Disable. If it is disabled, the choice offered is Enable. You can also Ctrl+click (right-click) the layer mask and choose Disable/Enable.

Painting in the skin

You have the parts for the photograph. Now you put them together. You start by painting in Christina's skin.

1. **Shift+click the layer mask on Weird Dreams Skin and Weird Dreams Background.**

   The original view of Christina is revealed and the layer masks on both Weird Dreams layers are enabled.

2. **Get a soft, 30-pixel brush.**

   See "Setting up your brush" earlier in this chapter.

3. **Set white as your foreground color. Type D for the default colors.**

   Type X to exchange them if needed.

4. **Click the layer mask of Weird Dreams Skin to make it active.**

   The active border appears. Refer to Figure 4-8.

5. **Brush in the new "pop art" over Christina's skin.**

   Paint in all of the skin except for her lips, nostrils, and eye. Your work looks similar to Figure 4-33.

Figure 4-33: Christina's new pop art skin.

When editing in Photoshop you want to work at 100% view or greater. Get there by choosing View⇨Actual Pixels. See Appendix B for more.

Bringing in the background

The skin is in. Now you bring in some, not all, of the background. Follow along:

1. **Activate the layer mask on Weird Dreams Background.**

2. **Paint in the background.**

   Starting as close to the parasol as you can, paint in the background to the left side of Christina. Continue along the top to the line that goes above her head and all the way to the right edge.

3. **In the options bar, click the blue button with a triangle in it next to the Opacity window. Move the slider to the left until the window displays 50%.**

   You see that opacity setting in Figure 4-34.

Figure 4-34: Lower the Brush opacity to 50%.

4. **Click in a blank area of the options bar or press Enter to close the slider.**

5. **Paint in the rest of the background and Christina's dress.**

   The 50% opacity brush allows part of the Weird Dreams Background to be revealed. The lighter background at Christina's back gives the composition a sense of motion. The pattern on the dress adds interest.

6. **Option+click (Alt+click) Weird Dreams Background layer mask.**

   The photograph is replaced by the contents of the layer mask in black, white, and shades of middle gray. Your mask looks similar to what you see in Figure 4-35. The areas painted with white with the brush at 100% opacity are white on the layer mask. Those painted with the brush's opacity set at 50% are middle gray.

7. Option+click (Alt+click) the Weird Dreams Background layer mask again when you are done.

When painting with a 50% brush (or any opacity lower than 100%), releasing the mouse button, then clicking again and continuing to paint adds another 50% of gray over the existing paint. This results in a darker area of gray that allows less of the effect to show through the double painted area.

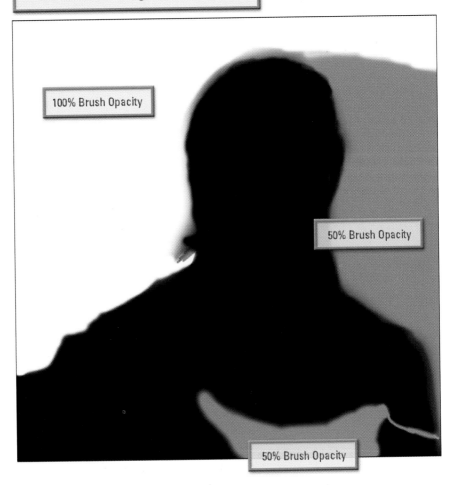

Figure 4-35: The layer mask on Weird Dreams background.

If you see gaps in the mask, you can paint on it in the Layer Mask view. If the white area shows portions of black, paint over them with 100% white. If black areas appear in the places painted with gray, do these steps:

1. **Set the brush at 100% opacity.**

2. **Option+click (Alt+click) the gray in the large layer mask window to sample it.**

3. **Paint over the black places.**

White on a layer mask reveals what is on the layer. Black on the mask conceals or hides the contents of its layer. Shades of gray reveal the layer up to their value of gray. Light gray reveals more. Dark gray reveals less.

Finishing touches

The photograph in Figure 4-36 so far shows stark contrast in color between Christina and the background. This is an "in-your-face" expression of the Weird Dreams idea. Toning down Christina's skin will help a lot.

Figure 4-36: A heavily pop-art photograph.

TIP

It is very good to play

Playing in Photoshop is very good. It helps you discover what happens if you do something different. It stimulates your creativity, feeds your heart, and makes you smile when you see something you like. Smiling is also very good.

1. **Click the Weird Dreams Skin layer thumbnail.**

2. **Click+drag the Opacity triangle in the Layers palette to the left until it reads 30%.**

   You can see this in Figure 4-37. The skin tone now has a tattoo-like appearance and is easier on the eye. See Figure 4-38. Understand more by playing with the opacity of the Weird Dreams Background layer.

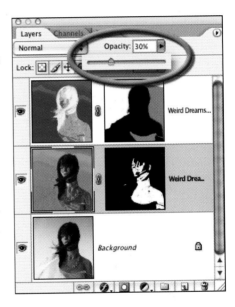

Figure 4-37: The Opacity slider lowers the opacity on the layer Weird Dreams Skin.

Figure 4-38: The finished photograph from my mind for your eyes.

Book V

Preserving Pixels

The 5th Wave

By Rich Tennant

"I think you've made a mistake. We do photo retouching, not family portrai....Oooh, wait a minute – I think I get it!"

Good practices are involved with everything you do. Photoshop is no different. Book V guides you through nondestructive image editing in Photoshop. You discover how to retouch portraits, whiten teeth, brighten eyes, and smooth lines under and around the eyes. You do these things in ways that always allow you to change your mind (no matter when you change it). You create stunning black and white from your color digital photographs and you understand how Photoshop works its black and white magic. You create an easy way to preview conversions for your own black and white photographs. You have a peek into how to get the color on your screen to be the color on your print.

Chapter 1: Understanding Nondestructive Editing

*C*hange. Count on it. Change is the only constant. This chapter is all about change, as in changing your mind and not having to work hard to make a change. You read how to store all of your edits to a Photoshop file in layers, beginning by creating a backup of the Background layer. You understand how destructive tools work and how to replace them with safe ones. You use layers to store adjustments, modifications, and retouching. You discover how to rework an overedited area without having to redo the whole file. You begin to think about editing in a way that always lets you go back and . . . change your mind. Think of this chapter as revealing how to have unlimited do-overs forever!

Artist Matt Lamb says that, "a painting is finished when a dealer takes it out of [my] studio by force and hangs it in the house or office of a client." That works for painters, sculptors, and other artists who deliver one-of-a-kind works. Imagine how life would be for them if they didn't know when a work was done.

Now understand that as a digital photographer, your life is that of an artist whose work never has to be finished. The reason for the possibility of the neverending story is, of course, Photoshop. A properly executed work done in layers is one that can be changed as many times as whim or inspiration strikes.

Erasing the Evil Tools

The Eraser Tools — Eraser, Background Eraser, and Magic Eraser — do exactly what their names say they do. They erase pixels. That's why they are "evil." There needs to be a big red DON'T USE symbol like the one in Figure 1-1 when they are clicked.

Okay. They aren't really evil in the horror movie or serial killer sense. They are evil because they destroy or permanently alter pixels. These kinds of methods in Photoshop are arguably fine as long as the file is open and no more than 20 steps have been done. After a pixel has been erased, for example, and 20 more changes are made on the file, the change is permanent. When a file is saved, closed, then opened again, the history is cleared and the ability to undo an edit is gone.

Figure 1-1: Don't use these tools.

The default number of history steps or undos in Photoshop is 20. This setting can be changed in Photoshop's preferences.

Hiding versus Erasing

Here are quick demonstrations of what the Eraser does and how to do exactly the same thing by hiding pixels instead of erasing them.

Erasing

The mission of the project is to make the roof of the car interior blend with the corrugated tin roof so no black from the car photograph extends into the sky.

1. **Download the folder for Book V, Chapter 1 from www.amesphoto.com/ learning.**

   The code to go to the login/registration page is 4D59776. If you have already registered, type in your user name (your e-mail address) and password.

2. Navigate to the sample folder in Bridge.

3. Double-click Eraser.psd to open it in Photoshop CS2.

The file has three layers: the Background layer of a corrugated tin roof and rafter, the Eraser layer of the interior of an old, deserted car, and a duplicate Hide Pixels layer of the same old car. As you see in Figure 1-2, the layer Hide Pixels is hidden. The lack of an eye tells you that.

4. Choose the Eraser Tool from the toolbox.

5. In the Brush window in the options bar, click the triangle to open the settings.

6. Make the eraser 60 pixels in size by moving the Master Diameter slider until the window reads 60 px.

Refer to Figure 1-3.

7. Make the hardness 0% by either dragging the Hardness slider all the way to the left or typing 0 in the window.

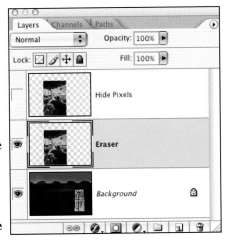

Figure 1-2: Hide Pixels is hidden.

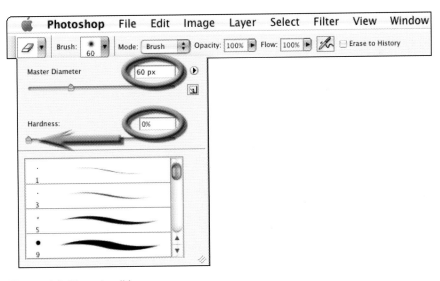

Figure 1-3: Move the slider.

8. **Click anywhere in the options bar to close the Brush window.**

9. **Working in the Eraser layer, erase the black portion of the layer that extends into the sky.**

   Use one stroke of the mouse to follow the roof line. When you finish, your work looks like Figure 1-4. Compare the thumbnails in the layers Eraser and Hide Pixels. Notice that the pixels in the Eraser layer are gone.

Figure 1-4: Your work will look like this.

10. **Click the Background layer's eye icon to hide it.**

    You see only the car interior and the soft edge where the pixels were erased. See Figure 1-5.

11. **⌘+Z (Ctrl+Z) to undo the erasing.**

    The erased pixels come back on the screen and in the Eraser layer's thumbnail. See Figure 1-6. If you did several strokes to erase the top of the car interior, ⌘+Option+Z (Ctrl+Alt+Z) until all the erased pixels return.

12. **If you did the erasing with one stroke of the mouse, type ⌘+Z (Ctrl+Z) to redo the Eraser.**

    If you used several strokes to do the original erasing, you have to redo each stroke. ⌘+Shift+Z (Ctrl+Shift+Z) until your screen looks like Figure 1-5.

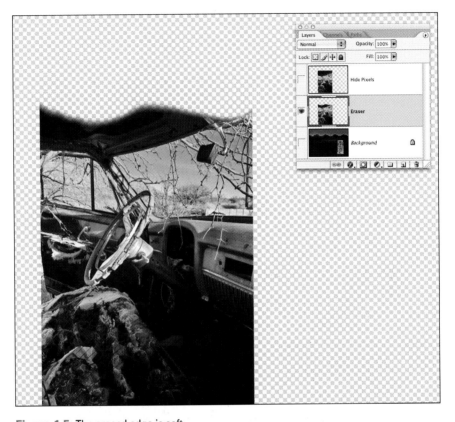

Figure 1-5: The erased edge is soft.

13. **From the Photoshop menu, choose File⇨Save, then choose File⇨ Close.**

14. **Select File⇨Open Recent⇨Eraser.psd or double-click Eraser.psd in Bridge.**

    See if you can undo the erased pixels. Typing the undo keystrokes are all for naught. Those pixels are outta here, never to return. Keep this file open and work through the following section.

Hiding

This part of the project introduces you to adding and using a layer mask to an image. Layer masks on photographs work exactly as they do on adjustment layers. (If you haven't already done the projects in Book IV, Chapter 4, you may want to do so now. Those projects help you understand layer masks and bring you up to speed for this one.)

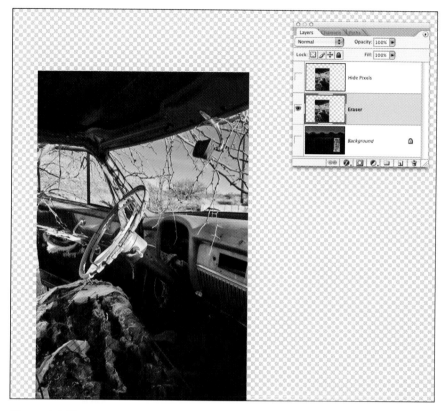

Figure 1-6: The erased pixels are back.

1. **In Eraser.psd, click the eye icon on Eraser to hide the Eraser layer.**

2. **Click the eye icons on the Background and Hide Pixels layers to make them visible.**

3. **Click the layer thumbnail of Hide Pixels to activate that layer.**

   Your layer stack looks like Figure 1-7.

4. **Click the Add Layer Mask icon in the Layers palette.**

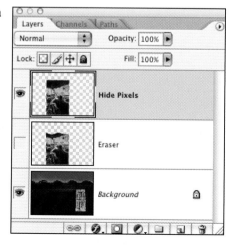

Figure 1-7: This is your layer stack.

Clicking the Add Layer Mask icon puts a reveal all layer mask on the layer Hide Pixels. The icon is circled in red in Figure 1-8. A reveal all layer mask is filled with white. A hide all layer mask is filled with black. Refer to Figure 4-1 in Book IV, Chapter 4 for the identification of the icons at the bottom of the Layers palette.

Figure 1-8: Add Layer Mask icon and reveal all layer mask.

5. **Select the Brush Tool from the toolbox.**

6. **Move the Master Diameter slider until the window reads 60px and type 0 into the Hardness textbox. Opacity should be 100%.**

When you finish you have a soft-edged, 60-pixel brush. Appendix B has keyboard shortcuts for brush size, edge hardness, and more.

7. **Set the foreground color to Black.**

If the toolbox colors are not white and black, click the default color's icon or type D. If white is the foreground color, click the exchange colors icon or type X. Find the icons in Figure 1-9.

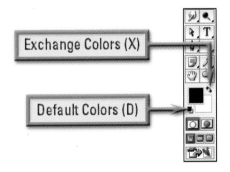

Figure 1-9: Exchange Colors and Default Colors icons.

Photoshop's painting tools use the foreground color in the toolbox. You can change the color by double-clicking in the foreground color box to open the picker or by clicking a color in the Swatches palette.

8. **Paint on the layer mask with black over the parts of the car interior that are in the sky above the roofline.**

When you finish, your screen and Layers palette look like Figure 1-10. Notice that an area of black is on the layer mask. The pixels are still visible on the layer thumbnail. They are hidden from the screen by the black on the layer mask.

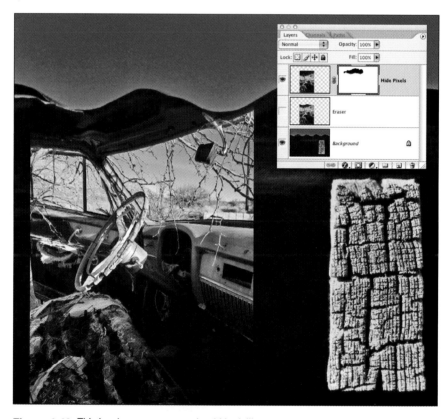

Figure 1-10: This is what your screen should look like.

9. **Click the eye icon on the Background layer to hide the layer.**

   The Hide Pixels layer looks like the Eraser layer, as you see in Figure 1-11. The pixels are hidden by the layer mask. Bring them back.

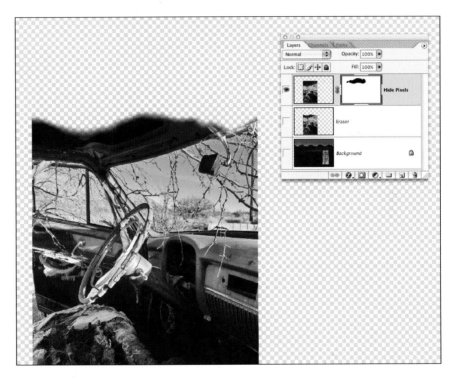

Figure 1-11: Hide Pixels and Eraser look the same.

10. **Disable the layer mask by Shift+clicking inside the layer mask on the layer Hide Pixels.**

    A red X is displayed in the layer mask and the pixels that were hidden appear on the screen, as shown in Figure 1-12.

11. **Enable the layer mask by Shift+clicking inside the layer mask.**

    The red X is removed and the pixels on the screen are hidden where there is black on the layer mask.

12. **Choose File⇨Save and then choose File⇨Close.**

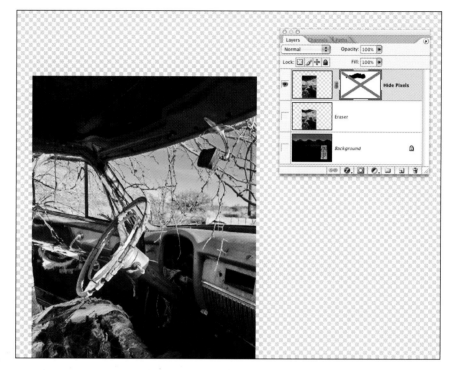

Figure 1-12: Hide Pixels is disabled.

Cashing in on unlimited undos

Here's the big difference between using a layer mask and the Eraser Tool. Put back the left half of the pixels along the roofline.

1. **Reopen Eraser.psd by choosing File➪Open Recent➪Eraser.psd or double-click its preview in Bridge.**

2. **Activate the layer mask by clicking its icon on the Hide Pixels layer.**

   The active border appears around the Layer Mask icon, as in Figure 1-13.

3. **Click the Background layer's eye icon to reveal the layer.**

Figure 1-13: The Layer Mask icon is active.

4. **Click the Exchange Colors icon (see Figure 1-9) or press X.**

   You made white the foreground color.

5. **Paint at the upper-left edge of the interior of the car above the roofline.**

   The black part of the car's roof appears above the corrugated tin, as you see in Figure 1-14. Even after the file was saved and closed, the pixels are still there. And there's more. The Eraser Tool only lets you undo the whole stroke. Remember when you did ⌘+Z (Ctrl+Z) to undo the Eraser? The entire stroke was undone.

   Using a layer mask and painting with white allows you the control of bringing back any part of the pixels hidden by black on the mask. How? Simply paint with white.

Figure 1-14: The black part appears.

Protecting the Background Layer

The first *best practice* in Photoshop is to always protect the Background layer. Make it a habit to never, ever make edits on this layer. You make a duplicate of the Background and edit that layer. This serves two purposes: First, it protects the Background layer. Second, it gives a before and after comparison of the work you have accomplished by simply clicking the duplicate layer's eye icon on and off.

Make notes of the work you want to do in Photoshop while you are making photographs. Often a few quick steps in Photoshop are all you want, as in the case of the building in Figure 1-15. I saw the leaves, the sunspot, and the crane in the viewfinder. I knew I would have to do simple fixes to give a clean view of this unique architectural angle. Figure 1-15 shows the retouching for this photograph of a building whose sides meet at an acute angle.

Figure 1-15: These are the things I want to fix.

Backing up the background

Here's how you protect your Background layer:

1. **Download the folder for Book V, Chapter 1 from www. amesphoto.com/learning.**

   The code to the login/ registration page is 4D59776.

   If you have already registered, type in your user name (your email address) and password.

2. **Open the file by double-clicking it in Bridge.**

3. **Select Layer➪New➪Layer Via Copy from the Photoshop menu bar to duplicate the Background layer.**

TIP

More keyboard shortcuts! Woohoo! ⌘+J (Ctrl+J) makes a duplicate of the highlighted layer and places the new layer directly above the one copied. If the highlighted layer has a selection, only the selection is copied onto a new layer.

4. **Rename the Background layer duplicate by double-clicking the words Layer 1 (immediately to the right of the layer thumbnail).**

5. **Type in** Retouch **and press Enter.**

    Your layer stack looks like Figure 1-16. All of the retouching in the next steps takes place on the layer named Retouch. Keep your file open for the next section.

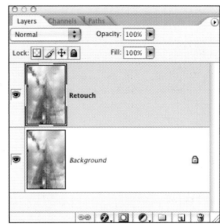

Figure 1-16: Your layer stack looks like this.

Doing the minor fixes

The healing tools copy the tone and texture of the sampled area to the area being healed. The underlying color of the healed area is maintained.

Removing the leaves

Just for fun and to give you a brief introduction to a few great retouching tools — Clone Stamp and Healing Brush and Patch Tools — finish the fixes shown in Figure 1-15.

1. **Click the Clone Stamp Tool icon shown in Figure 1-17.**

    The flyout menu shows you the other tool available: Pattern Stamp.

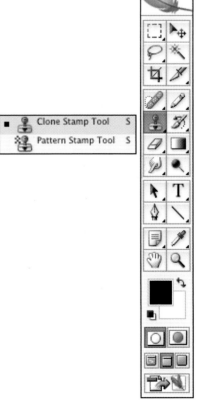

Figure 1-17: Clone Stamp is the way to go.

2. In the options bar, choose a 70-pixel, soft-edge brush.

The options bar is shown in Figure 1-18.

Figure 1-18: The Clone Stamp options bar.

3. Option+click (Alt+click) in the clouds to the right of the leaves, as you see in Figure 1-19.

4. Clone the blank clouds over the leaves.

The Clone Stamp Tool works just like a brush except that instead of using paint, it copies the sampled area over the leaves. Figure 1-20 shows the cloning in progress. The cloned area is very obvious. Now you use the Healing Brush to blend it together.

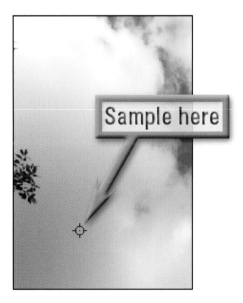

Figure 1-19: Sample the clouds . . .

Figure 1-20: . . . and clone the clouds.

5. Click and hold the Spot Healing Brush icon.

The healing tools menu appears.

6. Choose the Healing Brush.

The Spot Healing Brush is the default choice of the toolbox you see in Figure 1-21.

7. Again, Option+click (Alt+click) in the clouds shown in Figure 1-22.

This samples the area of clouds to the right and below the cloned area.

8. Heal the mismatched cloned area by painting over it with the Healing Brush.

The result while you are working looks, well, wrong! See Figure 1-23. When you release the mouse, the healing happens automatically. Ta da! The cloning is fixed. Remember to heal where you cloned over the leaves in the brighter areas of the cloud, too.

Keep your file open for more fixes.

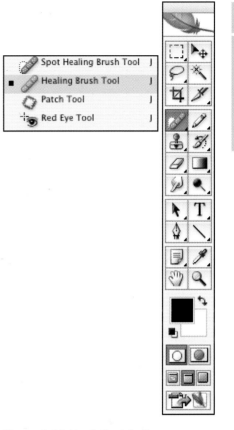

Figure 1-21: Here's the default.

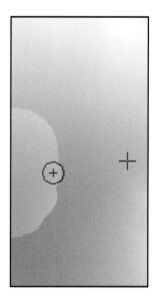

Figure 1-22: Sample the clouds . . .

Figure 1-23: . . . and the clouds are healed.

Fixing the sunspot

The sunspot is really a specular highlight. *Specular* means mirror. What you are seeing is the sun reflected in the granite . . . the mirror in this case.

1. **Click and hold the Spot Healing Brush icon and choose the Patch Tool.**

   See Figure 1-21 for the icons.

2. **Draw a selection around the sunspot.**

   Be careful to avoid the centerline or the left edge of the stone. Your selection wants to look like the one in Figure 1-24.

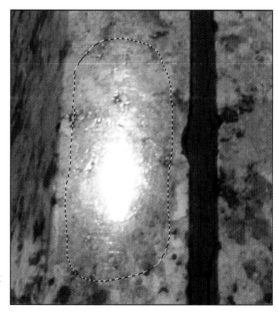

Figure 1-24: Avoid either edge.

3. **Click inside the selection and drag it across the centerline.**

   Check Figure 1-25 for positioning. The area you drag the selection over replaces the original selection as you drag, giving you a real-time preview of what will be patched over the original pixels.

4. **Release the mouse button to patch the selection.**

5. **Choose Select⇨Deselect from the menu bar or press ⌘+D (Ctrl+D).**

   Notice that the pattern of the granite is duplicated in the patched area in Figure 1-26. This is a dead giveaway that Photoshop has been used.

Fixing the fix

The goal of great work in Photoshop is to be undetected by the viewer.

1. **Get the Healing Brush from the toolbox.**

   See Figure 1-21.

2. **Option+click (Alt+click) in an area of the stone that is free of distinguishing marks.**

   Now heal in the area of the repeated pattern.

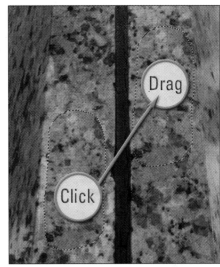

Figure 1-25: Position your sample like this.

Figure 1-26: A duplicate pattern: a dead Photoshop giveaway.

Book V
Chapter 1

Understanding
Nondestructive
Editing

3. Brush over the obvious duplicates of pattern.

Each time you release the mouse button, Photoshop heals the area. When you are finished, your retouch is like Figure 1-27. Look Ma! No patterns! Keep going . . . .

Fixing the crane

This one is easy and demonstrates a cool way to use the Healing Brush.

1. Sample on the edge of the building above the crane.

You want to sample the building's edge and the sky together, as you see in Figure 1-28. For clarity's sake, the figure shows the diameter of the brush. The sample point is the crosshairs.

2. Click the building edge next to the crane; drag down the edge of the building and over the entire area of the crane. Release the mouse.

Magic! The crane is gone in one stroke! The trick is to make certain that the sample point and beginning of the Healing Brush stroke are centered on the edge, as in Figure 1-29.

Figure 1-27: Healing stone.

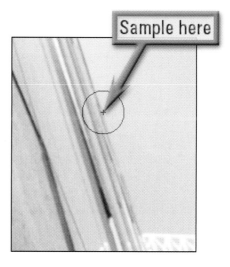

Figure 1-28: This is your sample spot.

The great part about this style of using Photoshop is you get to see the work you have done and compare it to where you started. Click the eye icon on the layer Retouch so it's off. You see your work disappear. Now click the eye icon again. All of the flaws — the leaves, sunspot, and crane — vanish. Figure 1-30 shows the result. There you have the basics. Making a copy of the background layer and always working only on that layer means you can always go back.

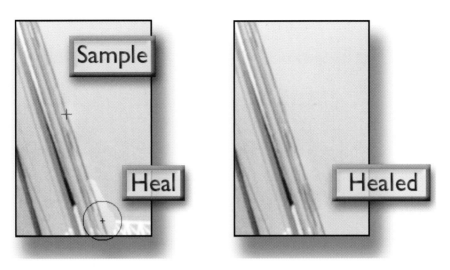

Figure 1-29: Center the Healing Brush on the edge of the building.

Figure 1-30: Before and after.

Recovering from Big Mistakes

A big mistake is when a lot of work has been done on a retouch layer and part of it isn't right. A client changes his mind and the fix he wants looks like it would require doing all of the work on the Retouch layer over again.

Here is an example: Figure 1-31 shows a retouching strategy map for this headshot of actress Tiffany Dupont. Notice that the map calls for plumping up her lip a little bit. (You read how to do this in Book V, Chapter 3, by the way.) Figure 1-32 shows the lip before, on the Background layer, and after, on the Retouch layer. You see that all the other retouching has been done, including removing hair below her chin and from across her eye. A lot of work has been already accomplished to bring the image this far.

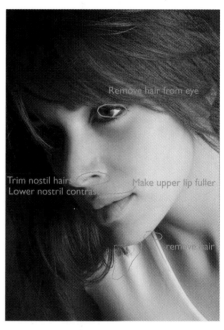

Figure 1-31: The strategy map.

Figure 1-32: Before and after.

At the point in a retouch where something drastic is to be done, duplicate the layer and rename it with the procedure.

Had this example been properly executed, Retouch would have been duplicated and renamed Liquify Lip. In this example, the work on the lip makes it look too exaggerated. So it has to be redone. Sometimes you get caught up in the heat of the work and forget to follow procedure. There was a time when this kind of do-over meant starting completely over. Here is how to recover from this boo-boo:

**Book V
Chapter 1**

**Understanding
Nondestructive
Editing**

1. **Download the folder for Book V, Chapter 1 from www. amesphoto.com/learning.**

    The code to go to the login/registration page is 4D59776. If you have already registered, type in your user name (your e-mail address) and password.

2. **Open the file Tiffany.psd by double-clicking it in Bridge.**

3. **Click the eye icon on the layer Strategy Map to hide the layer.**

4. **Click the Retouch eye icon on and off several times, leaving it on.**

    You see how much work has been done. It would be no fun at all to do it over. Leave this eye icon on.

5. **Click inside the layer thumbnail for the layer Retouch.**

6. **Select the Lasso Tool from the toolbox shown in Figure 1-33.**

7. **Draw a selection around the exaggerated lips.**

    Your selection looks like Figure 1-34.

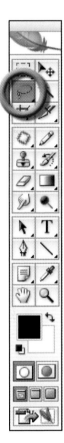

Figure 1-33:
The Lasso
Tool.

Figure 1-34: Circle the lips.

8. Click in the thumbnail of the Background layer.

Your layer stack looks like Figure 1-35. Now you make the selection into a separate layer

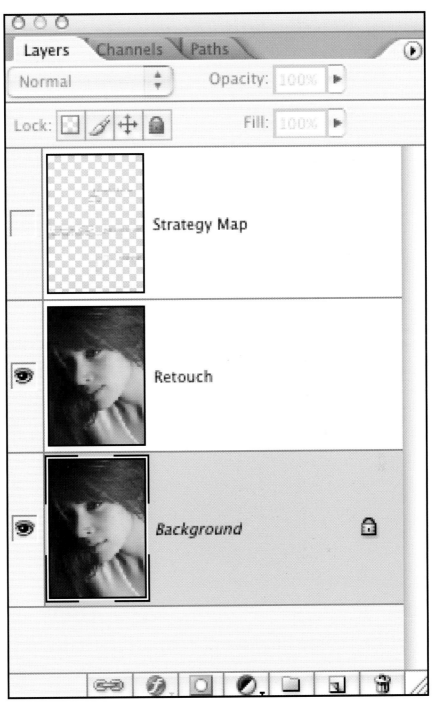

Figure 1-35: Your layer stack looks like this.

9. Choose Layer⇨New⇨Layer Via Copy, shown in Figure 1-36.

The selection is now a new layer named Layer 1.

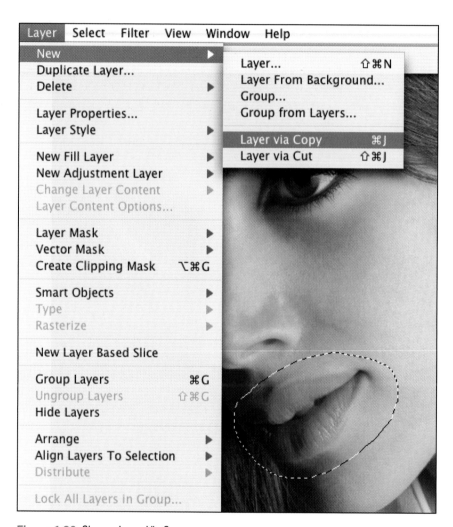

Figure 1-36: Choose Layer Via Copy.

10. **Click+drag the Layer 1 thumbnail up the layer stack until it is above Retouch.**

    When you see a solid bold line between the layers Retouch and Strategy Map (as you see in Figure 1-37), release the mouse button. The lips from the Background layer now cover the exaggerated ones. All that's left is to merge Layer 1 with Retouch.

11. **Click the flyout disclosure triangle at the top right of the Layers palette. Select Merge Down from the menu, as in Figure 1-38.**

12. **Use the Healing Brush on the skin above her upper lip and below her lower one.**

    Your layer stack is shown in Figure 1-39.

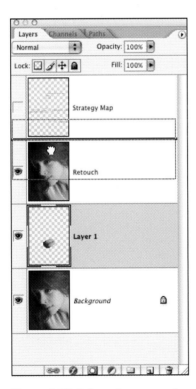

Figure 1-37: Release the mouse when you see this bold line.

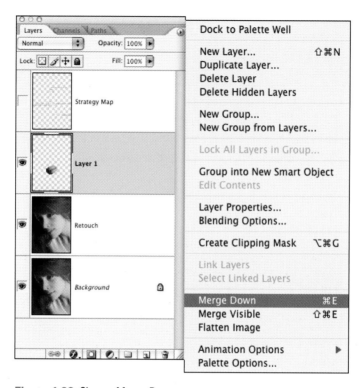

Figure 1-38: Choose Merge Down.

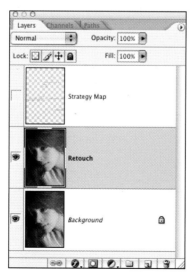

Figure 1-39: Here's your layer stack again.

Chapter 2: Creating Stunning Black and White

In This Chapter

✓ **Understanding the ways Photoshop converts to black and white**

✓ **Exploring the Channel Mixer adjustment layer**

✓ **Boosting the highlights**

When color film was introduced, the buzz on the streets was that it would kill black and white. Well, 60 or so years later we are still enthralled with what those "colorless" photographs convey. Black and white is everywhere. You see it in fashion magazine advertisements not because it is less expensive; you see black and white because it carries drama, impact, and mood. Brides are choosing black and white for part, if not all, of the photographic coverage of their special day. Fine-art black and white adorns the walls of prestigious offices, hotels, and homes. Black and white is here to stay, which is more than the outlook for color film in this age of digital capture.

In this chapter you read about what Photoshop does when converting color to black and white. You see how the most popular conversion methods give drastically different results and, in understanding how they work, you know a new way of thinking about the information in a digital photograph — especially when it comes to black and white. You discover how to selectively boost the highlights and create an amazing high-fashion black and white look.

Making Color Happen

Figure 2-1 is a set of overlapping circles of primary colors Red, Green, and Blue. The overlaps form the complements of the primary colors: cyan, magenta, and yellow. The middle, where all three circles overlap each other, is white.

Color in Photoshop is comprised of three individual channels; one each for Red, Green, and Blue are shown in black and white. Figure 2-2 shows them, and a composite channel of all three (labeled RGB) displays the color circles in full color. The Red channel shows the red circle as white, while Green and Blue are black. The Green channel displays Green as white and red and blue as black. The Blue channel's Blue circle is white and its Red and Green circles are black. You work with these channels later in this chapter.

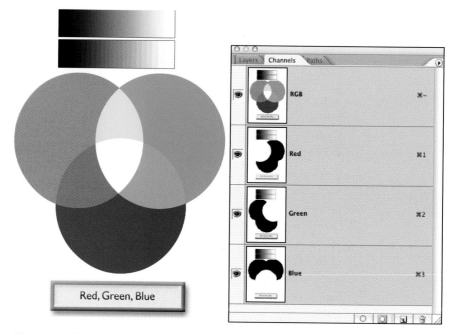

Figure 2-1: The primary colors Red, Green, and Blue and their complements.

Figure 2-2: Channels in Photoshop.

Converting Color to B&W Three Ways

As with most things Photoshop, converting color to black and white can be achieved many ways. You are exposed to three of them in this chapter. The emphasis is on the one that offers the most control and is an adjustment layer to boot. You can make your black and white conversions and re-convert them later if you choose. And you knew I would show you that!

Grayscale

The most popular black and white conversion seems to be converting a file to grayscale by simply letting Photoshop throw away the color. A *grayscale* image has only one channel: gray.

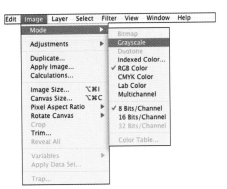

1. **Download the sample folder from www.amesphoto.com/ learning.**

   You're asked to register if you haven't already done so. The code for the login/registration page is 4D59776.

2. **Open the file Color Circles.psd in Photoshop.**

   Work along to see how different conversions produce very different results.

3. **Select Image⇨Duplicate.**

4. **Name the file** Grayscale.psd **and click OK.**

5. **Choose Image⇨Mode⇨ Grayscale, as shown in Figure 2-3.**

6. **Click OK when the Discard color information? box appears.**

   The box is shown in Figure 2-4.

7. **Save the file.**

   Your conversion looks like Figure 2-5.

Figure 2-3: Convert the file to grayscale.

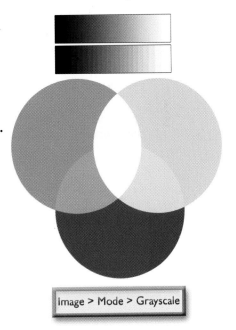

Figure 2-4: Yes, Photoshop. It's OK to get rid of the color.

Figure 2-5: A grayscale conversion.

Desaturate

This method is also popular. It can be done with an adjustment layer or from the Image⇨Adjustments menu.

1. **Download the sample folder from www.amesphoto.com/learning.**

   You're asked to register if you haven't already done so. The code for the login/registration page is 4D59776.

2. **Open the file Color Circles.psd in Photoshop.**

3. **Select Image⇨Duplicate and name this file** Desaturate.psd.

4. **Choose Create a New Adjustment Layer icon⇨ Hue/Saturation.**

5. **Drag the Saturation slider all the way to the left until the Saturation window reads −100.**

   This setting is highlighted with a red arrow in Figure 2-6.

6. **Click OK.**

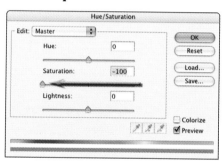

Figure 2-6: The image is desaturated when the entry window reads −100.

The layer stack looks like the one in Figure 2-7. The desaturated file is a lot different from the grayscale conversion. *Desaturating* makes all of the colors gray, as you see in Figure 2-8.

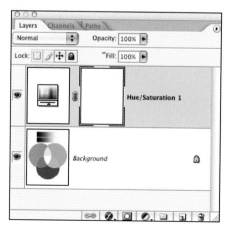

Figure 2-7: The layer stack and the Hue/Saturation layer.

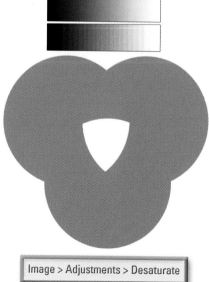

Image > Adjustments > Desaturate

Figure 2-8: Conversion by desaturation.

Channel Mixer

Channel Mixer does exactly what its name says. It mixes the channels according to your specification. It is a latecomer to the tools for making black and white in Photoshop. Grayscale and Desaturate go all the way back to Photoshop 1.0.

Channel Mixer, which made its debut in Photoshop 5, offers far and away the most control, and since it's available as an adjustment layer, is the perfect choice for black and white conversion.

The Blue channel in digital photography is important to make colors work. It is also the channel that carries the most *noise,* or *artifacts,* produced by the DSLR camera's sensor. Noise is generated when the computer in the camera can't interpret information from the pixels on the sensor. When working with black and white, the Blue channel is often left at 0%.

1. **Download the sample folder from www.amesphoto.com/learning.**

   You're asked to register if you haven't already done so. The code for the login/registration page is 4D59776.

2. **Open Color Circles.psd.**

3. **Click the New Adjustment Layer icon at the bottom of the Layers palette and choose Channel Mixer.**

   See Figure 4-1 in Book IV, Chapter 4 for the Layers palette icons.

4. **Click the Monochrome checkbox in the lower-left corner of the dialog.**

   The checkbox is circled in red in Figure 2-9. 100% Red is the default setting for Channel Mixer layers.

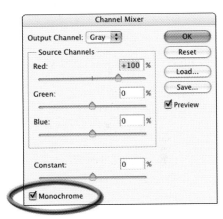

Figure 2-9: Monochrome makes it black and white.

5. Click OK.

6. Rename the new adjustment layer Red 100%.

The effect of the Channel Mixer adjustment layer at 100% Red with Monochrome checked is shown in Figure 2-10. Compare it to the Channels palette in Figure 2-2.

100% of any of Red, Green, or Blue renders that color in the channel pure white.

7. Make another Channel Mixer adjustment layer.

8. Make these settings:

- **Red:** 0%.

- **Green:** 100%.

- **Blue:** 0%.

9. Click the Monochrome checkbox and click OK.

Your dialog is shown in Figure 2-11.

10. Rename the new adjustment layer Green 100%.

11. Click off the layer Red 100% eye icon.

As soon as Red 100% is hidden, the black circle representing the color Red reappears; the Green circle becomes white. You see this effect in Figure 2-12.

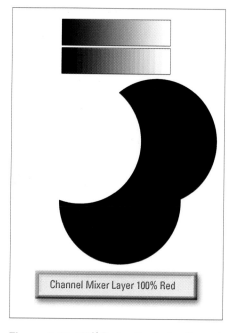

Figure 2-10: 100% Red setting in the Channel Mixer adjustment layer.

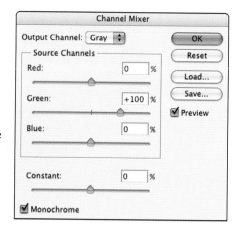

Figure 2-11: The dialog for the Channel Mixer Layer Green 100%.

12. **Make another Channel Mixer adjustment layer.**

13. **Set this one up as follows:**

    - **Red:** 70%.
    - **Green:** 30%.
    - **Blue:** 0%.

14. **Click the Monochrome checkbox and click OK.**

15. **Rename the adjustment layer** Red 70% Green 30% Hide Green 100%.

    The newest version of Color Circles.psd is shown in Figure 2-13. Now the different amounts of the colors mixed together by the Channel Mixer layer shows varying gray tones in the Red and Green channels. There is no Blue so it remains black.

16. **Make another Channel Mixer adjustment layer.**

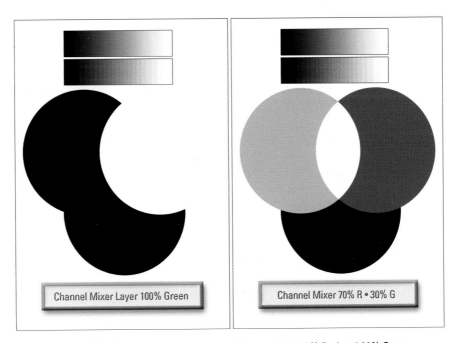

Channel Mixer Layer 100% Green

Channel Mixer 70% R • 30% G

Figure 2-12: 100% Green setting.

Figure 2-13: 70% Red and 30% Green.

17. **This time make these settings:**

    - **Red:** 40%.

    - **Green:** 60%.

    - **Blue:** 0%.

18. **Click the Monochrome check-box and click OK.**

19. **Rename the layer** Red 40% Green 60%.

20. **Click the eye icon to hide the layer Red 70% Green 30%.**

21. **Save Color Circles.psd.**

    Keep the file open. You use it in the next project.

 TIP

The total percentage of all of the channels combined in Channel Mixer does not want to be more than 100%. Your new version of Color Circles.psd is shown in Figure 2-14.

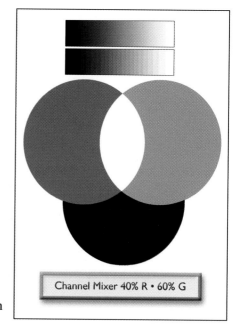

Channel Mixer 40% R • 60% G

Figure 2-14: 40% Red 60% Green Channel Mixer adjustment layer.

Mixing It Up Right

You see how Channel Mixer affects colors in a photograph when it converts them to black and white. Now you choose the right mix for a color photograph.

Selecting multiple layers

Figure 2-15, a photograph of a house of signs and a windmill sitting toward the end of Main Street in Idaho City, Idaho, has lots of color and a blue sky with some clouds. Making another set of the Channel Mixer adjustment layers on this photograph would give you a good range of choices. And that would be a lot of extra work. Here's a more efficient way.

 ON THE WEB

1. **Open Idaho City.psd and Color Circles.psd.**

   The files are in the sample folder you downloaded earlier in this chapter. If you skipped the first project, go to www.amesphoto.com/learning. The code for the login/registration page is 4D59776. You're asked to register if you haven't already done so.

2. **Click the header bar of Color Circles.psd to make it the active document.**

   Your desktop and Photoshop work area look similar to Figure 2-16.

Figure 2-15: Idaho City color.

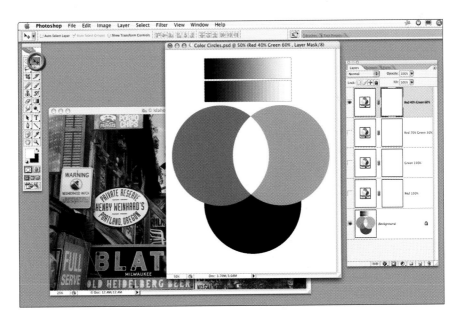

Figure 2-16: Idaho City.psd, Color Circles.psd, and the Move Tool circled in the toolbox.

3. **Choose the Move Tool from the toolbox.**

   It's circled in red in Figure 2-16.

4. **Make active the top layer in the layer stack: Red 40% Green 60%.**

   This selects all of the Channel Mixer adjustment layers in Color Circles.psd.

5. **Shift+click the bottom Channel Mixer layer: Red 100%.**

   All of the Channel Mixer layers are selected, as shown in Figure 2-17. The ability to select more than one layer in the layer stack is new to Photoshop CS2.

   When a layer is active in the layer stack, Shift+click another layer to select all of the layers between the active layer and the one clicked. To select layers that are not immediately above or below the active layer, ⌘+click (Ctrl+click) the layer you want to select.

6. **Click inside one of the selected layers and drag all of them onto Idaho City.psd. Release the mouse button.**

   Figure 2-18 shows how the outlines of the layer stack show up as dotted lines when you successfully drag them to the color file. The layer stack for that file is in Figure 2-19. Once you release the mouse button, the effect of the visible layer shows on the screen.

7. **Click the eye icon on Red 100%.**

   Notice that the image changes.

8. **Click it off to compare it to Red 40% Green 60%.**

9. **Now show Red 70% Green 30%; hide and show Red 100%.**

   Which one do you like best?

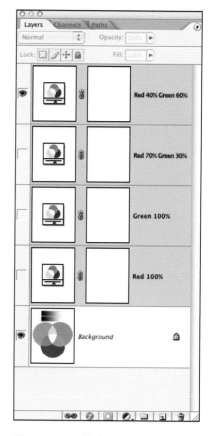

Figure 2-17: All Channel Mixer layers are selected.

Figure 2-18: The outlines of the layers appear when they are moved to another file.

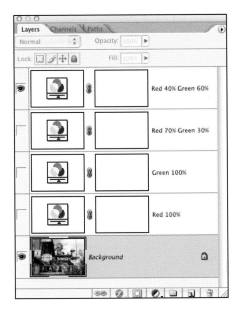

Figure 2-19: Idaho City.psd's layer stack
with four Channel Mixer adjustment layers.

The Channel Mixer layer that is closest to the Background layer takes prece-
dence when its eye icon is on.

Comparing the mix results

The black and white versions represented by the four different Channel
Mixer adjustment layers are shown in Figures 2-20 through 2-23.

Choose which one you like best. Look closely at the Neighborhood Watch sign.
See how it changes in all four versions in Figure 2-24? Look at Figure 2-15 to
see the color of the sign. You see the amazing control Channel Mixer offers
when making color into stunning black and white.

You can use the Channel Mixer layers you created and saved in Color
Circles.psd. Choose the Move tool. Then simply open the new photograph in
Photoshop CS2 and drag the Channel Mixer layers on it. You now have a
standard starting point for creating your very own stunning black and white
photograph. Make new Channel Mixer layers and play with different settings.
See which ones you love.

Red 40% • Green 60%

Figure 2-20: Red 40% and Green 60%.

Red 70% • Green 40%

Figure 2-21: Red 70% and Green 40%.

Green 100%

Figure 2-22: All Green.

Red 100%

Figure 2-23: All Red.

| Red 100% | Green 100% | R 70% • G 30% | R 40% • G 60% |

Figure 2-24: Comparing the four Channel Mixer adjustment layers.

Chapter 3: Retouching Photographs of People

In This Chapter

↙ **Understanding why retouching happens**

↙ **Making retouching strategy maps**

↙ **Enhancing eyes, whitening teeth**

↙ **Copying visible layers**

*T*his chapter introduces you to retouching people. You discover why retouching happens in the first place and its importance to portraits. You see the difference that professional makeup adds to a photograph. You discover how to make your own retouching strategy maps. You explore techniques to enhance eyes, whiten teeth, and smooth skin. You consolidate your efforts by copying the visible layers to a new layer before continuing the edits.

Debunking the Vanity Myth

Why are photographs retouched? The answer that comes immediately to mind is, "Vanity." And I am sure that can be part of it. Another reason is the very nature of a photographic portrait. It is a frozen moment in time that is enlarged to nearly life size and sometimes even bigger. It does not move. It can be examined very close up (much closer than you would dare look at the person in a social situation) for as long as the viewer wants to and even with a magnifying glass, for heaven's sake. This doesn't happen in any other photographic medium. Videos, television, and motion pictures control how long we see the people on the screen and how close we are to them as well. Add to that the distractions of movement and dialog. We can't notice imperfections readily. The same holds true in life. When you talk to a person, she or he is at least a couple of feet away. You look at the eyes and lips. You concentrate on what is being said. You don't really notice the little imperfections of circles under the eyes, or crow's feet next to the eyes, or deep laugh lines.

A photograph removes social distance, viewing time, verbal personality, and motion from the experience. The viewer is free to examine the photograph and the "flaws" that aren't seen for the distractions in life as close and for as long as she or he wants. You, the viewer of the photograph, could even use a magnifying glass — something you would not consider doing in person with someone you know casually.

Figure 3-1: Pre-makeup clean face and hair.

Making Up a Difference

Professional makeup is really important when taking photographs of women — and it doesn't hurt when shooting men. Women understand the value of makeup. Younger men in their twenties and early thirties are getting the idea as well. Men who are older see it as an affectation or even effeminate behavior. Sometimes you can get them to hold still for powder at least. Sometimes not.

A large makeup brush with powder brushed over a man's face not only reduces shine, it gentles them, too. Most men have never experienced how good a makeup brush feels on the face. Do it with a clean brush! The men will love how good it feels. They might even let you put a little powder on the brush.

Figure 3-2: With makeup.

Face and hair start clean. Figure 3-1 shows a well-rested model ready for the makeup chair. Starting clean lets the makeup artist build the look without compromise. Figure 3-2 is of the model after hair and makeup. Already you see a big difference! Finally, look at Figure 3-3. Here the retouching is finished. The model is beautiful in all three photographs. The retouched version gives a view of who she would be were you chatting with her at a party.

Figure 3-3: After retouching.

Mapping Out Your Strategy

A *strategy map* shows the work you need to do on the photograph. The map is made on its own layer so it can be shown or hidden. Strategy maps serve three important purposes:

✔ When made with a client present, it is an agreement on the work being done.

✔ It serves as a guide for the work to be completed.

✔ It is a reference that shows if the work has been completed. You see how this works later in the chapter.

Now you open the photograph shown in Figure 3-2, create your own strategy map, and make a retouching layer.

1. **Go to www.amesphoto.com/learning and download the files for Book V, Chapter 3.**

   The code to go to the login/registration page is 4D59776. If you have not registered, you are asked to. Your user name is your valid email address. If you have already registered, you are asked for your password.

2. **Open the file Cheryl.psd.**

   Navigate to the downloaded folder in Bridge. Double-click the file's thumbnail to open it in Photoshop CS2.

3. **Click the New Layer icon at the bottom of the Layers palette.**

   The function of each of the icons at the bottom of the Layers palette is shown in Figure 3-4.

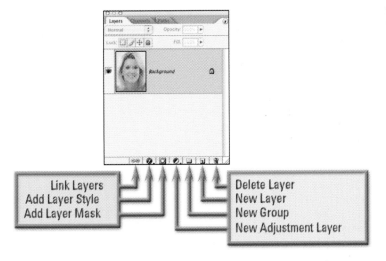

Figure 3-4: The icons at the bottom of the Layers palette.

4. **Double-click the words Layer 1, type in** Strategy Map, **and press Enter.**

5. **Click+hold the Brush palette. Choose the Pencil Tool, as shown in Figure 3-5.**

6. **Double-click the foreground color in the toolbox to open Photoshop's Color Picker.**

7. **Enter these settings:**

   • **R:** 0.

   • **G:** 255.

   • **B:** 0.

   Figure 3-6 shows the settings circled in red.

8. **Click OK.**

9. **Click the Brush menu in the options bar.**

10. **Drag the Master Diameter slider until the window says 5 px and press Return.**

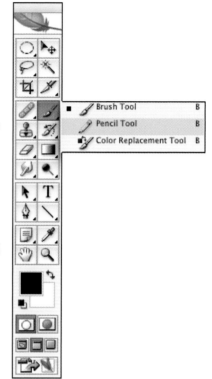

Figure 3-5: Choosing the Pencil Tool.

Alternative to the slider, you could type **5** in the textbox. Pressing Return (or clicking a blank area of the options bar) closes the Brush menu. The Pencil Tool, whose diameter you just set, is always hard edged.

11. **Choose View⇨Actual Pixels and enter** 100% **in the Navigator palette.**

    As an alternative, you can press ⌘+Option+0 (Ctrl+Alt+0).

12. **Draw around the areas that will be retouched.**

    You've just created your strategy map. Refer to Figure 3-7 for the areas you will be retouching. Now you make a retouching layer.

    It is important to protect the Background layer. Always make a copy of the Background layer and work on the copy. Book IV, Chapter 4 tells you how to do this.

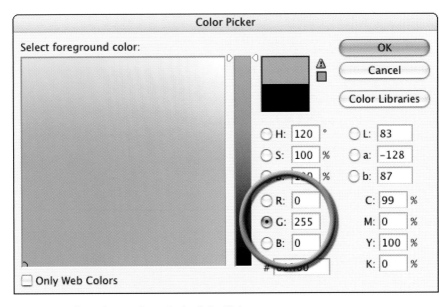

Figure 3-6: Selecting 255 Green in the Color Picker.

13. **Click the Background layer thumbnail to make it active.**

14. **Choose Layer⇨New⇨Layer Via Copy.**

    Alternatively, you can press ⌘+J (Ctrl+J).

15. **Double-click the words Background Copy and type** Retouch; **press Enter.**

    Continue with this file through the next section.

TIP

On retouching

Retouching is meant to be subtle. You see in this chapter how easy it is to overdo brightening eyes and teeth and removing lines. Use good judgment in applying the techniques you read here. If that little voice inside says, "That's a little much...," pay attention and back off a bit. The reward is knowing how much you have helped the photograph while no one else notices.

Figure 3-7: The strategy map.

Outlining How It's Done

Lines on the face are really shadows. Removing them is fine for women in their twenties. Later in life, getting rid of them completely looks fake and plastic. So you start by getting rid of them completely. You bring them back later in the project.

Softening lines

The layer Retouch is active. Get started:

1. **Choose the Healing Brush from the toolbox.**

   The icon is shown in Figure 3-8.

2. **Choose these settings in the options bar:**
   - **Hardness:** 100%.
   - **Brush:** 10.
   - **Mode: Normal.**
   - **Source radio button: Selected.**
   - **Aligned checkbox: Not selected.**
   - **Sample All Layers checkbox: Not selected.**

Figure 3-8: The Healing Brush's options bar settings.

Healing the lines

The following steps show you how to sample an area of clear skin, stroke, and the direction of each healing operation used on her left (your right) eye. Each step has two figures. A figure with a number 1 circled in red shows the healing brush sample point with a + sign and the point where you begin the healing stroke (circled +). A figure with a number 2 circled in red shows the end of the stroke. The + sign shows where the healing stroke is sampling. As you stroke with the healing brush, the + moves in alignment with the brush.

Enter Photoshop's preferences by typing ⌘+K (Ctrl+K). From the menu in the upper-left corner, choose Display & Cursors. (It says General when you first open preferences.) Click Show Full Size Brush Tip and Show Crosshair in Brush Tip. In the Other Cursors section, click the Precise button.

The Sample cursor, shown in Figure 3-9, appears when you press the Option (Alt) key. Move the cursor over the point you want to sample — usually an area of clear skin — and then click the mouse button.

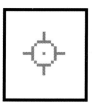

Figure 3-9: The Sample cursor.

1. **Click the eye icon of the layer Strategy Map to hide the layer.**

2. **Make sure that the layer Retouch is active.**

   Your layer stack looks like the one in Figure 3-10.

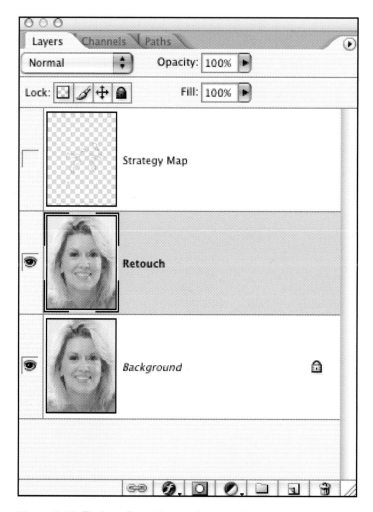

Figure 3-10: The layer Retouch ready for retouching.

3. **Sample the point shown in Figure 3-11.**

4. **Position the Healing brush as indicated by the brush cursor. Brush over the line and stop at the point shown in Figure 3-12.**

   Refer to Figure 3-13 for the sample point and Healing brush starting position.

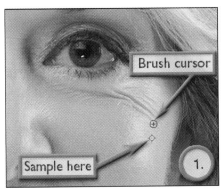

Figure 3-11: Begin the retouch.

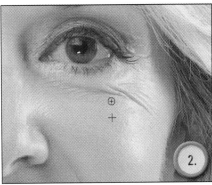

Figure 3-12: The healing stroke.

5. **Heal along the line, stopping as shown in Figure 3-14.**

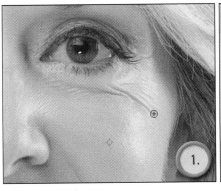

Figure 3-13: Sample . . .

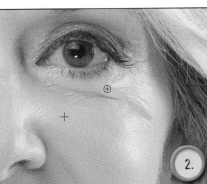

Figure 3-14: . . . and heal.

6. Heal under Cheryl's eye.

Refer to Figure 3-15 for the starting positions and to Figure 3-16 for where to stop.

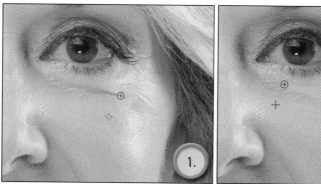

Figure 3-15: Sample . . .   Figure 3-16: . . . and heal under Cheryl's eye.

7. Heal the texture under Cheryl's eye.

Figures 3-17 and 3-18 illustrate the sample point and the healed area. Now you heal the artifact left by the healing brush from Step 4. *Artifacts* are unwanted results from retouching. Now sample on the edge of the highlight on Cheryl's cheek.

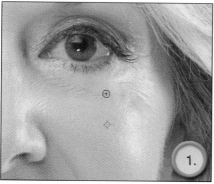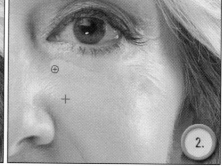

Figure 3-17: The sample begins here.   Figure 3-18: Healing the artifact from Step 4.

8. **Position the Healing brush at the right edge of the artifact, move the brush over it until it's covered, and release the mouse button.**

   Sample and starting points are shown in Figure 3-19. The completed Healing stroke is depicted in Figure 3-20. Now you heal the line to the right of Cheryl's eye.

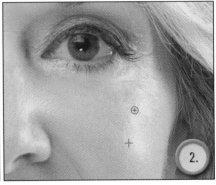

Figure 3-19: The sample of clear skin is at the edge of the highlight.

Figure 3-20: Center the cursor on the edge of the highlight and heal the line.

9. **Position the cursor on the edge of the shadow and sample, as shown in Figure 3-21.**

10. **Move the Healing brush into the eyelid and release the mouse button, as shown in Figure 3-22.**

    Next you sample on Cheryl's cheek. See Figure 3-23 for the sample point.

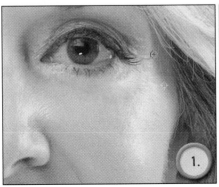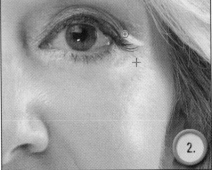

Figure 3-21: Sample on the edge of the shadow . . .

Figure 3-22: . . . and heal into the eyelid.

11. Place the Healing brush on the line you see in Figure 3-23 and heal to the right.

The stroke is shown in Figure 3-24.

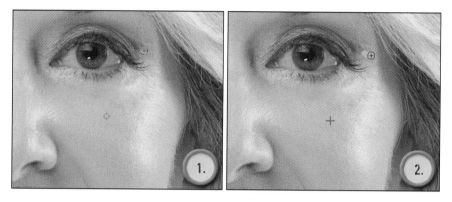

Figure 3-23: Sample clear skin on Cheryl's cheek . . .   **Figure 3-24:** . . . and heal the eyelid here.

12. Heal the other eye.

By now you have a good idea of how the Healing brush works. On your own, heal the lines on Cheryl's right (your left) eye. This is great practice. When you finish, your work will look like Figure 3-25. Keep this file open to continue working through the next section.

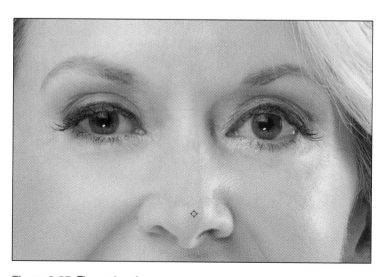

Figure 3-25: The work so far.

Bringing back some lines

As I said before, no lines on a person's face at all is really unbelievable. You want some of them and you want to be able to change your mind, especially when you show your model your work. This is nondestructive Photoshop, remember? The layer Retouch is active in the layer stack if you followed the instructions in the preceding section.

1. **Click the triangle in the blue box next to Opacity in the Layers palette.**

2. **Move the Opacity slider to the left until its window reads 65%.**

   Your Layers palette looks like the one in Figure 3-26. The Opacity window and slider are circled in red. Look at your screen and Figure 3-27. There are subtle traces of the original lines. This is what you would expect to notice subliminally if you were talking to Cheryl in person.

3. **Rename the Retouch layer** Soften Lines—Eyes.

   You do this since the Retouch layer really only softens the lines around Cheryl's eyes. Keep your file open to continue working.

Renaming layers with descriptive information helps you remember what each layer does when you want to reedit a photograph. This saves lots of time and brain work.

Figure 3-26: Lower the opacity to bring back a hint of the lines.

Figure 3-27: Soft lines are beautiful.

Softening Laugh Lines with Nondestructive Editing

The laugh lines in Figure 3-2 are also a bit pronounced. You use a similar technique after setting up a new Retouching layer. You need to copy the visible layers to a new layer. There are two ways to do this technique: the Hard Way and the Way Easy Way.

Copying visible layers the hard way

First, a new retouch layer the Hard Way:

1. **Be sure that the layer Soften Lines—Eyes is active.**

2. **Click the Create New Layer icon at the bottom of the Layers palette to make a new layer.**

   Look back at Figure 3-4 to locate the icon.

3. **Press Option+click the Layers palette menu disclosure triangle.**

4. **Choose Merge Visible.**

   The disclosure triangle is circled in red in Figure 3-28. Keep your file open as you work through the next section.

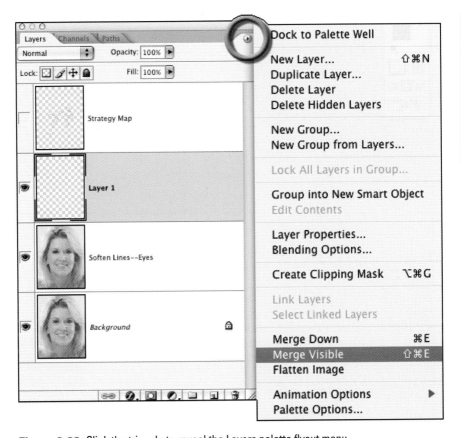

Figure 3-28: Click the triangle to reveal the Layers palette flyout menu.

Copying visible layers the way easy way

Copying the visible layers to a new layer doesn't have to take all the work of the previous steps. There is a keyboard shortcut. I know by now you are totally surprised that I would mention shortcuts. Anyway, it's done by holding down the entire left side of the keyboard and typing E. Alright, maybe it isn't the entire left side of the keyboard, and it is a great way to remember.

To copy visible layers to a new layer, press ⌘+Option+Shift+E (Ctrl+Alt+ Shift+E). Memorize this one. It's an amazing timesaver and is one of my top-10 shortcuts.

Okay, choose your favorite method and move on:

1. **Rename Layer 1** Retouch.

   The layers Background and Soften Lines—Eyes have been copied to the new layer, which you renamed Retouch. Your layer stack looks like the one in Figure 3-29.

2. **Set the Healing brush to a 20-pixel size.**

3. **Sample on Cheryl's right (your left) cheek at the bottom of the laugh line.**

   Figure 3-30 shows you the starting point for the Healing brush, too.

4. **Heal the area shown in Figure 3-31.**

   This only works for the most recent stroke of the Healing brush (or any other tool in Photoshop, for that matter). Do all of your work without lifting the mouse button until you have covered the entire area to be healed.

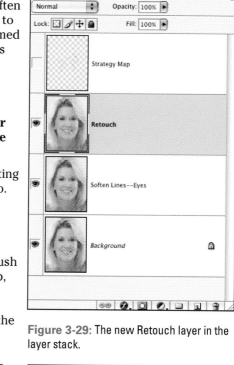

Figure 3-29: The new Retouch layer in the layer stack.

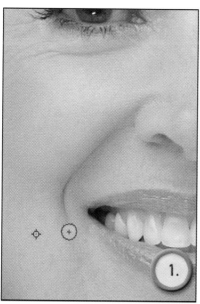

Figure 3-30: Start here . . .

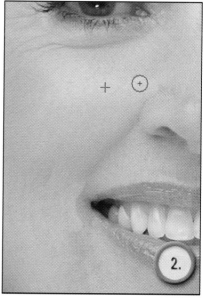

Figure 3-31: . . . and heal here.

5. Select Edit➪Fade Healing Brush from the Photoshop menu.

Refer to Figure 3-32.

6. Set Opacity to 40%.

Notice that you can preview the effect by clicking the Preview checkbox shown in Figure 3-33.

7. Heal the laugh line on Cheryl's left (your right) side and sample Cheryl's cheek to the right of the bottom of the laugh line.

Begin healing from the bottom, all the way up the line to the edge of her nose. Keep your file open to continue working in the next section.

The light comes from your right, so the laugh line on that side is already lighter. The fade amount will be less. In this case it is around 50%. Work the slider until the effect looks right to you.

**Book V
Chapter 3**

Retouching Photographs of People

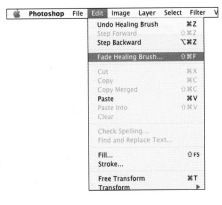

Figure 3-32: Choose Fade Healing Brush.

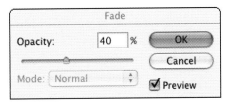

Figure 3-33: Check the effect by selecting Preview.

Removing a flyaway or two

It is a very good idea to examine your portraits at 100% pixels. Get there with View➪Actual Pixels or ⌘+Option+0 (Ctrl+Alt+0). At that magnification you are well within the subject's personal space. This close-up view shows you the retouching you want to do. See the two blonde hairs that cross Cheryl's eyebrow in Figure 3-34?

This Healing brush technique requires careful choice of the sample point and precise alignment of the brush afterwards.

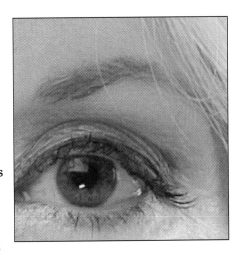

Figure 3-34: The two flyaway hairs.

1. Click the Navigator palette tab or choose Window➪Navigator.

The Navigator palette is grouped with the Info and the Histogram palettes.

2. **Enter** 200% **in the size window and press Enter.**

   The Navigator's preview shows the area of the screen in the red rectangle in Figure 3-35.

3. **Get a 10-pixel brush. Sample on the top edge of Cheryl's eyebrow.**

4. **Heal into the eyebrow on the first part of the stroke; go back over the eyebrow and heal into the skin on Cheryl's forehead.**

TIP

   Figure 3-36 shows the sample point and where to begin healing. Heal into the eyebrow on the first part of the stroke; go back over the eyebrow and heal into the skin on Cheryl's forehead as you see in Figure 3-37. The sample point of the Healing brush stays aligned with the brush tip as you go over an area. Healing down into the eyebrow, back up over the same

Figure 3-35: 200% view in the Navigator palette.

area, and out into the forehead does not cause overhealing, or a *build up,* of the effect in the eyebrow as long as it is a single stroke.

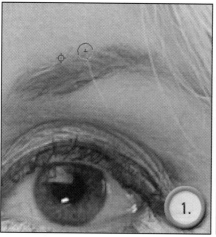

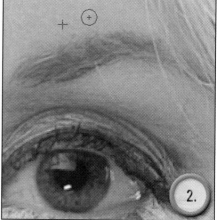

Figure 3-36: Sample on the eyebrow's edge, center the brush on the edge over the hair . . .

Figure 3-37: . . . and heal into the eyebrow, then out and into the skin in one stroke.

5. **Sample at the bottom edge of Cheryl's eyebrow; heal down into the upper part of skin over Cheryl's eye.**

Refer to Figure 3-38 for the sample and starting points. Figure 3-39 shows the healing points.

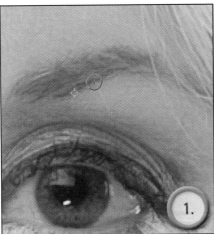

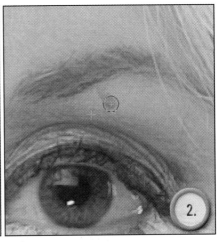

Figure 3-38: Sample on the lower edge of the eyebrow . . .

Figure 3-39: . . . and center the cursor over the hair on the edge and heal into the skin.

6. **Repeat the process on the remaining hair; heal the hairs to just below the other hair.**

Your finished part of this section looks like Figure 3-40.

7. **Heal the line on the bridge of Cheryl's nose.**

Sample in the middle just below the line. Start in the middle and heal back and forth. These are the finishing touches.

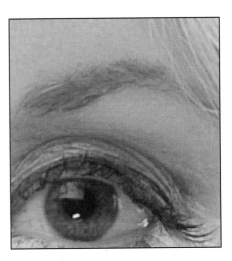

Figure 3-40: The finished eyebrow.

Checking Your Work with the Strategy Map

Now check what you have accomplished using the strategy map. Here's how:

1. **Choose View⇨Actual Pixels.**

   Alternatively, you can ⌘+Option+0 (Ctrl+Alt+0).

2. **Click the eye icon on the layer Strategy Map to reveal the layer.**

3. **Click the eye icon on each of the Soften Lines—Eyes and Retouch layers to hide those layers.**

   Your screen and layer stack are like the one in Figure 3-41. Look closely at Figure 3-41. You see the strategy map overlaying the Background layer. This is the Before retouching view.

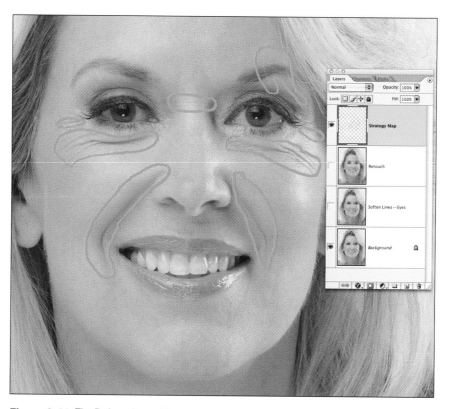

Figure 3-41: The Before view with strategy map.

4. **Click the Retouch layer's eye icon to show the layer.**

5. **Look carefully at the areas circled in the strategy map in Figure 3-42.**

   Every circle will change if all of the work is finished.

6. **Click on and off the eye icon of layer Retouch.**

   You see the circled area jump, indicating the work is complete. If nothing happens inside a circle, hide the strategy map and finish retouching.

7. **Check your work using the before and after technique you have just used.**

8. **Save your work.**

   Your work here is done. The final is shown in Figure 3-43.

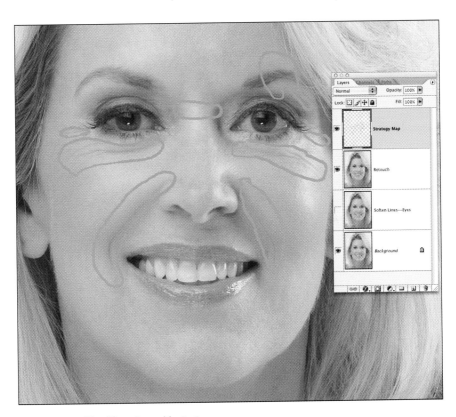

Figure 3-42: The After view with strategy map.

Figure 3-43: Your work here is done!

Cleaning up the Windows to the Soul

When the art historians of a future time look back on the dawn of digital retouching they will shake their heads at most of the work and say, "Didn't they know that the whites of the eyes are really gray?"

Eye enhancement is about contrast and brightness. The pupil wants to be as dark as possible (while remaining believable) and the irises want to be brighter, again believably. This project shows you how to do both. You use the photograph of Gabriella.

Darkening the pupils

You use an adjustment layer and the multiply blending mode to increase the contrast of the pupils.

1. **Go to www.amesphoto.com/ learning and download the files for Book V, Chapter 3 if you haven't already.**

   The code to go to the login/ registration page is 4D59776. If you have not registered, you are asked to. If you have already registered, you are asked for your password.

2. **Open Gabriella.psd.**

3. **Make your layer stack look like the one in Figure 3-44. Make sure the layer Retouch is active.**

4. **Click the New Adjustment Layer icon at the bottom of the Layers palette.**

   Refer to Figure 3-4 for a description of the icons at the bottom of the Layers palette. Read more about adding adjustment layers in Book IV, Chapter 4.

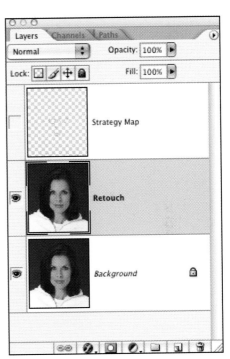

Figure 3-44: Gabriella.psd's layer stack.

5. **Choose Curves and click OK in the Curves dialog.**

6. **Rename the Curves 1 layer Pupils.**

7. **Choose Blending Mode⇨ Multiply.**

Multiply is circled in red in Figure 3-45, which shows what your layer stack looks. Don't freak! Yes, the photograph of Gabriella got really dark. That's the effect of the Curves layer in the Multiply blending mode. It makes everything darker. This is good to know and great to remember.

8. **Choose Edit⇨Fill⇨Black.**

9. **Set the Opacity at 100% and click OK.**

The Fill dialog settings are shown in Figure 3-46. The photograph of Gabriella looks normal again.

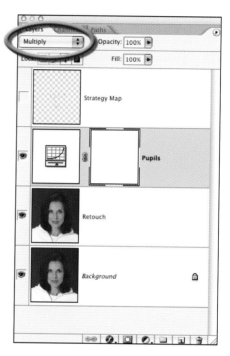

Figure 3-45: Setting the layer Pupils blending mode to Multiply.

10. **Zoom in 400% by choosing ⌘+Option+0 (Ctrl+Alt+0), then pressing ⌘++ (Ctrl++) three times.**

You see the zoom percentage in the Navigator palette circled in Figure 3-47.

11. **Select the Brush Tool and set it at 10 pixels.**

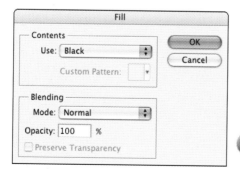

Figure 3-46: The Fill dialog.

Figure 3-47: The 400% view.

12. **Click the Brush drop-down menu in the options bar. Type** 50 **in the Hardness window.**

    You see the Hardness window circled in red in Figure 3-48.

13. **Click in a clear area of the options bar to close the menu.**

14. **Set the brush opacity to** 100% **in the options bar.**

15. **Set the foreground color to white.**

    If you've followed the preceding steps, you really know a lot about Photoshop by getting this far. Congratulations. From now on steps will be worded something like this: "Get a 10-pixel brush with 50% hardness at 100% opacity. Set white as the foreground color."

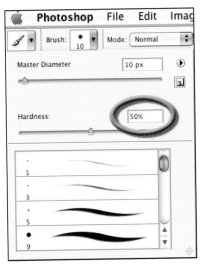

Figure 3-48: The Paint Brush options.

16. **Paint with white over Gabriella's pupil.**

    Her pupil gets really dark, as shown in Figure 3-49.

17. **Darken her other pupil.**

18. **Get a 2-pixel brush, set Opacity to** 50%, **and set Hardness to** 0%.

19. **Paint white on the layer mask of Pupils over the black line, around the iris.**

    Use a single stroke to go all the way around the iris, which you see in progress in Figure 3-50. If you lift the mouse button, there will be a darker area where the strokes overlap. Not good.

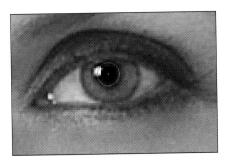

Figure 3-49: Darkening Gabriella's pupil.

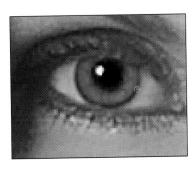

Figure 3-50: The 50% line darkens the edge of her pupil.

20. Repeat on the other iris.

Continue working on this file through the next section.

Blending the enhancement of the pupils and iris edge

Now you blend the pupil work.

1. Option+click (Alt+click) inside the layer mask.

The layer mask replaces the photograph of Gabriella on the screen. You see the paint you have applied and how the enhancement looks in the photograph in Figure 3-51.

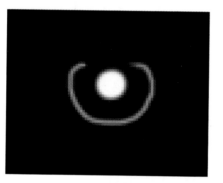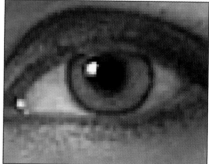

Layer mask as painted

Figure 3-51: The layer mask revealed.

2. Choose Filter➪Blur➪ Gaussian Blur.

3. Enter .9 in the Radius window of the dialog shown in Figure 3-52.

4. Click OK.

The filter subtly blurs the paint on the layer mask. Compare the effect shown in Figure 3-53 to the original layer mask in Figure 3-51. Keep on going with this file.

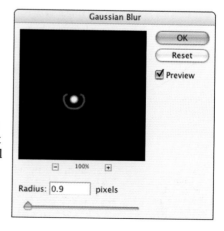

Figure 3-52: Blurring the line and pupil, too.

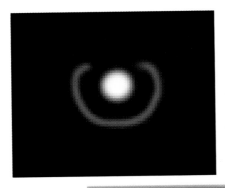
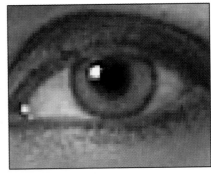

Layer mask blurred .9 pixels

Figure 3-53: Softer and more subtle.

Brightening the irises

This section is almost exactly like darkening the pupils. The blending mode of the Curves layer changes, as does where you paint. Everything else is the same. The steps that follow are combined. If you don't remember exactly how to do a step, refer to the previous section.

1. **Make a new Curves adjustment layer. Rename it** Irises.

2. **Change the blending mode of Irises to Screen.**

   The photograph of Gabriella gets instantly brighter. The Screen blending mode makes the image on the screen a lot lighter. Your layer stack looks like Figure 3-54, which shows Screen circled in red.

3. **Change the layer mask of Irises from white to black.**

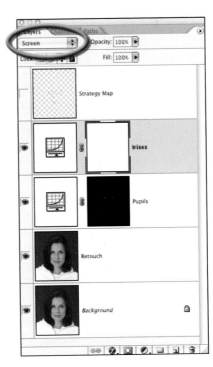

Figure 3-54: The Curves layer Irises set to the Screen blending mode.

Here is another way that is a lot faster than filling the layer mask with black: Choose Image⇨Adjustments⇨Invert or press ⌘+I (Ctrl+I). You knew I would tell you the keyboard shortcut, didn't you?

4. **Set the brush opacity to** 100%, **with white as the foreground color.**

5. **Paint in the catch lights on both eyes.**

   Catch lights are reflections of the lights in the eye. They are circled in Figure 3-55. You won't see much change in the catch lights.

6. **Lower the brush opacity to** 50%.

7. **Paint in each iris using a single stroke to avoid paint buildup.**

   Check out Figure 3-56 to see the paint brightening up the irises.

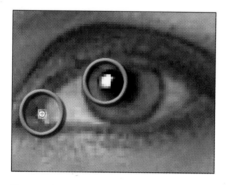

Figure 3-55: Brighten the catch lights with a 100% brush.

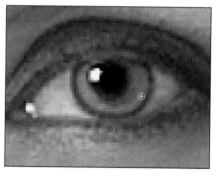

Figure 3-56: Brighten the iris with a 50% brush.

8. **Paint along the lower eyelid, from tear duct to outer eye, along the top edge of the lower lid.**

   Figure 3-57 shows you where to paint.

9. **Show the layer mask on Iris by Option+clicking (Alt+clicking) it.**

10. **Choose Filter⟹Blur⟹Gaussian Blur.**

    The .9 pixel blur is still in the Radius window.

11. **Click OK.**

    Again, the difference is very subtle. Keep moving with this file.

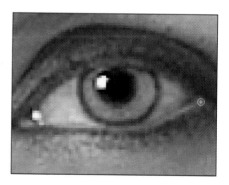

Figure 3-57: Lighten the top edge of the lower eyelid.

Photoshop is capable of making drastic and dramatic changes to a photograph. Usually that results in a poor image. Compare the layer mask as painted to the one blurred .9 pixels in Figure 3-58. Hard to see a difference? Good. That's what you want. Resist the temptation to overdo things.

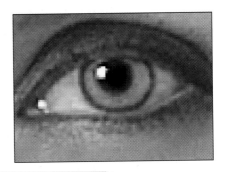

Layer mask as painted

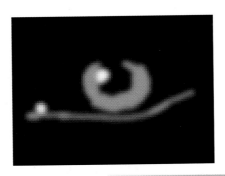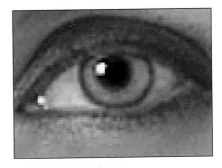

Layer mask blurred .9 pixels

Figure 3-58: Before and after blurring Irises's layer mask.

Reducing the intensity of the enhancements

In Figure 3-59, Gabriella's eyes look too bright and almost unworldly. This section is more of the subtle-is-better approach to Photoshop.

Figure 3-59: The too-bright eyes effect.

1. **Click the layer Irises.**

2. **Enter 50% in the Opacity window.**

   The window is circled in red in Figure 3-60. Alternatively, use the Opacity slider to set it at 50% — or use my favorite, the keyboard shortcut!

Use the keyboard to change the layer opacity. Start by choosing the Move tool from the toolbox; see the tool circled in Figure 3-61. The keyboard can set the opacity: 1 is 10% and 2 is 20%, so 5 is 50%. Numbers in between are set by typing the numbers quickly — 7 5 is 75%.

Figure 3-62 shows the before enhancement, full enhancement (100% opacity on the layers Pupils and Irises), and reduced eye enhancement (with the two layers at 50% opacity).

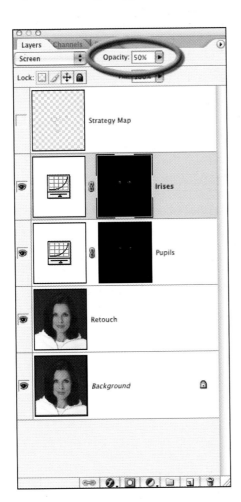

Figure 3-60: The Opacity window.

Figure 3-61:
The Move Tool.

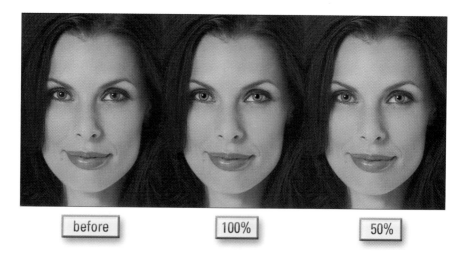

before   100%   50%

Figure 3-62: Eye enhancements compared.

Bucking the Dentist: Whitening Teeth

Getting white teeth used to require a trip to the dentist or Crest White Strips, at the very least. Now there's Photoshop. Whitening teeth is a two-part process using what you know about layer masks if you've followed along, and introducing you to a new adjustment layer: Hue/Saturation.

Brightening

This technique is the same as with brightening the irises in the previous section.

1. **If you haven't already go to www. amesphoto.com/learning and download the files for Book V, Chapter 3.**

   The code to go to the login/ registration page is 4D59776. If you have not registered, you are asked to. If you have already registered, you are asked for your password.

2. **Open Terry.psd.**

   Terry has a great smile in Figure 3-63. His teeth want a little work. They have a yellow cast and are dull in the photograph.

Figure 3-63: The teeth.

3. **Choose New Adjustment Layer icon⇨Curves⇨OK.**

4. **Rename Curves 1 Brighten.**

5. **Change the blending mode of Brightening to Screen.**

6. **Press ⌘+I (Ctrl+I) to invert the layer mask from white to black.**

   Your layer stack looks like the one in Figure 3-64, which circles the blending mode in red.

7. **Get a 10-pixel, soft-edged brush at 100% opacity.**

8. **Set white as the foreground color.**

   Work at 200% view when painting the layer mask.

9. **Paint over Terry's teeth.**

   They become very bright.
   Remember, you paint on a layer mask and lower the layer's opacity to the appropriate brightness later. Paint carefully. This layer mask is used on another adjustment layer later in the project. Your work looks like Figure 3-65 when you are finished.

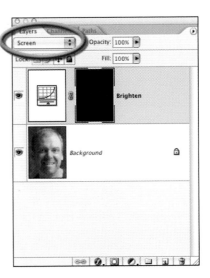

Figure 3-64: The Brighten layer set to Screen blending mode.

Figure 3-65: Bright teeth layer mask.

When you "paint outside the lines," press the X key to exchange the colors in the toolbox, making black the foreground color. Paint out the mistake. Type X again to make white the foreground color and continue.

Whitening

Now that the brightening mask is finished, you use a new adjustment layer: Hue/Saturation.

1. **Choose New Adjustment layer icon⇨Hue/Saturation⇨OK.**

2. **Rename the new adjustment layer** Whiten.

3. **Ctrl+click (right-click) the layer mask.**

   This brings up the contextual menu.

4. **Choose Delete Layer Mask, as shown in Figure 3-66.**

   Now you copy the layer mask on Brightening to Whiten.

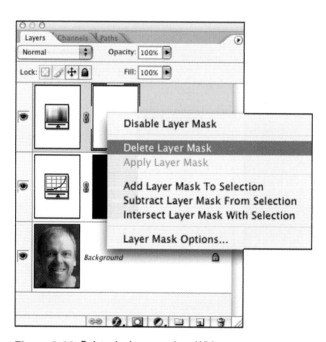

Figure 3-66: Delete the layer mask on Whiten.

5. **Option+click (Alt+click) inside the layer mask icon on the layer Brightening.**

6. **Drag the layer mask to Whiten.**

A double-arrow cursor shows that you are copying the layer mask. A black border appears around the layer Whiten when it is ready to receive the new layer mask. This black border is shown in Figure 3-67.

7. **Click Brighten's eye icon to hide it.**

Your layer stack now is shown in Figure 3-68.

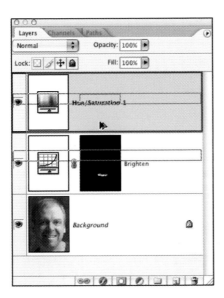

Figure 3-67: Copying a layer mask.

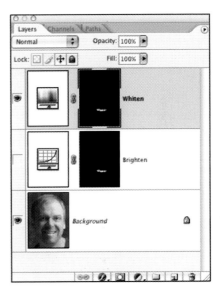

Figure 3-68: The layer stack ready to whiten Terry's teeth.

8. **Double-click the Whiten thumbnail to open the Hue/Saturation adjustment layer dialog.**

9. **Drag the Saturation slider to the left until it reads –35, as you see indicated in Figure 3-69.**

10. **Click OK.**

Terry's teeth no longer have that yellowish cast.

Figure 3-69: Lower the saturation.

Brightening and whitening

Together at last.

1. **Show the layer Brighten.**

   Whoa! Way too bright! See Figure 3-71.

2. **Lower the opacity of Brighten to** 20%.

   That's better. The layer stack is shown in Figure 3-70. The completed brighter-, whiter-toothed photograph of Terry is shown in Figure 3-72!

The watchword for quality retouching is *subtle.* This chapter opens the doors to several useful techniques that when applied lightly make your photographs appear as if the person were in the room with you.

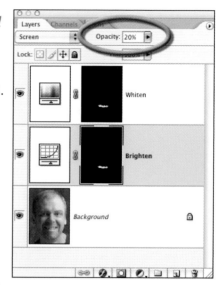

Figure 3-70: Lower the opacity of the layer Brighten.

Figure 3-71: A smile so bright you have to wear shades!

Figure 3-72: White and bright.

Chapter 4: Getting What You See Onscreen to Come Out in Print

In This Chapter

✔ **Calibrating your monitor**

✔ **Understanding color profiles**

✔ **Applying color profiles in Adobe Photoshop CS2**

*T*his chapter is color management lite. It is the absolute minimum you want to know in order for your prints to look like your screen. You discover your monitor type and how to calibrate it and discover why calibration is important. You read about color profiles, as well as discover what you need to make your own, have them made for you, or download them from web sites. You apply the color profile to a copy of the photograph before you print it.

Calibrating Your Monitor

Monitor calibration is important. Once a monitor is *calibrated,* Photoshop knows how it displays color and can present the colors of your photograph on the screen accurately. Popular calibration software is manufactured by Gretag Macbeth and X-rite. I show you calibration using the X-rite Pulse package, which calibrates monitors either glass screen (CRT) or flat panel (LCD). To get this right, first install the software that came with your monitor calibration package.

Color monitors come in two types. They are *CRT (cathode ray tube)* and *LCD (liquid crystal display).* The CRT is big, deep, and has a screen made of glass. The LCD is a flat panel and sports a delicate plastic cover over the liquid crystals. Knowing if your monitor is CRT or LCD lets you know how to attach the calibration sensor to the screen.

Calibration sensors, or *pucks,* have a suction cup for use on the glass screen of a CRT. They also come with a weight that allows you to gently (and I do mean gently) hang the puck against the LCD panel.

Never, never, never, ever use a suction cup on an LCD panel! You will ruin the LCD monitor if you do.

Follow the onscreen instructions presented by the software calibration package. For Gamma, choose 2.2. *Gamma* is how the monitor translates digital information for the viewing environment. Over time, a Gamma of 2.2 has become standard. For white point or color temperature, choose D-65. This is a slightly bluer white point and, again, has evolved into an accepted starting point. Figure 4-1 shows a puck reading a patch on an LCD panel. The software displays a series of known color patches that the puck reads. The information about the actual color the monitor displays is compared to the color of the patch. The software can then produce a profile or color translator that Photoshop uses to present accurate color on the monitor.

Turn off any energy-saving settings for your monitor before you begin calibration. You do not want your screen saver to activate while you're calibrating. Talk about a confused puck. Also, calibrate in a darkened room with as little ambient light as possible.

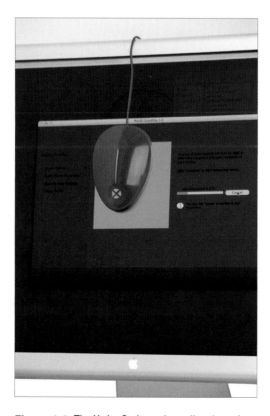

Figure 4-1: The X-rite Optix puck reading the color patches on an LCD monitor.

Understanding Color Profiles

Color profiles are simply translation packages that tell your printer what to do with the color Photoshop sends it. You can make your own with packages with the X-Rite Pulse or the Gretag Macbeth Eye-One.

The profiling systems include a *spectrophotometer,* which reads the colors your printer prints, and software to build a profile. Figure 4-2 shows the X-rite Pulse spectrophotometer reading a printer's color patches in preparation for creating a profile.

You can also contact color management experts in your area to build a profile for your printer and paper. Search the Internet with **color management** for more. The most popular way to get a profile for your printer and paper is to download it. Go to your printer manufacturer's web site for more information. These profiles are the least accurate. They are much, much better than no profile at all!

Figure 4-2: Reading color patches with the X-rite Pulse.

Applying Color Profiles and Printing

You have finished shooting and choosing, and all of your editing in Photoshop is finished. It's time to make a print. Here's how:

1. **Choose Image⇨Duplicate from the Photoshop menu to duplicate your file.** The dialog is filled in with the name of your file and adds the word *copy.*

You never apply a profile to your working file. *Profiles* change the color of the file to what the printer needs to see to make a print that looks like what you see on your screen. This color shift is great for output and very bad for your working file. Always apply the profile to a copy of the working file.

2. **Click OK.**

3. **Choose Layer⇨Flatten Image.**

That puts all of the layers into the background layer. That's why you want to work on a copy. If you did this to your original, all of your nondestructive work is lost. Book V, Chapter 1 talks more about nondestructive editing.

4. **Choose File⇨Print with Preview from the Photoshop menu bar.**

5. **Click the More Options button if you don't see the whole dialog.**

The button is circled in red in Figure 4-3.

6. **Choose Color Management Options from the menu directly under the preview pane.**

7. **Choose these settings in the dialog:**

   • **In the Print area, click the Document button.**

   • **In the Options area, set Color Handling to Let Photoshop Determine Colors.**

8. **For Printer Profile, choose the profile you created, had made, or downloaded from the Printer Profile menu.**

9. **Set Rendering Intent to either Relative Colorimetric or Perceptual. Select the Black Point Compensation checkbox.**

Relative Colorimetric maps the colors as closely as possible from the original to the printer. Perceptual maps the colors according to the way you see the world with your eyes. Make a print with each one and decide which works better for you.

10. **Click Print.**

This brings up the Print dialog.

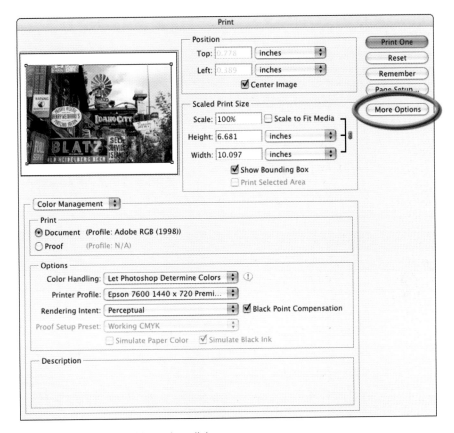

Figure 4-3: The Print, with preview, dialog.

11. **Select your printer from the Printer menu.**

    Different printers bring up different selections in the menu below the
    Presets menu.

12. **Look for Color Management or Color Options (or something else color
    related) in the Copies & Pages drop-down menu.**

13. **Choose No Color Adjustment, None, or Off depending on who makes
    your printer.**

14. **Click Print.**

This is an overview of how to get your photographs onto paper accurately.
Many books discuss how to manage color from camera to monitor to printer.
It is important to know that resources exist to help you realize the quality of
print that you want from your photo-quality printer.

Book VI
Appendixes

The 5th Wave   By Rich Tennant

©RICHTENNANT

IMAGE editor   PHOTO MAKER   GRAPH Accent   CAMERA SOFT   PICTURE CLICK   PHOTO

"...and here's me with Cindy Crawford. And this is me with Madonna and Celine Dion..."

These are the parts of a book that nobody reads and you are going to want to read anyway. Here you find the essential keyboard shortcuts that make using Photoshop fast and efficient. You find resources and links to manufacturers you read about in the book and where to go to further your understanding about digital photography and Adobe Photoshop CS2.

Appendix A: Resources

This compilation of the web sites I've listed throughout the book should be helpful when you're ordering equipment, want to read more about your DSLR camera, or want to know more about photography.

- Ames Photographic Illustration, Inc. (for downloading files): www.amesphoto.com/learning
- Avery (CD labels): www.avery.com
- ExpoDisc (color references): www.expodisc.com
- Giottos (tripods, cleaning tools): www.giottos.com
- GretagMacbeth (ColorCheckers): www.gretagmacbeth.com/indes/products_color-standards.htm
- Hakuba (memory card cases): www.hakubausa.com
- The Killers (music): www.thekillersmusic.com
- LaCie (hard drives): www.lacie.com
- Lensbaby (lenses): www.lensbaby.com
- Lightware (memory card wallets): www.lightwareinc.com
- Lowepro (memory card wallets): www.lowepro.com
- Manfrotto (tripods): www.bogenimaging.us
- Memorex (CD labels): www.memorex.com
- nik multimedia (special effects program): www.nikmultimedia.com
- Other World Computing (hard drives): www.macsales.com
- Professional Photo Resources: www.ppratlanta.com
- Professional Photographers of America: www.ppa.com
- REI stores (cold-weather gear): www.rei.com
- Tamrac (memory card wallets): www.tamrac.com
- U.S. Government (copyright information): www.copyright.gov
- Visible Dust (cleaning tools): www.visibledust.com
- Weather forecasts (lighting): www.weather.com
- WhiBal (color references): www.whibal.com

Appendix B: Kevin's Essential Photoshop Keyboard Shortcuts

Menu Shortcuts

Task	Mac Shortcut	Windows Shortcut
Save File	⌘+S	Ctrl+S
Save File As	⌘+Shift+S	Ctrl+Shift+S
Close File	⌘+W	Ctrl+W
Don't Save (for Save changes before closing dialog)	D	D
Close All Open Files	⌘+Option+W	Ctrl+Alt+W
Levels	⌘+L	Ctrl+L
Repeat Previous Levels Settings	⌘+Option+L	Ctrl+Alt+L
Curves	⌘+M	Ctrl+M
Repeat Previous Curves Settings	⌘+Option+M	Ctrl+Alt+M
Invert	⌘+I	Ctrl+I
New Document	⌘+N	Ctrl+N

Layers Palette

Task	Mac Shortcut	Windows Shortcut
New layer with New Layer dialog	⌘+Shift+N	Ctrl+Shift+N
New layer	⌘+Option+Shift+N	Ctrl+Alt+Shift+N
Merge down	⌘+E	Ctrl+E
Merge visible layers	⌘+Shift+E	Ctrl+Shift+E
Merge visible layers to active layer	⌘+Option+Shift+E	Ctrl+Alt+Shift+E
Copy a selection to a new layer	⌘+J	Ctrl+J
Cut a selection and paste to new layer	⌘+Shift+J	Ctrl+Shift+J
Cycle forward through blending modes (in the Move Tool)	Shift++	Shift++
Cycle backward through blending modes (in the Move Tool)	Shift+-	Shift+-

continued

Layers Palette *(continued)*

Layer opacity (in the Move Tool)	1 = 10%, 2 = 20%, . . . 0 = 100%. Two keys in rapid succession for numbers between (e.g. 24 = 24%).	
Create new layer and copy all visible layers to it	⌘+Option+Shift+E	Ctrl+Alt+Shift+E

Selections

Task	Mac Shortcut	Windows Shortcut
Select All	⌘+A	Ctrl+A
Deselect	⌘+D	Ctrl+D
Feather Selection	⌘+Option+D	Ctrl+Alt+D
Inverse Selection	⌘+Shift+I	Ctrl+Shift+I
Hide Selection	⌘+H	Ctrl+H
Luminosity Selection from RGB Composite	⌘+Option+~	Ctrl+Option+~

Tools

Shortcut	Tool
V	Move Tool
M	Marquee Tools
L	Lasso Tools
W	Magic Wand
C	Crop Tool
J	Healing, Patch, and Red Eye Tools
B	Brush and Pencil Tools
S	Clone and Pattern Stamp Tools
G	Gradient and Paint Bucket Tools
A	Path and Direct Selection Tools
P	Pen Tool and Freeform Pen Tool
T	Type Tool
U	Shape Tools
I	Eye Dropper, Color Sampler, and Measure Tools
Q	Quick Mask Mode

Shortcut	Tool
F	Full screen with menu bar (gray background) Full screen (black background) Standard (document window)
3 = 30%, 0 = 100%, 24 = 24%	0–9 changes tool opacity (instead of layer opacity) when available
[	Brush Size Smaller
]	Brush Size Larger
Shift+[	Brush Edge Softer (25% per stroke)
Shift+]	Brush Edge Harder (25% per stroke)

Here is a cool way to customize tool selection to eliminate having to hold down the Shift key to cycle between tools:

1. **Type ⌘+K (Ctrl+K) to open the General Preferences pane.**
2. **Deselect the Use Shift Key for Tool Switch checkbox.**

Here is a cool way to move between rectangular and elliptical Marquee tools:

1. **Press the M key.**
2. **Press the M key again.**

This is a huge timesaver.

Bonus Chapter 1: Beating the Shoebox Syndrome via Cataloging

In This Chapter

✓ **Keywording your digital negatives**

✓ **Creating a catalog**

✓ **Finding and seeing what you want**

*F*ace it. If you took photographs before digital came along, you have a shoebox somewhere on a shelf with prints and negatives in it. So how do you find that one print of Auntie Tilley's 69th birthday celebration in Lowman, Idaho, when your daughter was 9 and sat on the porch of the Southfork Lodge in, oh, was it 1985?

This question plagues photographers: How do I find that one print? Unfortunately, in the analog world of film and photographs, finding it meant you had to create and maintain a physical filing and cataloging system. The really very good news is that in these days of digital capture, cataloging and locating photographs is as simple as dragging and dropping if you set it up right in the first place.

This chapter confronts the demon of finding your digital photographs. You discover how to use simple words as keys to future searches. You create a catalog for your photography in Extensis Portfolio 7.0. You explore how to search for a cataloged photograph. Finally, you find out about the other options available in cataloging software.

Wording Is the Key

In Book II, Chapter 2, you read about naming image files and adding descriptions to the folders that hold them. These names and descriptions are a simple and powerful form of keywording. *Keywords* are indicators that computers use to find specific information.

When you drag your discs of digital negatives onto the cataloging window of any cataloging program (like Extensis Portfolio or iView Media Pro), the software automatically reads and records the keywords included in the image names and their folders. Additionally, the software adds the metadata created when you shoot the photograph. It can also include some data that you may add in Bridge.

The Metadata panel boxed in red in Figure 1-1 appears when you click the Metadata tab under the Preview pane in Bridge. It has submenus for File Properties, Camera Data (EXIF), and IPTC Core, and it adds a menu for Camera Raw when a RAW file is selected.

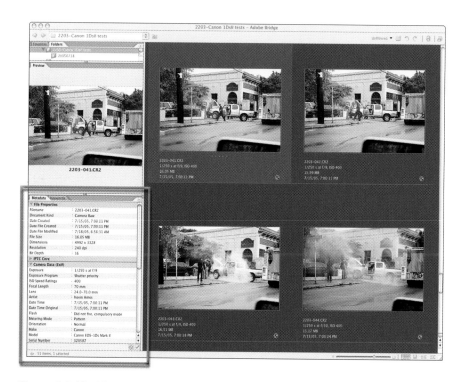

Figure 1-1: The Metadata panel.

Metadata is defined as data about data. In the context of digital photography, metadata is simply information about your image file. Digital cameras add information about the photographs you take, including the date and time it was shot, the aperture, shutter speed, format, file size in pixels, and more. Metadata added by your camera is called *EXIF (Exchangeable Image File Format)* data.

The Keywords tab has presets included by Adobe in Bridge. The preloaded keywords can be modified in the palette's flyout menu (shown in Figure 1-2). This is where you add information like Lowman, Southfork Lodge, and Aunt Tilley. You can keyword a group of files in Bridge by selecting a group of photographs, then clicking the check boxes to all the keywords you wish to use. The keywords are added to the file's metadata. You can remove keywords by unchecking the boxes.

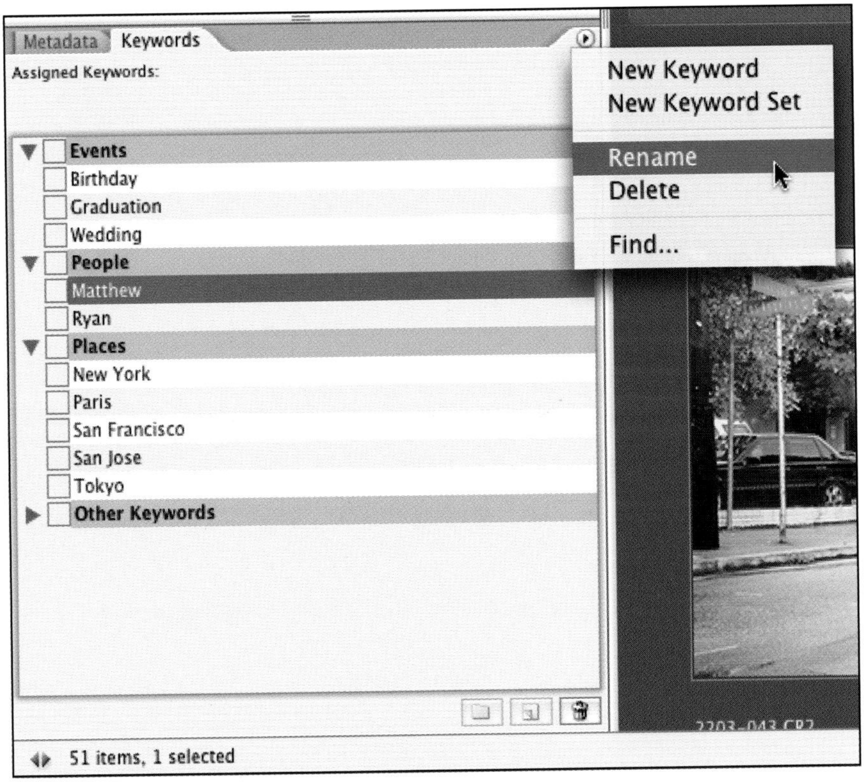

Figure 1-2: The Keywords tab.

Flipping Through the Catalog

It's easy to create a catalog of your digital photographs — and at least for 30 days it's free. Extensis has a trial version of its most excellent cataloging software, Portfolio 7.0, available on its Web site. Portfolio 7.0 works on both Mac and Windows.

It's easy to create your own catalog:

1. **Go to www.extensis.com and create an Extensis user account.**

   You have to create a user account to download the free trial. No credit card required!

2. **Click Download a Free Trial (in the I want to. . . section).**

3. **Open the trial version of Portfolio by double-clicking its icon.**

4. **When the software asks for a serial number, click the Demo button.**

   The Open dialog opens automatically, as shown in Figure 1-3.

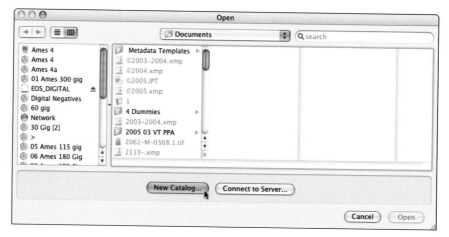

Figure 1-3: The New Catalog option in Portfolio's Open dialog.

5. **Click the New Catalog button.**

6. **Type a name for your new catalog in the Save As textbox; choose a place to save the catalog from the Where drop-down menu and click Save.**

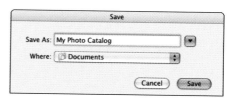

Figure 1-4: The Save dialog.

   Figure 1-4 shows the Save dialog.

7. **Leave the Enable Screen Previews checkbox selected and click Done, as shown in Figure 1-5.**

   Screen previews are very useful when reviewing your catalog. They allow you to preview the actual JPEG file you have cataloged. This is one use of many for the JPEG proofs created in Book III, Chapter 1.

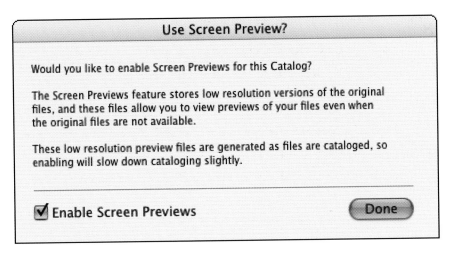

Figure 1-5: Choose to see screen previews.

8. Choose Catalog⇨Catalog Options from the Portfolio 7.0 menu bar to open the dialog in Figure 1-6.

Once this dialog is set up, click the Don't Show This Dialog When Cataloging checkbox. Otherwise, the dialog opens every time you catalog more photographs. You can get back to it from the Catalog menu.

Figure 1-6: The Portfolio 7.0 Cataloging Options dialog.

9. Click the Advanced button.

10. **Click the Thumbnail Size drop-down menu and choose 256 × 256.**

Figure 1-7 shows the Thumbnail Size menu circled in red.

11. **Make sure that Extract Thumbnails from Files and Do Not Catalog Items That Cannot Be Thumbnailed are unchecked. Click OK.**

You would think you'd want to extract the thumbnails from a file. And in fact that's what happens when this checkbox is left unchecked. Portfolio goes to the actual image data of the file and makes a brand new thumbnail. When selected, it pulls the thumbnail from the file's embedded thumbnail file, resulting in a really poor-quality preview.

12. **Click and drag the disc or folder onto the cataloging window shown in Figure 1-8.**

You're done. The Cataloging Status window appears; see Figure 1-9. It displays the files cataloged, which image is being cataloged, and where the file is stored.

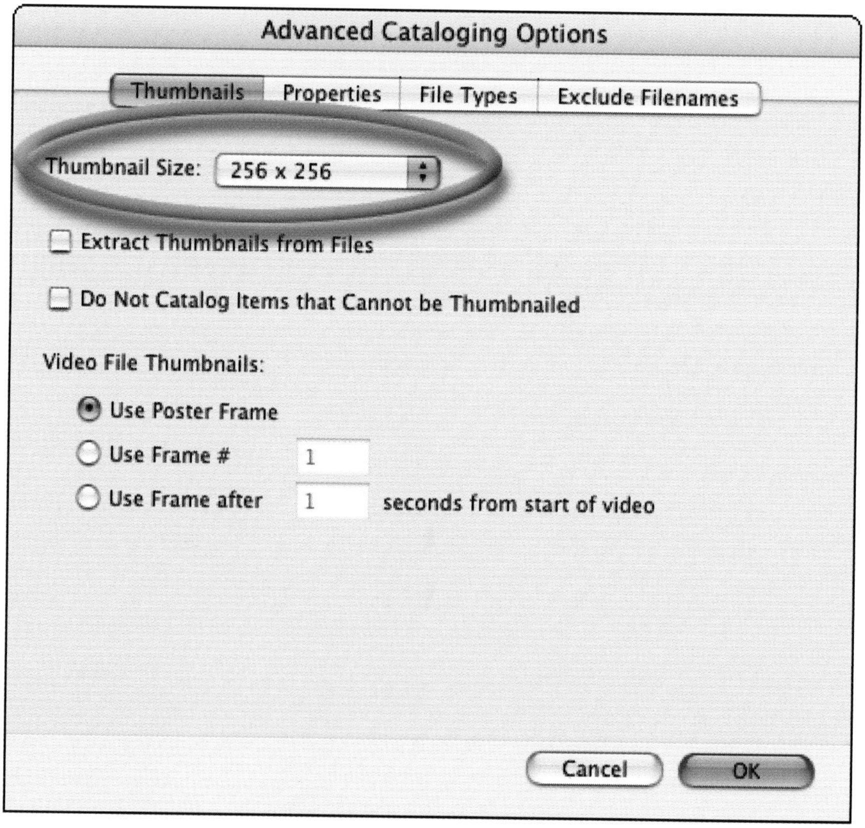

Figure 1-7: Choosing a thumbnail size.

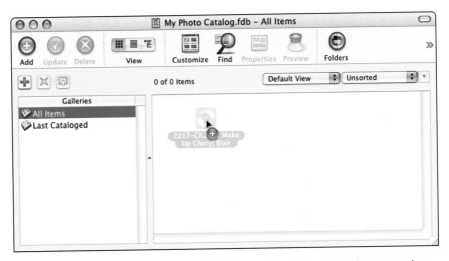

Figure 1-8: The cataloging window receiving dragged files, indicated by the green + sign.

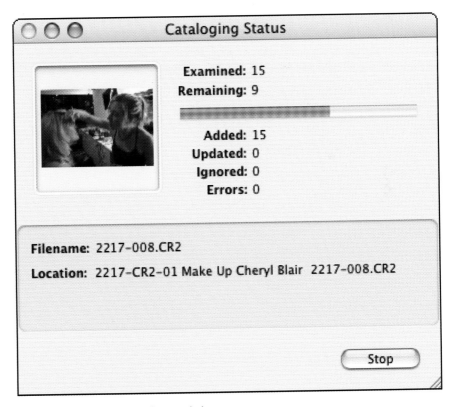

Figure 1-9: The Cataloging Status window.

13. Once cataloging is complete, click the Customize icon at the top of your catalog interface.

The Customize dialog looks like the dialog in Figure 1-10.

14. In the Size drop-down menu under Show Thumbnail, choose 256 × 256.

You can experiment with different looks by changing the border. Click Apply to see how the new border looks in your catalog. Your new catalog is finished and only just begun, all at the same time. You can continue adding images to your catalog. As you do, its value as a sorting tool grows.

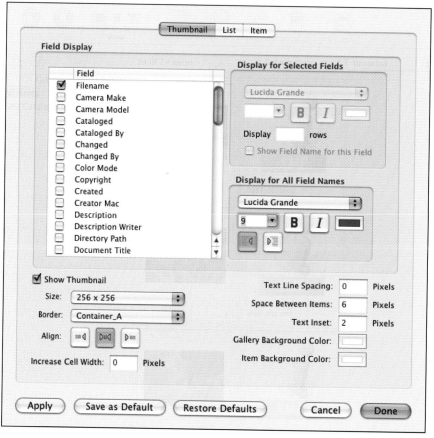

Figure 1-10: Experiment with the border settings.

When cataloging RAW files renamed in Bridge that have had the Preserve Current File Name in XMP Metadata box checked (or have had settings made in Camera Raw), the accompanying XMP *sidecar* file is also cataloged. Group all of the XMP sidecar files together by choosing Extension next to the Custom View menu; see Figure 1-11. Make sure the triangle next to the word Extension is pointed up; change its direction by clicking it. All of the images are first in the catalog, followed by the sidecar files. For more information on these metadata carriers for RAW files, see Book III, Chapter 2. Portfolio reads and retains the sidecar .xmp metadata in the catalog of RAW files. Portfolio creates previews of RAW files made with most DSLR cameras.

Figure 1-11: Images first, then sidecars.

Remember, the trial version of Extensis Portfolio 7.0 is good for 30 days. You might not want to put a lot of work into cataloging your photographs if you plan not to buy the full version. Cataloging done in the trial version is transferable to a fully licensed version. That's nice to know. You can start working and not have to do it over if you decide to purchase Portfolio.

Finding, Sorting, and Reviewing Photographs

The whole purpose of having a catalog of anything is to find what you want when you want it. Book II, Chapter 2, along with this chapter, show you how to get everything set up so you can do just that. Now you put it all together to find your photos!

Locating

Computers are great at keeping track of lots of needles in multiple haystacks. Tell it which needle you want and it will tell you which haystack, right down to the exact piece of straw the needle you want is resting on.

1. **Click the Find icon in the Portfolio 7.0 toolbar.**

   The Find icon is a magnifying glass. It's circled in Figure 1-12. (This is my catalog of RAW files and has almost 15,000 entries.) The Find dialog opens with keywords already selected.

2. **Change the middle drop-down menu from Starts With to Contains. See Figure 1-12.**

3. **Enter what you remember about the photograph.**

   In my example, I want to find photographs of a model named Cheryl having her make up done. When I enter *Cheryl* in the search field I get all the photographs of every model named Cheryl. This isn't bad since it lets me review some other work that might not be in the front of my mind.

   If you aren't in a hurry to find that one photograph, use general search criteria and review all of the results. You'll be delighted at what you find!

4. **Click Find.**

   All the photographs of Cheryl are displayed in the gallery window.

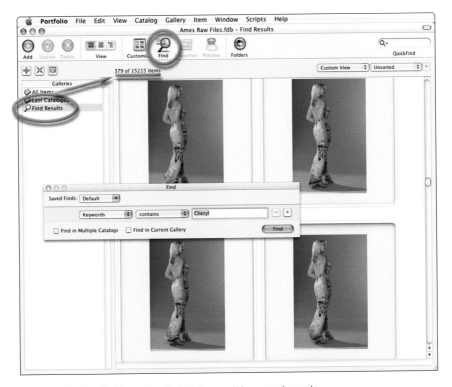

Figure 1-12: The Find icon, the Find dialog, and the search results.

Sorting them out

The gallery in Figure 1-12 has 379 photographs of Cheryl. If I am in a hurry, the simplest way to get to just the photos of her in make up is to modify the search.

1. **Click the Find icon to open the Find dialog (if it's not already open).**

2. **Add a new search field by clicking the + sign at the end of the search window.**

   The sign has a red circle around it in Figure 1-13. A new search line is added below the original in which I searched for Cheryl. When I add Make Up to the Contains search window, I'm now searching for all photographs that have the keywords *Cheryl* and *Make Up* in their metadata.

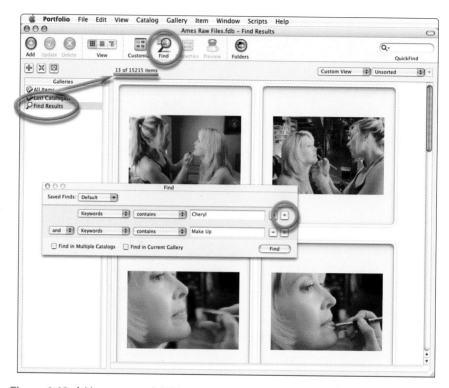

Figure 1-13: Add a new search field.

3. Click Find.

In this example, the search returns only 13 of the 379 photographs of Cheryl, as you see in Figure 1-13.

Reviewing

Now you can take a closer look at the photographs in the Find Results gallery in Portfolio 7.0.

1. Click the first thumbnail, scroll to the last thumbnail, and Shift+click the last thumbnail.

You've selected all the photographs in the Find Results gallery. All the thumbnails are now bordered in color like the two in Figure 1-14.

Figure 1-14: Bordered thumbnails and the Preview icon.

2. Click the Preview button (circled in red in Figure 1-14).

The Preview dialog opens. At the bottom of the dialog are direction arrows; they're underlined in red in Figure 1-15. Clicking the right arrow moves you to the next image, while the left arrow changes the view to the previous preview. The left and right arrows that point to a vertical bar move the view to the first or last selected photograph, respectively.

The toolbar at the top allows you to zoom in or out, fit the image in the window, view actual size, and even go to the original if the disc is on your computer. The last icon, a red circle with a white x, deletes the image. Don't use this icon ever.

As you review your photographs, write down the names of the previews whose originals you want to work with. You can zoom in to check focus and detail. Preview is showing you the actual JPEG files you cataloged. Since they are full-sized versions of their RAW file, the detail is very good. Close the Preview window after you have finished choosing from your catalog of found images by pressing ⌘+W (choosing X). Click outside the border to deselect the thumbnails of photographs from your search.

Figure 1-15: Preview window direction arrows.

Where is the original photograph, anyway?

Reviewing is finished and I've chosen the photograph I want to use. Now I have to know exactly where the digital negative is on which disc. Here's how: Highlight the thumbnail of the chosen photograph in the Catalog. Click the Properties button in the toolbar. It's circled in red in Figure 1-16.

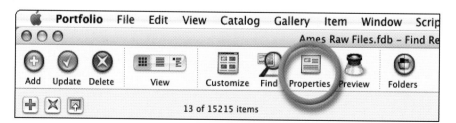

Figure 1-16: The Properties button.

The information appears in the Properties dialog shown in Figure 1-17. It shows a thumbnail of the image, and at the bottom it shows that the photograph is located in my event or job jacket number 2217 on a disc labeled 2217-CR2-01 Make Up Cheryl Blair. The image number on the disc is 2217-020.CR2. Perfect. Book III, Chapter 2 talks more about naming files and discs.

Bonus Chapter 1

Beating the Shoebox Syndrome via Cataloging

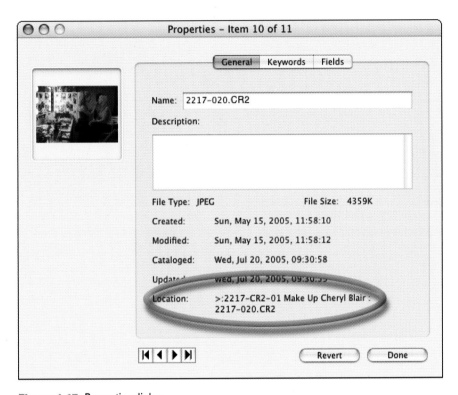

Figure 1-17: Properties dialog.

 Event or *job jackets* are 10 × 13 inch manila envelopes with a label showing the event number in the upper-left corner, as shown in Figure 1-18. These jackets are filed by event number. The project name helps if you insist on finding photos the old-fashioned way . . . by working at it. The jacket also holds paperwork (in this case, Cheryl's model release). The disc with her photographs is stored there as well.

Figure 1-18: An event or job jacket, model release, and labeled disc of RAW files.

Opening the file

The photograph in Figure 1-19 shows all of the . . . well er, stuff professional make-up artist Ransom uses to prepare a model for photography. (The glass of water in the foreground has a straw in it. Models use straws to drink so they won't mess up their oh-so-carefully applied lipstick and liner!) And yes, the color looks better. You read about that in the next chapter.

Figure 1-19: The photo I was looking for.

Bonus Chapter 2: Presenting Electronic Proofs

In This Chapter

✔ Setting up the workspace

✔ Password-protecting your presentation

*Y*ou have fabulous photographs that, if you followed along in Book III, Chapter 3, you exhibited on paper proof sheets. Another way to show your files is to create self-running PDF presentations that can run on any computer running Adobe's free Acrobat Reader software. This chapter shows you how to do that.

Digital Presentations via PDF

Paper prints are great. They work much better on refrigerator doors than an iPod Shuffle hanging from a magnet. They work without a computer or other special viewing device (unless you call a table lamp a special viewing device). They are really tough to e-mail or post on a web site. That's why Photoshop CS2 has PDF presentations and Web Photo Galleries.

These are handy *portable document format (PDF)* files that you can create in Photoshop. Anyone with Adobe Acrobat Reader can open and view the presentation. Here's how to make your own:

1. **Open your folder of photographs in Adobe Bridge.**

2. **Select 8–10 of your favorite photographs by ⌘+clicking (Ctrl+clicking) each one.**

   In keeping with the live music performance in Book III, Chapter 3, I use photographs of Tom Petty for my presentation. You can use your own photographs for this project.

3. **Still holding down the ⌘ (Ctrl) key, type 5, then 8.**

   Five stars appear under the selected thumbnails. The stars are highlighted in green like those in Figure 2-1.

4. **If you are working with RAW files (and I hope you are because it is a good thing), press ⌘+R (Ctrl+R).**

   This opens the Camera Raw dialog.

Figure 2-1: The stars are highlighted green.

5. **Set up the workspace section (shown in Figure 2-2) by changing Space to sRGB IEC61966-1, Depth to 8 Bits/Channel, and Size to the smallest setting.**

   After you make the PDF presentation, you can (and should) change them back.

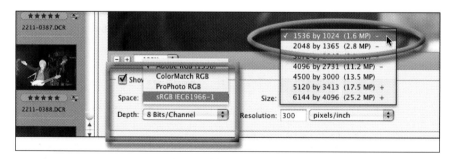

Figure 2-2: Copy these settings.

6. **Click Done.**

7. **In Bridge, choose Tools⇨Photoshop⇨PDF Presentation, as shown in Figure 2-3.**

   You can see the PDF Presentation dialog in Figure 2-4. Now you set up the presentation. The Source Files section of the dialog lists the path of the photographs you chose in Bridge.

Figure 2-3: Choosing PDF Presentation.

8. **Click the Presentation button in the Output Options section.**

   The Presentation Options section becomes editable.

9. **Set a time for advancing to the next image.**

   The default is 5 seconds.

10. **If you want the presentation to play until the user presses the Escape key, click the Loop after Last Page checkbox.**

    The transitions in this version of PDF Presentation are a bit clunky. None is my favorite. It is the default setting.

11. **Click Save.**

12. **Type a name for your presentation in the Save box.**

    I chose to call mine Tom Petty.pdf and save it to the Desktop; see Figure 2-5. You will probably want to call yours something else unless you were one of the 50 or so photographers in the pit with me that rainy night. (Gee did we ever get wet!)

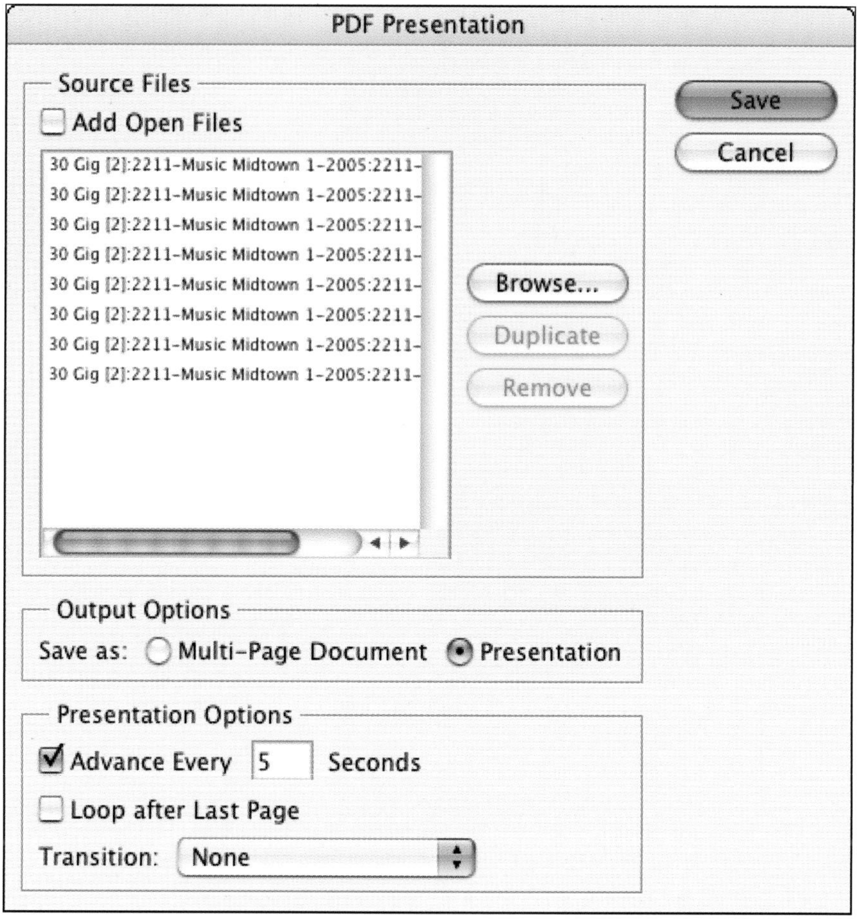

Figure 2-4: Choose the settings that suit your needs.

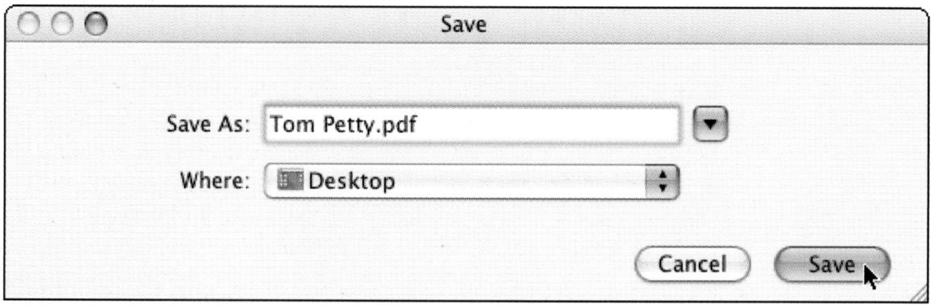

Figure 2-5: Saving Tom Petty to my Desktop.

13. **Set up the PDF presets and tell your presentation to play itself.**

   The finished dialog looks like Figure 2-6.

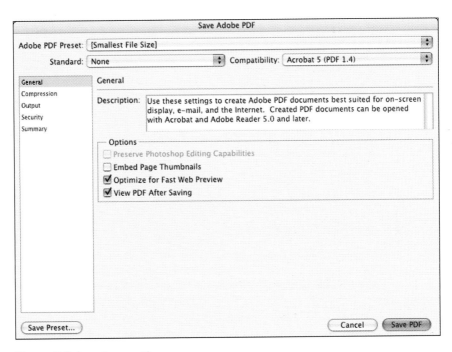

Figure 2-6: Copy these settings.

14. **Click the View PDF After Saving checkbox.**

   This launches Acrobat Reader and plays your presentation when it's finished.

15. **If you want to e-mail your presentation go to Step 16. If not, click Save PDF.**

   The default settings for PDF presentations will create a file sometime close to 50MB (megabytes) in size. That's so big it would choke a horse, let alone an e-mail server. And imagine having to download that big boy. No thanks. The Save Adobe PDF dialog allows you to make your presentation small enough that it can be e-mailed. You find it under the Compression section on the left side.

16. **Click the word Compression, highlighted in blue on the left in Figure 2-7.**

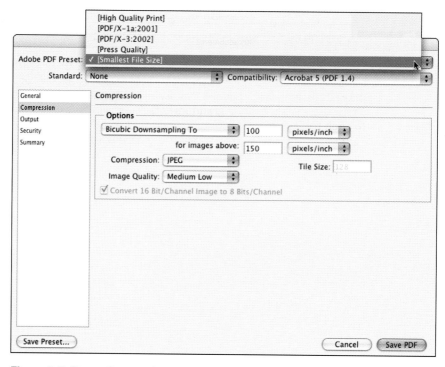

Figure 2-7: Choose Compression, then Smallest File Size.

17. Select Smallest File Size from the Adobe PDF Preset menu.

18. Click Save PDF.

Where are you going?

A *path* is the location of a file on a computer. On a Windows computer a path looks something like this: C:\My Documents\Pictures\2221-Music Midtown 1-2005\2211-0520.dcr. The drive is C:\. The folder My Documents has a subfolder inside it named Pictures. Inside that folder is one called 2221-Music Midtown 1-2005. The RAW files are in that folder. The first image chosen is 2211-0520.dcr.

The example illustrated in Figure 2-4 is the Macintosh version of a path — :2211-Music Midtown 1-2005:2211-0520.dcr. The hard drive is an external one named 30 Gig [2]. Living inside that drive is a folder named 2221-Music Midtown 1-2005. As in Windows, the image files, including 2211-0520.dcr, are in that folder.

You can password protect your PDF presentation so it can be viewed only. Click the word Security in the Save Adobe PDF dialog.

Photoshop opens your chosen photographs, reduces them in size, and places them in a self-running PDF document. It even opens Acrobat Reader and plays it for you. Now you can make a slick slideshow of Bobby's Birthday Party and e-mail it to the grandparents. They will be thrilled that you went to such trouble to show them their darling grandson's special day. Go on. Take the credit and cash in a bit on the hard-work part. I'll never tell.

Bonus Chapter 2

Presenting Electronic Proofs

Index

E

G

Notes

Notes

Notes

Notes

Notes

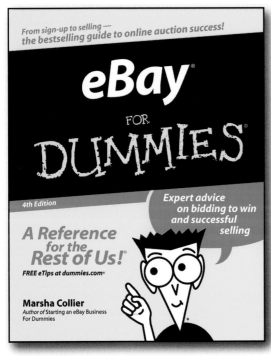
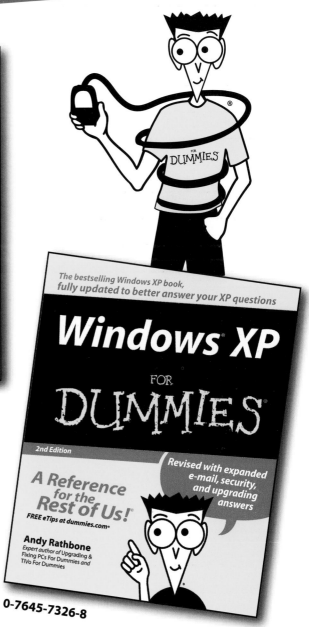

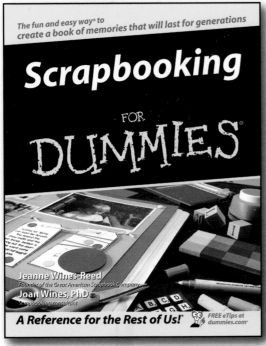

Don't forget about these
bestselling For Dummies® books!

*The fun and easy way®
to let the music play!*

iPod® & iTunes®
FOR
DUMMIES®

2nd Edition

**Includes coverage
for both Windows®
and Mac® users**

**A Reference
for the
Rest of Us!®**

FREE eTips at dummies.com®

**Tony Bove
Cheryl Rhodes**
*Coauthors of iLife® '04 All-in-One Desk
Reference For Dummies*

0-7645-7772-7

*The bestselling guide, now updated!
Pick up the techniques you need to play—starting today*

Guitar
FOR
DUMMIES®

2nd Edition

Bonus audio CD:
Play-along exercises
Songs, riffs, chord
progressions,
and more

Mark Phillips
Former music director, Cherry Lane Music

Jon Chappell
Editor in Chief, Guitar magazine

A Reference for the Rest of Us!™

FREE eTips at
dummies.com®

0-7645-9904-6